Scandinavians in Chicago

Scandinavians in Chicago

The Origins of White Privilege in Modern America

ERIKA K. JACKSON

UNIVERSITY OF ILLINOIS PRESS
Urbana, Chicago, and Springfield

Publication of this book was supported by funding
from Colorado Mesa University Social and
Behavioral Sciences Department.

© 2019 by the Board of Trustees
of the University of Illinois
All rights reserved
1 2 3 4 5 C P 5 4 3 2 1
∞ This book is printed on acid-free paper.

Library of Congress Cataloging-in-Publication Data
Names: Jackson, Erika K., 1978– author.
Title: Scandinavians in Chicago: the origins of white privilege in
    modern America / Erika K. Jackson.
Description: [Urbana, Illinois]: University of Illinois Press, [2019]
    | Includes bibliographical references and index.
Identifiers: LCCN 2018018108| ISBN 9780252042119 (hardcover :
    alk. paper) | ISBN 9780252083822 (pbk. : alk. paper)
Subjects: LCSH: Scandinavian Americans—Illinois—Chicago. |
    Scandinavian Americans—Race identity—Illinois—Chicago.
    | Whites—Race identity—Illinois—Chicago.
Classification: LCC F548.9.S18 J33 2019 | DDC 977.3/11004395—
    dc23 LC record available at https://lccn.loc.gov/2018018108

Ebook ISBN 978-0-252-05086-2

Contents

List of Tables   vii

Acknowledgments   ix

Introduction   1

1   When Scandinavians Were Swarthy:
    Migration and the Origins of "Scandinavian Stock" in Chicago   18

2   Vikings and Dumb Blondes: The Construction of
    American Discourse on Nordic and Scandinavian Whiteness   47

3   The "Swedish Maid": "Strong" Nordic Workers
    in an Elite American World   79

4   Scandinavians Behaving Badly: Vice, Representation,
    and Reform in Early Twentieth-Century Chicago   109

5   World War I, Nativist Rhetoric,
    and the "White Man Par Excellence"   136

6   The New Nordic Man of the 1920s   155

    Conclusion: The Contemporary Importance of Nordic
    Whiteness   179

Notes   191

Index   223

List of Tables

Table 1.1:   Emigration from Sweden, 1851–1890   28
Table 3.1:   Percentage of manual workers, Chicago, 1890   84
Table 3.2:   Percentage of manual workers, Chicago, 1900   85
Table 3.3:   Wives at work, Townsend District, 1890   86
Table 3.4:   Occupational structure in 1900 of adult Scandinavians   88
Table 5.1:   Citizenship of foreign-born white males, Chicago, 1910   145
Table 5.2:   Number and percent naturalized, 1920   150
Table C.1:   Ethnic Groups in the United States
             by Household Income, 2015   183
Table C.2:   List of Colleges and Universities in U.S.
             with Nordic Studies Programs   184

Acknowledgments

In the course of this project, I have benefited from the guidance and support of countless colleagues, archivists, family, and friends. It is with sincere gratitude that I acknowledge some of them here.

My motivation in writing this book began out of a desire for self-identity. Growing up as an adopted child, I listened intently to stories my Grandpa Swanson told of his ancestors from Sweden. My family accepted me as one of their own; there was never a question that I was not also Swedish. When I grew older, I began to understand that ethnicity is not something you simply adopt by proximity. All my life I noted a distinct sense of interest whenever I told someone that I was Swedish. I became fascinated with this sense of privilege, though why was my perceived ethnicity a point of interest? Some questions people asked exposed American stereotypes regarding race: "If your family is Swedish, then why don't you have blonde hair?" I was often afraid that questions like these would expose me as an "adopted" Swede, rather than a biological one. Then again, why did it matter? Years later, my mom would come across my adoption paperwork, which indicated I was Norwegian, not Swedish. As one can imagine, it created quite the renegotiation of identity.

Because many of our ancestors lived in Chicago during the early twentieth century, I also wanted to live there and learn more about them. My graduate advisors, Susan Hirsch and Lewis Erenberg, introduced me to the work of professional historians and instilled in me a love of archives. I had the privilege of working as an intern and museum educator at the Swedish American Museum, which made my interest in my family's past grow even more. Years later, I went on to pursue my PhD at Michigan State University, and it was there that my interest in the history of Scandinavians in Chicago deepened. At MSU, I had the opportunity to work with outstanding scholars and mentors. The late David Bailey inspired me to go further and think deeper—I miss him deeply. I am grateful for my colleagues, Kate Caccavaio, Jason Friedman, Ted Mitchell, and Elise Wagner McCurties, who encouraged me to keep going and to escape the confines of Morrill Hall, and to Dionicio Valdes, who bravely took a group of us to Växjö, Sweden, as part of a scholar exchange. I owe a special and profound gratitude to my graduate advisor, Lisa Fine, who first ignited my love for history as an undergraduate at Michigan State. There is no one in my professional life whom I respect or admire more than Lisa. She demonstrates that it is possible to achieve a balanced academic and personal life and taught me how to be a professor and a historian. Morrill Hall is gone, but I will always treasure my time there.

At my current position as associate professor of history at Colorado Mesa University, I am grateful to work with a dynamic community of teacher-scholars. Over my years at CMU, my historian colleagues have provided me with comradery, support, and guidance through this process: Sarah Swedberg, Steve Schulte, Adam Rosenbaum, Vince Patarino, Doug O'Roark, and Justin Liles. I thoroughly appreciate all of my fellow colleagues who imparted camaraderie along the path to tenure and promotion. Jay Ballenberger graciously accepted my offer to give my manuscript another look through the eyes of a librarian, Steve Merino and Brenda Wilhelm provided sociological insight, Michelle Sunkel shared coffee and laughter, and Tim Casey instilled encouragement during lunchtime visits. Finally, I would like to thank my students at Colorado Mesa for always challenging me to think differently and for inspiring me with your growth.

Through the life of this project, I have benefited from multiple sources of financial support: Colorado Mesa University's Faculty Professional Development Fund; Trans-Atlantic Summer Institute at the University of Minnesota; the Dagmar and Nils William Olsson fellowship at the Swenson Swedish Immigration Research Center; and the Department of History at Michigan State University. Jessica Herrick, department head of the social and behavioral sciences at Colorado Mesa, graciously provided funds to help with the completion of this book. I would like to thank the many archivists and librarians who helped me navigate archival collections for this project. Thank you to Steve Spencer, Anna-Kajsa Echague, and Anne Jenner at the Swedish-American Archives of Greater Chicago at North Park University for the painstaking efforts you put into helping me locate materials, gather permissions, and select images. The staffs at Augustana College's Swenson Swedish Immigration Research Center; Newberry Library; Kenilworth Historical Society; and Pacific Lutheran University Archives and Special Collections were essential.

My book's argument deepened through the insight of fellow colleagues at conferences and seminars over the years who motivated me to formulate and share my research, including conferences held by the Society for the Advancement of Scandinavian Studies, Social Science History Association, and Loyola University Chicago. I am indebted to Dag Blanck and Daron Olson, who at the SASS conference in 2013 gave me the courage to submit my book proposal to the University of Illinois Press. UIP was my first choice and when I sent my book proposal to acquisition editor Dawn Durante, admittedly, I thought my goal was a long shot. She gave me the greatest thrill of my professional career by responding that she wanted to read more. This process has undoubtedly made me a better writer and I have her to thank for that. Dawn, you are everything I could have asked for in an editor. I am highly appreciative of the work my two external reviewers put into the final stages of the book. They provided me with tangible feedback, employed depth and focus, but also were kind and supportive.

I owe my success and completion of this book to my friends and family, who are too numerous to list. I have immense gratitude for Amanda Bynum and Betsy Chafee, who are stunning; and for Rick Northrup and the Martinich family, who have always supported my work. To my parents, Jeff and Kathy Jackson, who, admittedly, did not agree with my decision to attend graduate school in the first place and gave me the shock of my young adult life when they refused to pay for my continued studies. I love and respect them every day for giving me the harsh dose of reality I needed in order to grow up and achieve my goals on my own. In the process of this project, I gained two of the best in-laws anyone could ask for, Rick and Tamara, who welcomed me into their family with open arms.

In the time I spent on this book, I gave birth to my daughter, Svea. When I was finishing the first draft, Svea would kick and nudge me from inside my belly— my constant reminder to keep going, as difficult as it was. I first discovered her name in my research, and it stuck with me until my husband and I decided to have her. As babies do, she added time to the end of the project, but I would not trade the time I was able to spend with her in her first years for anything. She is a precocious and sassy little redhead; I know she will achieve great things as she inspires me every day. Finally, to my husband, Derek, who is the best partner, father, and support system I could ever want. He has provided feedback, talked through various incarnations of ideas that went into the book, and supplied the emotional strength I needed to see this book to the end. I dedicate this book to my family—Derek and Svea, you are my everything.

Scandinavians in Chicago

Introduction

In 1908, the *Chicago Daily Tribune* announced a so-called international search for "the world's most beautiful living woman" through a photographic newspaper contest. This method of entertainment, which was a product of newly acceptable forms of urban commercialism, invited women from Western European countries, including France, Italy, and Germany, as well as contestants from the United States. The implicit goal of the competition was to attract suitable migrants and businesses to Chicago by creating positive associations of the city with physical beauty. A pseudoscientific racial hierarchy that placed Nordic people at its apex weighed heavily upon the opinions of Americans during the early twentieth century. Therefore, it was no surprise that the *Tribune* operated under the assumption that the winner would be located in either Sweden or Norway. Focused solely on the predictions of two Scandinavian newspapers—*Idun*, a leading Swedish woman's periodical, and *Norsk Familie Journal of Christiania*—the article translated announcements of the pageant from Swedish and Norwegian for Chicago's readership. In an effort to establish credibility for the contest, both countries selected a "beauty jury" comprised of famous literary and artistic representatives who could judge aesthetic feminine qualities, which included Norway's Bjørn Bjørnson, director of the National Theater, and Daniel Fallstrom, described as "Sweden's favorite modern poet."[1] According to Laura Fitinghoff of *Idun*, Sweden's national pride hinged upon the public's social perceptions of Nordic femininity, which illustrated the larger potential of Scandinavians from an international perspective.

Figure 1: Image that accompanied the *Chicago Daily Tribune* article, "Will the World's Most Beautiful Woman Be Found in Sweden or Norway?" on January 19, 1908.

The *Chicago Daily Tribune*'s focus on the International Beauty Contest offers an essential view of the ways in which Scandinavian and American writers participated in the intricate social construction of Nordic whiteness. During the nineteenth century, Victorian Americans eschewed such unrefined public displays of the female body. P. T. Barnum's introduction of the portrait beauty contest embraced the mantra of the public and private spheres and invited respectable women to submit photographs of themselves that were commissioned into portraits. This particular contest illustrated the ways in which individual countries used the more modern practice of women's independence in public as a way of determining respectability.[2] Fitinghoff used gendered language to exaggerate the expected physicality and habits of desired Nordic contestants and to purposely contrast their humility with the "vanity" of women from the "darker" European races. "As a matter of general knowledge," Fitinghoff wrote, Swedish women possessed an element of racial fitness "better preserved than the degenerated countries of the south." In contrasting the qualities of Nordic women with races many deemed unfit, Fitinghoff both stereotyped their ethnicity and emphasized their hyper-whiteness. Due to their modesty, such "beautiful blonde daughters" of Sweden who embodied "loveliness, grace, symmetry, and piquant daintiness" would be difficult to locate given the assumed vulgarity of beauty contests. *Idun*'s original article was not written for an American audience and therefore presents a more authentic representation of the diversity of

Nordic whiteness from a Scandinavian's perspective. Fitinghoff ultimately does not identify assumed blond physicality as most beautiful, but instead describes the "typical northern beauty" of Västerbotten, stereotyped as having dark blue eyes and heavy, dark hair.[3] Despite their brunette tresses, she emphasized that their fair complexions and tall, slender bodies fit into idealized racial categorizations of anthropological study.

The *Chicago Daily Tribune*'s coverage of the International Beauty Contest of 1909 illustrated transnational understandings of racial capital informed by public musings on the importance of Nordic whiteness. The concept of Nordic whiteness was an essential racial construct that embodied hyper-whiteness—a set of assumed, interconnected ethnic characteristics—and granted social privilege to those who could claim Scandinavian heritage. This theory was a product of the dangerous progression of late nineteenth- and early twentieth-century anthropological discussions of "race" nativists later employed as a means of determining fitness for American citizenship. In 1899, William Z. Ripley shifted the ideological focus away from subdivided national races to categorize European peoples into three groups (Teutonic, Alpine, and Mediterranean) defined by physical characteristics. Ripley determined that Teutons were universally the most "ideal," the fairest of all white races, characterized by blondeness, a tall stature and bony frame, and dolichocephalic traits (or a long, narrow head—a marker of intelligence). The further away one's race is from Teutonic, the darker, and thereby more problematic, their features.[4] Ripley's preference for the term *Teutonic* contrasted with anthropologist Joseph Deniker's term *nordique*, which he used to distinguish as northern European "ethnic groups" with the same physical characteristics described by Ripley.[5]

Matthew Frye Jacobson argued that this "fracturing of whiteness" meant race became a biological determinant that signaled destiny.[6] Yet, the fluidity of race also created a diverse language to gauge levels of whiteness and formulate it into a possession. American writers and the general public made use of this language in order to analyze nearly every aspect of the millions of new immigrants, from their racial physicality to their behaviors and cultural practices. Ethnic stereotypes became a staple of American culture, reflecting the fears and anxieties of negative social change to accommodate the flood of "strange" folk. Most often, negative assumptions centered upon those immigrants deemed unable to assimilate because of darker complexions or ethnic practices judged as incongruent with American culture. Like the Irish of Noel Ignatiev's study, whiteness could be attained but often through conflict, even violence. The power of racial politics gave the imagined spectrum of whiteness a certain fluidity, especially if a group fell into an in-between category.[7]

4 · *Introduction*

Until recently, the study of American ethnic history focused almost entirely on groups who fought for legitimacy, operating under the premise that those with uncontested whiteness required no further study. Such uncontested, or normative, whiteness, according to Ruth Frankenberg, is a location of "structural advantage" and based upon an assumption that one's whiteness is normalized, invisible, and unproblematic.[8] Yet, just as it is vital to study the history of groups who fought to identify as white, so too is it essential to investigate the process by which those who achieved racial hegemony were able to do so. Analysis of the reception of Scandinavians in America illustrates the vast complexities of whiteness during the late nineteenth and early twentieth centuries. Jørn Brøndal argued that historical assumptions often categorize Scandinavians as "indisputably white," despite the fact that racial thinking on Nordics indeed shifted over time. A modification in anthropologic, nativist, and historical discourse of American and Scandinavian writers in essence manufactured the "relatively safe spot" of Scandinavian immigrants and their children within the evolving hierarchy of whiteness.[9] According to nativists, Scandinavians were more willing (and racially able) to assimilate because the group provided the least amount of difference from the Anglo-American "old stock."

The etymology of the words *Nordic* and *Scandinavian* illustrates a more complex categorization of racial and ethnic difference that similarly shifted along with the historical discussion of whiteness. According to Arne Lunde, the *Nordic* category most often connoted the imagined biology of race (skin pigmentation, the color of one's eyes and hair, the length of one's head, and height) while the *Scandinavian* category signaled ethnicity and difference (foreignness in culture, gender roles, language, class, and so on).[10] Yet, what these categories do not consider is the extent to which these terms were used interchangeably by both Americans and Scandinavians regardless of critical thinking about the dichotomies of race and ethnicity. Furthermore, the definition of *Nordic* does not take into consideration the importance of gendered physicality most often understood in racial, rather than ethnic, terms by Americans. Within the American cultural consciousness, Nordic whiteness translated into ideal, universally gendered concepts. The American press stereotyped the racial features of Scandinavian men and women in static constants. According to racialized discourse, Nordic women and men could be identified in America by their ideal racial qualities (blonde hair, blue eyes, and tall statures). Americans employed terms such as *hard-working*, *virile*, and *trustworthy* as exhibitive feminized and masculinized ethnic traits. Historical considerations of Nordic whiteness cannot be fully understood apart from the social construction of gender as part of the larger process of defining race and ethnicity.

Scandinavians in Chicago explores ideological, gendered concepts of Nordic whiteness and Scandinavian ethnicity employed by native-born Americans in Chicago during the late nineteenth and early twentieth centuries to construct societal hegemony. The focus of this book sets out to advance a more comprehensive understanding of the Scandinavian American experience by examining the process by which Nordics became the embodiment of whiteness. The aim of this study is to emphasize the significance of an intricate cultural interplay between native-born Americans and Scandinavian immigrants within the process of constructing Nordic racial hegemony. Influenced by earlier nativist rhetoric, in the 1890s anthropologists set out to create a racial dogma that positioned all of the European peoples upon an imagined, yet static, hierarchy that affixed Nordics at its apex. American historians, newspaper editors, and other writers repeated and expanded upon the language of Nordicism. The common response of most immigrant newspapers was to defend their race within the press. As both Thomas Guglielmo and Peter Vellon demonstrate, immigrants such as Italians in both New York and Chicago used the ethnic press to manufacture positive arguments for their whiteness.[11] In contrast, Scandinavian immigrant newspapers, historians, and writers repeated and mirrored ideal racial and ethnic perceptions of its people created by the mainstream American press. Rather than constructing an authentic persona of the common Nordic immigrant, Scandinavians chose to play upon the observations of the American media as a means of benefiting their cause. By the end of the twentieth century, this exaggerated image of the idealized Nordic man and woman loomed as an inauthentic, sexualized stereotype from which Scandinavian Americans sought to separate themselves. In this unique perspective, the Scandinavian struggle for racial and ethnic legitimacy occurred in reverse.

Chicago provides a fitting backdrop for the study of the significance of Nordic racial hegemony and the experiences of Scandinavians and Scandinavian Americans. From its very origins, Chicago was inherently multicultural. By 1890, immigrants and their children comprised 79 percent of the population of the city.[12] The city's uniqueness as a midpoint between the East and West Coasts, coupled with the fact Chicago's population was comprised of nearly every immigrant group in America, makes it an essential site of analysis regarding the imagined racial hierarchy. Rural midwestern areas or cities such as Minneapolis and St. Paul are most often associated with large Scandinavian populations, yet Chicago was one of the largest Scandinavian cities in the world by 1900. Due to massive immigration, by 1900 Chicago became the second-largest Swedish city in the world (second to Stockholm); Swedes represented 10 percent of Chicago's immigrant population and constituted the third largest ethnic group in the city

6 · *Introduction*

after the Germans and the Irish.[13] Similarly, in 1900, there were 41,551 Norwegian residents; Chicago's immigrant community of "Little Norway" made up the third-largest Norwegian population internationally after Oslo and Bergen. By 1910, there were also 18,500 first- and second-generation Danish immigrants living in Chicago's Humboldt Park region.[14] Previous studies of Scandinavian Chicago focused on the individual group dynamics of Norwegians, Danes, and Swedes of Chicago and little on interactions with those of non-Scandinavian origin. Instead, the goal of this study is to draw attention to the discussions created by both Americans and Scandinavians of Chicago as a unique conversation in which an immigrant community supported and maintained racial and ethnic stereotypes as a means of achievement.[15]

Scandinavians in Chicago is one of the first attempts to place the Scandinavian American experience within the context of the historical study of whiteness. Until recently, relatively few historians sought to describe the racial status of Nordics in America. Articles by Jørn Brøndal, Dag Blanck, and Gunlög Fur in the spring 2014 issue of *Journal of American Ethnic History* began to rectify historiographic gaps. Brøndal's examination of filiopietistic and nativist literature of the late nineteenth and early twentieth centuries confirms the "messiness" of the racial hierarchy, though systematically locates order through an ideological division of "romantic" and "scientific" traditions of race.[16] Scandinavian American academics, newspaper editors, Lutheran ministers, and amateur historians fashioned the romantic tradition, which "aired various rather cocksuresounding assumptions about the Scandinavian Americans, their past, and their racial makeup that seemingly meshed well with an emergent American nativist discourse," wrote Brøndal.[17] Such filiopietistic venerations of Scandinavian American history emphasized the unsullied racial characteristics of Nordics as a whole.[18] In this framework, historians were able to embrace the more positive Anglo-Saxon elements of their racial identity while creating distance from other groups.[19] The focus of such studies was on white, "heroic," male migrants functioning as separate groups (Danes, Norwegians, and Swedes) rather than as an ethnic whole (Scandinavians). As late as the 1970s, the continued insular study of Scandinavians in America gave a certain antiquity to the historiography as other immigration scholars had begun to explore concepts of national heritage and connections across ethnic cultures. In her evaluation of the field in 1987, Kathleen Neils Conzen warned against "a historiography content to talk only to itself and debate only within its own context"; aside from a few notable exceptions, no vital historiographic shift toward a more critical analysis of Nordic whiteness occurred.[20]

As a poststructuralist work, this book does not suggest a return to the top-down approaches of dusty lore. Instead, a closer analysis of the racial identities Nordics manufactured within America offer a greater understanding of social awareness of hegemony and autonomy. An understandable avoidance of discussions that connote white privilege remain in considerations of the history of Scandinavians in America. The historiographic focus has been on the victimization of groups who fought to win racial legitimacy and far less on those whose whiteness was not a point of deliberation.[21] Conversely, the more tangible contestations of whiteness experienced by the Irish, Italians, and other "undesirables" of immigration history tend to discuss the benefits of white privilege without using such terms. By creating false racial identities as a means of attaining social status, such groups lost the unique markers of race and ethnicity. Similarly, for Scandinavians, the false social expectations that went along with Nordic identity presented the issue of façade over the course of the twentieth century—becoming what Americans saw as the physical embodiment of "Nordic" or "Scandinavian" but not based in an authentic heritage or persona. Such assumptions of uncontested whiteness miss a vital opportunity to problematize the meanings of whiteness. This study focuses on immigrants who were able to attain success because they did not encounter roadblocks reserved for other groups by way of racial and ethnic prejudice, nativist rhetoric, or stereotyping. However, this study should not be taken as one that merely focuses on the privileges afforded to white people. The process by which Nordic and Scandinavian whiteness came to be understood in America is vital to the study of race and ethnicity as it looks at the other side of such categorizations. Nordic and Scandinavian whiteness still involved the process of racial profiling, and while, admittedly, racial preference does often result in privilege, such an emphasis is still significant to the study of how Americans used stereotyping to distinguish European immigrants from one another.

The historiographic avoidance of topical analysis that connotes white privilege is a direct product of internal conflict among scholars of whiteness studies. The perceived ranking of Nordics at the top of an imagined social hierarchy constructed a central dimension of the whole notion of race, with material and psychological implications for the "wages of whiteness" earned.[22] Yet, critical analysis of such inferences to the collateral of race continue to spark embattled debates. In "Whiteness and the Historians' Imagination," Eric Arnesen charged the field with reducing the ideological study of whiteness to a "blank screen onto which those who claim to analyze it can project their own meanings" and that, overall, the field suffered from "a number of potentially fatal methodological

8 · *Introduction*

and conceptual flaws."[23] His position sharply conflicted with Roediger's, that by making whiteness, rather than white racism, the focus of historical study, we could gain a more valuable perspective on the ways that white Americans "think of themselves, of power, of pleasure, and of gender."[24] More particularly, the historical implications of discussing the "scientific truth" of white superiority creates additional problems in its study; the myth of the Germanic "Aryan" and Nordic race still remains intertwined with the image of Scandinavians as the "whitest of all whites."[25] However, one could argue that the basic methodology behind the study of history employs analysis intended to portray a particular point of view, which is always subject to the perspective of the author. What most historians can agree upon is that whiteness and the ideological formation of race is based upon a powerful set of myths that were set into motion by American culture, historical study, and political agenda.

Therefore, it should be made clear that this book does not argue that Nordics underwent a process of "becoming" white, as their whiteness was seldom questioned. Early historical references to Scandinavians as "swarthy" made by such notable Americans as Benjamin Franklin were more indicative of an unwillingness to assimilate into Anglo-Saxon society rather than a threat to their racial stock.[26] If Scandinavians did occupy a certain category of "in-betweenness," it was for a brief period of time prior to the publication of nativist tracts of the 1840s, which created "a fundamental revision of whiteness itself."[27] During this period, Scandinavians embraced an Anglo-Saxon identity as a means of racial positioning as "old stock." In Chicago and across America, as Dag Blanck pointed out, an awareness of the benefits from belonging to this category emerged as immigrants and native-born Americans engaged in a process of incorporating Scandinavians into the fold of a shared Anglo-Saxon heritage.[28] Later on, anthropological works of the 1880s in essence created an imaginary social hierarchy of race. Resulting legislation favored the continued arrival of "desirable" Nordics and curtailed larger numbers of "problematic" "Alpines" and "Mediterraneans" by providing a clear message of those European immigrants who were wanted and those who were not.

Due to anthropologic discussions that framed the Nordic race as the whitest of all races, Scandinavians exhibited an ability to both retain and embrace "true" elements of ethnicity without the threat of nativist backlash. So long as Scandinavians identified with this comprehensive racial identity that combined an expected physicality with American values of liberty, republicanism, and prosperity, nativists granted them ethnic freedoms not avowed to other immigrant groups.[29] To better understand the historical significance of race and ethnicity on display, the second chapter of this study investigates the World's

Columbian Exposition of 1893 as the most blatant depiction of racial progress and expansion of white civilization. In the civilized White City, intended to suggest the millennial future of advanced white races, delegates from the Swedish, Danish, and Norwegian coalitions presented the Nordic race and ethnic Scandinavianism in highly beneficial and strategized terms.[30] The most infamous of these displays was an exact replica of an ancient Viking long ship, which was constructed by a group of Norwegians. They then set sail toward Chicago in an effort to argue the heroism of Leif Erickson and that he—not Christopher Columbus—was the true "discoverer" of America. Due to the honorable manliness of Erickson, Scandinavians proved their ancient roots in America and therefore were able to claim their Nordic heritage within the context of an intense pressure to assimilate. This ideological "homemaking myth" employed by a privileged immigrant group connected to further ethnic displays in order to prove Nordic superiority within the context of the fair.[31]

By studying the process by which Scandinavians maintained racial hegemony during the twentieth century, this book provides further perspective on the historical construction of both race and gender. Prior to the cultural turn, male scholars dominated the field of Scandinavian American history. Such narratives pored over the masculine Viking traditions of yesteryear and, while filiopietistic in scope, offered a vital analysis of Nordic masculinity and racial

Figure 2: The Norwegian replica Viking ship photographed as it arrived at the harbor of the World's Columbian Exposition in 1893, sailed by Captain Magnus Andersen. Courtesy of Wikimedia Commons.

hegemony. In recent years, two major trends emerged within the historiography of Scandinavian immigration: a focus on the significance of single, independent wage-earning immigrant women and the study of singular ethnic, linguistic, and religious groups apart from one another.[32] A number of published monographs and anthologies support the topic of this study, though they do not fully explore gendered whiteness, especially within the framework of Chicago or other urban spaces.

Despite Joan Scott's first translation of poststructuralism to analyze the language of gender using historical analysis, internal divisions continue among historians who argue the study of gender and whiteness only advances the history of heterosexual, white men further. In support of Scott's call, Joanne Meyerowitz asserted that the goals of gender history are vastly similar to those of whiteness studies: to "provide critiques of earlier theories of women's subordination (or subordination of 'lower' races), introduce historians to deconstructionist methods, and lay out an agenda for future historical studies."[33] Furthermore, the language of gender offers a multiplicity of meanings when studied together with the social construction of race and ethnicity. Studying the gendered language used to describe Nordic and Scandinavian features over the span of nearly a century illustrates significant shifts in etymology that cannot be replicated in other racial contexts. For instance, the singular term *Viking* connotes a natural synonym for masculinity in itself, in addition to virility, strength, violence, passion, aggression, and savagery. Yet, as other historians argue, the influence of the language of gender on experience, behavior, and decision-making over time remains difficult to determine. Studies of race, particularly of the African American experience, and of masculinity pushed historians to recognize the significance of gender to convey an emergent notion of difference.[34] Such wide-ranging and changing meanings of masculinity and femininity are particularly apparent in the modern era.

Studies of whiteness and gender both constitute elements of the relationship between power and privilege. From the sexualized, exotic "other" embodied in Orientalist literature to the "swarthy" immigrant who is neither masculine nor feminine, gendered understandings of race and ethnicity offer a multitude of complex new perspectives. When gendered concepts and language appear in considerations of ethnic groups, such examples tend to be used for the purpose of negating femininity or masculinity, such as depictions of the Irish and those of Jewish descent during the nineteenth century.[35] The study of Nordic whiteness and gender, particularly markers of physical attractiveness, complicates such depictions of ethnic groups in America. When sociologist Catrin Lundström compared perceptions of Swedish femininity in the United States versus

Singapore, she found that the contemporary association of hegemonic Nordic whiteness with feminine beauty is a wholly Western concept. In Singapore, the same markers of whiteness (blonde hair, fair skin) did not signal attraction, sexuality, or sin, but instead signified "westerner," "expatriate," and "foreigner," thereby weakening their femininity.[36] With that said, the entire notion of Nordic racial hegemony was a product of the American media during the modern era and is therefore essential to this study. Scandinavian Americans built and structured ethnic identity within a hierarchical framework that fashioned the Nordic race as part of the higher echelon of an imagined social ladder of immigrant groups. Men and women navigated within this hierarchy and benefited because of gendered language and socially constructed privilege.

The Significance of the Scandinavian American Press

The origins of discourse pertaining to Nordic white privilege began with the immense power of the immigrant and American press. As Scandinavian immigrants flooded into the rural and urban Midwest, they brought with them a unique culture shaped by a diverse literary and linguistic presence. Historically, Scandinavians were a remarkably literate group mainly due to the requirement of the Lutheran Church that all children be taught to read and write. Between 1899 and 1909, Scandinavian immigrants arriving in America had a literacy rate of 99.6 percent and were recognized by the U.S. Immigration Commission as the most literate of all European peoples in the United States.[37] In an effort to preserve, nurture, and promote linguistic retention and heritage, Scandinavian-language newspapers and publishing houses became prevalent throughout the cities and counties of the Midwest, producing more than one thousand Swedish newspapers and magazines.[38] The immense readership of the Scandinavian American press is indicative of both its influence and its success. Though most Scandinavian-language newspapers could not match the circulation figures of mainstream American newspapers, *Skandinaven* came close to equaling the Sunday edition of the *New York Times* during that same year.[39] While this comparison of circulation figures is notable, these rates underestimate actual circulation. Scandinavians distributed newspapers on city streets, exchanged publications in fraternal meetings, and frequented neighborhood bookstores, public libraries, and cafés to pore over weeklies that included American, Scandinavian, and local news.

Chicago was a city of great importance in its centrality to the establishment of a Scandinavian American press tradition in the late 1850s. During the antebellum era, Norwegians combined efforts with Danes and sometimes Swedes

12 • *Introduction*

to publish smaller religious, political, or independent newspapers for Scandinavians living in New York City, Chicago, and other developments throughout the Midwest such as Wisconsin and Minnesota.[40] Scandinavian American newspapers published in the United States between the 1840s and 1930s reflected a desire for information on politics, religion, and the communities in which Scandinavians lived, as well as the preservation of culture and language. The press reflected the clear religious, secular, and cultural divides within the Scandinavian community of Chicago and throughout the Midwest; therefore, this manuscript examines the vast diversity of such perspectives through careful selection of representative papers. Swedish Lutheran newspapers like *Hemlandet* and *Missions-Vännen* clashed openly with the more liberal weeklies such as *Svenska Amerikanaren, Svenska Kuriren*, and *Svenska Tribunen*, despite some shared Republican ideologies between the newspapers. The more mainstream, liberal newspapers saw higher rates of circulation with the Norwegian-language newspaper, *Skandinaven*, leading in popularity with an estimated circulation of 44,468 in 1900.[41] Danish-language newspapers like *Den Danske Pioneer* offer an intriguing contrast to the larger narrative produced by the Norwegian- and Swedish-language press in regard to region and political affiliation. Just under *Hemlandet* in circulation statistics, *Den Danske Pioneer* was published out of Omaha and reflected an independent Democratic voice in relation to the Republican-minded Swedes and Norwegians of the Midwest.

In a similar vein to the Scandinavian American press, Chicago's dailies reflected significant social and political divides among its readership during the nineteenth and into the twentieth century. Chicago's leading newspapers including the *Chicago Tribune*, the *Chicago Daily News*, and the *Chicago Times-Herald* reported widely on matters involving class conflict often perpetuated by racial and ethnic tensions. First published in 1847, the *Chicago Tribune* (which became the *Chicago Daily Tribune*) was popular among the city's elites, pushed an abolitionist agenda, and remained a staple of Republican politics for the whole of the nineteenth century while the *Chicago Times* (which merged with the *Chicago Herald* in 1895) took a pro-slavery, southern Democratic position.[42] Other newspapers like the *Chicago Daily News* strove for a wider general readership and took on more of an independent voice in reporting matters of social and political turmoil. Regardless of political affiliation, Chicago's newspapers focused more on matters regarding racial whiteness whereas the Scandinavian American press concentrated more on the connections of ethnicity and political activism and not nearly as much on issues of class. Amid growing nativist concern over the perseverance of ethnic identity, it makes perfect sense as to why the Scandinavian-language press focused on matters of cultural preservation.

Furthermore, as demonstrated in numerous articles, Scandinavian American editors had the added benefit of English acquisition, keeping them abreast of local conversations regarding their community. If any American editors or journalists slighted Scandinavians or their press in any way, the community was sure to hear of it, carefully concealed in the hidden discourse of diverse languages.

Historically, the immense power of the American media has often proven single-handedly responsible for perpetuating stereotypes and prejudices against diverse groups, particularly in times of social conflict. It is the most immediate source in constructing social attitudes toward race and ethnicity. Closer examination of the Scandinavian-language press provides one of the most valuable sites for understanding racial and ethnic identity outside of the influence of American rhetoric. Yet, the ways in which Scandinavian writers responded to the American narrative is equally important to this history of the social construction of Nordic whiteness. Although many historians have acknowledged the influence of the Scandinavian press in bringing about assimilation to American ways of life, few have compared the conversations raised by the community to those in the American media.[43] Through this comparison, we can explore how print media built ideologies regarding Nordic whiteness and Scandinavian ethnicity from all perspectives and points of interaction between the two sides.

Chicago is of great significance to the history of Scandinavian Americans in regard to demographics and culture, but also in comparison to other Scandinavian-centric areas of the country. Most commonly, the history of Scandinavians in America recalls their rural origins in the Midwest or the Pacific Northwest through a network of simple farming communities. Today, an American driving across the Midwest will travel past towns like Swedetown, Little Norway, Lindström, and Dannebrog. Remnants of Scandinavian ethnic heritage, albeit symbolic, shape significant portions of these areas and the history of its people is a sense of pride for Americans who self-identify as Scandinavian American. In fact, the most recent estimate illustrates that out of 11.9 million Americans who claim to have Scandinavian ancestry, a majority of those individuals live in the rural areas of the upper Midwest and Pacific Northwest.

It is important to note, however, that claims to ethnicity are not always accurate and often conflated with issues of racial identity. Recent U.S. census data show that among a diverse American population where 72.4 percent of the country self-report that they are racially white, a sizable percentage of that population claims Scandinavian or Nordic heritage (5.3 percent).[44] Controversy abounds when discussing estimates of the U.S. census, especially concerning the ways in which we perceive of racial and ethnic heritage. The significance here, however, lies in the issue of self-identification. In a modern world, where the consumer availability of DNA kits that promise to provide the buyer with the comfort of knowing their continental ancestry is one essential example of the continued weight of white privilege attached to the Nordic conception of race. When a person claims to be of Nordic or Scandinavian ancestry, there continues to be a self-perception of racial privilege attached to that identity. As this study emphasizes, Chicago was an instrumental site in the origins of public discussions of racial whiteness, privilege, and civilization, but it was not the only place in America where this conversation took place. Furthermore, as this study illustrates, American discourse created a barrier of exceptionalism that protected Nordics from labels other groups of European immigrants received. From the perspective of Scandinavians, writers systematically observed the ways in which constructs shifted between different societies. All Scandinavians looked the same in Scandinavia, but in America, they became the epitome of white—an observation that the press explored in great depth.

The process by which the foreign and American press gave Scandinavian Americans credence to their Nordic racial whiteness and Scandinavian ethnicity is the subject of the chapters that follow. The book's chapters take a thematic and chronological approach to the social construction of Nordic whiteness, focusing first on the origins of privilege granted to Scandinavians in Chicago. The topic of chapter one illustrates how Chicago's first Nordic settlers did not start out as an immigrant group with any form of hegemony during Chicago's booster years of the nineteenth century. Like their German, Irish, and Italian neighbors, Scandinavians built neighborhoods centered on cultural and religious institutions, garnered social networks, and gained tangible employment. In contrast to these particular immigrant groups, whom scholars have argued underwent a process of becoming white, Scandinavians used the language of American imperialists to not "become" white, but instead become "civilized."[45]

Chapter two explores this concept of civilization further in connection with the growing body of anthropologic and sociologic arguments for a hierarchy of the white races in America that gained momentum during the 1880s through the turn of the century. The World's Columbian Exposition of 1893 to 1894 provided a critical site for public discourse and ideological dissemination of the connections between Nordic racial whiteness, civilization, and fitness for American citizenship. The displays and publications of racial "theorists" positioned those originating from the Nordic race as the fittest in the world—a concept that is now called scientific racism, which has proved long-lasting. Scandinavians, unlike other European immigrants, were not placed in a defensive position but instead in one that could prove to be beneficial to their race. Swedish, Norwegian, and Danish publications and displays at the Exposition reinforced these racial stereotypes, depicting Scandinavians in gendered terms as intelligent, attractive, and most importantly, as the whitest of the white races. Positive stereotypes focused on the perceived physical and behavioral traits of Scandinavians were built into American culture through images, conversation, gossip, and commentary in news outlets like the *Chicago Daily Tribune*, magazines, and film. By the 1910s, the stereotype of the blonde-haired, blue-eyed Scandinavian was commonplace in popular culture.

Positive stereotypes regarding Nordic racial features evidently resulted in employment opportunities for Scandinavians in Chicago's varied industries, as chapter three details. A substantial majority of Scandinavian emigrants were employees or employers, and by the 1920s, a prominent class of Scandinavian American businessmen emerged. As early as the 1860s, a number of Scandinavians became involved in labor organization and unrest, resulting in class conflict between a volatile middle class and a politicized working class. In spite of class conflict, Scandinavians, together with Germans and Irish, constituted a group of foreign-born workers with the highest level of union affiliation in Chicago during the labor wars of the late nineteenth century.[46] While numerous Scandinavian workers saw substantial involvement in labor organizing and protest, they were protected by the narrative of Nordic *whiteness* and did not receive the same negative media attention as other immigrant groups such as Russians, Irish, or Germans. Instead, the American media focused more attention on the role of the "Swedish maid," illustrating the benefits provided by conversations regarding Nordic whiteness. The historiography on domestic service during the late nineteenth and early twentieth century focuses on the dangers and pitfalls of the position; yet this chapter contrasts how racial discourse led to a surprisingly beneficial social position for Scandinavian women.

Whereas the narrative on Nordic racial whiteness often worked in Scandinavian Americans' favor, the topic of chapter four investigates the darker side of white privilege within the context of Progressive-era fears over white slavery. In the early 1900s, Chicago witnessed a massive influx of young, single migrant women entering the city for employment at a time when the city became one of the most lawless in America. According to Progressive reformers, corruption and sexual danger threatened these innocents and posed the potential for white slavers to take advantage of them. Progressives exhibited concern for all women living "adrift" yet paid special concern to the women they considered the whitest, and therefore most valuable, on the white slave market. In contrast, Scandinavian Americans expressed a more progressive viewpoint on the dangers of vice and threats to female virtue, giving their youth agency and holding them accountable for the ramifications of their decisions, regardless of sex, social, or marital status. Rather than viewing immigrants as victims of their own circumstance, the focus of this chapter employs a feminist approach to explore the enlightened approach of the Scandinavian American community toward female agency.

Europe's entrance into World War I in 1914 provides another example of an important moment of negotiating Scandinavian identity in light of renewed discrimination against immigrants, as chapter five details. During wartime many of America's newest people adopted hyphenated ethnic identities or became "100% American" in an effort to prove allegiance to the American cause and embrace patriotism. Publicly, Scandinavian Americans in Chicago made use of such identities appropriated by American popular culture, which painted their group as endlessly loyal as a means of protection while privately keeping one foot in Scandinavia. The American public rewarded Scandinavians for their loyalties to the American cause following the war, most notably in the world of business. Using the language of nativism to their advantage, a rising elite class of Scandinavian businessmen benefited from the advantages Americans offered through acculturation and acceptance, as chapter six details. Conscious constructions of race and ethnicity gave rise to the "new" Nordic man—a masculine image built upon contemporary ideals of Nordic physicality, which emphasized the ethnic and cultural importance of nature, leisure, and consumerism during the 1920s. These affluent Scandinavians achieved success in the American business world while maintaining ethnic traditions through membership in fraternal clubs, notably the Nordic Country Club. However, the success of the new Nordic man shifted with the onset of the Great Depression.

Finally, the epilogue looks at some of the contemporary results of Nordic white privilege in dialogues about race and revisits the term *Nordic* in hindsight—a term that becomes problematic when used in the wrong context following Hitler's reign of terror in constructing the perfect Aryan race. Due to contemporary political correctness and matters of social appropriateness, you would *hopefully* never again see an organization calling itself the Nordic Country Club. The content of these chapters provides all of the essential contributions to the social construction of what it meant to be Nordic, and therefore worthy of unquestioned white privilege in America during the twentieth century. The purpose of this study is to provide a deeper understanding of the Scandinavian American experience by placing its context within a larger body of scholarship on critical whiteness studies. Thus far, relatively little work has been done concerning Nordic whiteness in this area, and from this perspective the book makes an important contribution. Gender provides a second point of departure as it explicitly discusses the gendered aspects of the social benefits provided by Nordic white privilege looking at the experiences of Chicago's immigrants. By better understanding the process by which Scandinavians became a privileged immigrant group in Chicago, we can further address the problems encompassed in contemporary viewpoints toward immigration, race, and ethnicity and how white privilege underlines such issues.

CHAPTER 1

When Scandinavians Were Swarthy

Migration and the Origins
of "Scandinavian Stock" in Chicago

Since the eighteenth century in America, continental ancestry and the social construction of race have made for strange bedfellows. From this early period, Americans illustrated variegated notions of whiteness that progressed well into the next century. For instance, in 1751, Benjamin Franklin expressed his concerns over Pennsylvania becoming a "colony of aliens" resistant to anglicizing, yet understood differences between race and ethnicity by noting it was no easier than acquiring "our complexion." In his opinion, the number of "purely white people" was quite small. Scandinavians (specifically Swedes) were not a part of this imagined racial grouping but instead were of "swarthy complexion," along with the Spaniards, Italians, French, and Russians. In his viewpoint, only Germans and the English comprised the "principle body of white people on the face of the earth," whose numbers he wished were increased.[1] Franklin, like other community leaders, viewed Scandinavians like other western Europeans migrating in small numbers to colonial America as outsiders unwilling to assimilate, and he linked whiteness to ethnic practices. Such racial variegations would not make their way into the 1790 naturalization law whose inclusivity of all "free white persons" allowed for the significant European migrations of the nineteenth century.[2]

By the 1840s, as the bonds of whiteness persisted in contrast to nonwhiteness, new racial divisions emerged that separated nativists from the European immigrants they viewed as competition or as a threat to Protestant society.

American travelers like John Lewis Peyton were eager to participate in the spirit of manifest destiny and recorded their observations on racial difference, religion, and ethnic character in grandiose, romantic narratives on the experience of the American West. Chicago, which during the 1840s emerged as a major transportation hub and site of commercial industry, witnessed an influx of Yankee entrepreneurs, passers-through, and immigrants from Ireland, Germany, Scandinavia, and the Netherlands eager to participate in the new western market. In this primitive town of temporary migrants who most likely resembled each other, Yankee observers like Peyton employed racial fragmentation to illustrate class dominance over the varied newcomers. Rather than the Anglo-Saxon stock who occupied North Carolina, in November 1848 Peyton encountered Swedish and Danish men in the "grimy" city who appeared "wild, rough, almost savage looking" with unkempt beards, clenching pipes in their teeth.[3] Like most Americans of the mid–nineteenth century, Peyton did not view Scandinavians as Anglo-Saxon like himself, but instead as part of a larger conglomerate of European races separate from their racial stock. Yet, by 1898, an emerging discourse of "civilization" changed the conversation away from questions of fitness to focus instead on new understandings of racial preference.

From Chicago's incorporation as a city in 1837 until the aftermath of the Chicago fire, Americans did not believe that Scandinavians were part of a preferred race of people. Categorically, they were white, but their endeavors and priorities did not yet make them fit for entrance into civilized American society. It was not until physical anthropologists and sociologists manufactured phenotypes of race informed by the new imperialism and social Darwinism during the 1880s that such positive connotations created a racial advantage for Scandinavians. Such new racial thinking combined with societal fragility in the fire's aftermath resulted in American acceptance of Chicago's Scandinavian newcomers. In other words, Scandinavians did not become *white*, they became "civilized" in the minds of Americans.

"Civilization," Gender, and Understandings of Whiteness

By the 1890s, white, middle- and upper-class Americans derived power from a widely shared discourse on civilization. According to Gail Bederman, the term took on a specific set of meanings due to the work of social Darwinists, who were informed by race, gender, and millennial assumptions about human evolution. According to hegemonic groups, through evolution, man evolved from the primitive savage to become "civilized" Anglo-Saxons in an advanced state of racial perfection and intelligence. Civilized men embodied "manliness," or white racial perfection linked to moral capital, control, and achievement in the labor force. Similarly, civilized women were delicate, unfit for hard labor, and relegated to the Victorian home.[4] In America, civilization was built upon an Anglo-Saxon racial heritage derived from the first heroic, English settlers. Yet, as Matthew Frye Jacobson pointed out, the term "Anglo-Saxon" was the product of a "political revision of whiteness," which occurred between the 1840s and the 1860s in response to nativist rhetoric regarding immigration.[5] Americans of Anglo-Saxon, Protestant "stock" viewed themselves as the most civilized of the white races, fit for governing the lower Celtic and Teutonic masses whom they believed needed their help in assimilating to American customs. From a national perspective, negative perceptions of immigrants from Ireland and Germany combined with fears of overpopulation. This intense focus on Germans and the Irish overshadowed concerns over the "swarthy" masses of Scandinavians whom nativists viewed as predominantly rural and therefore of little concern to those living in the Atlantic cities.

To native Chicagoans, however, Scandinavians were just as problematic as the Irish and Germans. From the 1840s until the 1880s, all three groups contributed to massive urban and social problems, such as poverty, slovenly living conditions, crime, and unwillingness to assimilate. Americans initially categorized these newcomers to the Midwest just as any other group of new European immigrants: insular, un-American, and a potential economic draw upon tax-paying citizens. Yet, the origins of their race went unquestioned in these early years. Scandinavians saw themselves, and Americans saw the new immigrants, as categorically white, though not Anglo-Saxon. In order to build racial legitimacy, some Scandinavians, such as community leader Carl Hjalmar Lundquist, used the term "Scandinavian stock" to homogenize the group as "one people, speaking the same language, and having the same religion, and the same historical traditions."[6]

The term, which made use of the same racial lexicon of Americans who spoke of "Anglo-Saxon stock," brilliantly associated racial fitness with social achievement. Because Americans saw them as part of an unidentifiable mass of white European immigrants, Scandinavians had to prove their fitness for settlement and citizenship through this unified racial and ethnic identity. By employing a pan-Scandinavian framework, even the newest immigrants could attain social, economic, and political success through charitable contributions, Republicanism, and entrepreneurship. Between the 1840s and the 1880s in Chicago, Scandinavians went from "swarthy" to "civilized" through social construction of a racial and ethnic identity that unified those of "Scandinavian stock" into a group separate from the "other white" immigrants of Europe. The process by which

Figure 3: The venerable Swedish community leader, Carl Lundquist. Courtesy of F. M. Johnson Archives and Special Collections, North Park University, Chicago.

Scandinavians achieving civilized status was a deliberate, successful attempt to create positive connotations between this identity and its representative people. Twenty years before racial "scientists" and anthropologists assigned Scandinavians to the "Nordic race," Chicago's Scandinavians illustrated an autonomous discourse on their racial heritage through romantic, filiopietistic accounts of the past.[7]

American Viewpoints on Scandinavian and Nordic Identity

In 1893, the spirit of ethnic celebration on display at the World's Columbian Exposition inspired a number of Scandinavian American scholars to begin detailing the historical narrative of their ancestors' past in America. In an effort to illustrate that Scandinavians originated from a civilized race, the resulting overly wrought historiography venerated previous generations with unnecessary details of the heroic yesteryear. Several authors like Olaf N. Nelson took on a deliberate tone of ownership and authority in recounting romanticized details of the history of Scandinavian Americans. Written in English, Nelson's multivolume work, *History of the Scandinavians* and *Successful Scandinavians in the United States*, was the first scholarly study to recount the story of Chicago's pioneer Scandinavians in filiopietistic fashion. The importance of Nelson's work, however, lies within the growing discourse on civilization that emerged during the late nineteenth century as it was the only work that clung to a truly pan-Scandinavian framework.[8]

While other studies detailed the history of Swedes, Norwegians, and Danes apart from one another, Nelson's work incorporated useful demographic data on Scandinavian emigrants in Chicago and included personal commentary on community dialogue and Nordic identity. Further studies focused on the formation of Scandinavian communities across the Midwest, telling and re-telling the story of the noble beginnings of these pioneers while stressing their commitment to church and community building.[9] These and other studies that followed examined Chicago's earliest Scandinavians from the perspective of Scandinavians and did not place that framework within the larger context of an American perspective or within multiple migratory cycles.[10] Examining the period between the 1840s and the 1880s in Chicago from the dual perspective of Americans and Scandinavian migrants highlights the significance of a rela-tively short amount of time that elapsed between emigration into slum condi-tions and upward social mobility. Within forty years' time, Scandinavians in Chicago went from swarthy, destitute beggars to civilized, gainfully employed immigrant elite in spite of an epidemic and the Great Chicago Fire.

Between the 1840s and the 1880s, immigrants from northern and western Europe poured into a young midwestern town not nearly ready for the massive population influx, resulting in urban sprawl, crime, and disease. Scandinavians initially contributed to the graft, living in an immigrant neighborhood also occupied by the Irish, Germans, and Italians along the polluted Chicago River. With goals of upward social mobility, a number of Scandinavians acclimated to foreign social structures. They also maintained a dominant cultural pres-ence through ethnocentric business ventures, while some openly clashed with their immigrant neighbors not aligned with their cultural standards or Protes-tant beliefs. After the devastation of the fire in 1871, rather than drawing upon public funds, a number of middle-class Scandinavians moved away from the unrestricted, and therefore dangerous, enclaves and established Scandinavian-centric communities centered upon cultural institutions. In a world of uncer-tainty, Scandinavians stood out to Chicagoans as exceptional foreigners. To Americans, Scandinavians held moderate political views and took favorable positions on issues like temperance. Furthermore, they embraced a capitalist model that placed homeownership as an end goal in moving up the social lad-der and practiced *tasteful* ethnic and religious traditions. But most importantly, they had separated themselves both physically and metaphorically from other immigrant groups in Chicago and could racially blend into civilized American society.

One could also attribute Scandinavians' easy transition to shared political and social ties within Sweden, Norway, and Denmark from the early nineteenth century to the beginning of mass immigration. Similarities in language and culture helped Scandinavians forge a bond that formed the basis of Nordic identity before arrival in Chicago. This is not to say that the founders of the earliest communities were always on common ground or in agreement. There were significant divisions among secular and religious Scandinavians that played out in the newspapers and even in city streets. What brought many Scandinavians together was the benefits offered to them because of their shared Nordic whiteness. By and large, Scandinavians who stayed in Chicago for two or three years gained the ability to migrate out of the shanties of the ethnic slums into homeownership, skilled jobs, and better economic conditions because of the value of their collective whiteness. Nordics came together with the goal of helping each other acclimate to the conditions of a foreign society and culture, forging a Scandinavian American identity that did not require the loss of culture, social practice, or even language in private or public use. The comparative ease in their transition into a new culture also contributed to the origins of a Nordic identity that these immigrants shared across country of origin and city space. By the turn of the twentieth century, Americans who shared the city with their Scandinavian neighbors came to prefer their presence to other immigrant groups due to a growing discourse on Nordic and Scandinavian whiteness.

One important source of information on ethnic identities and behaviors of Northern Europeans that shaped American attitudes on racial characteristics was the genre of travel literature made popular during the nineteenth century. Travel narratives offer unique, though often biased perspectives on foreign people coming to terms with the encroachment of the western industrial world. Just as John Lewis Peyton wrote about the "savage" Scandinavians he saw on the cobbled streets of Chicago, American writer Bayard Taylor offered a contrasting look at Scandinavians at home in Northern Europe. In artistic, widely published accounts, Taylor wrote of the "fresh, strong, coarse, honest, healthy people" he encountered in the land of the midnight sun who were "a thoroughly happy and contented race." Taylor complained about their slowness, though he described Scandinavians in wholly positive terms as men with "long yellow hair, large noses and blue eyes" and women "with the rosiest of cheeks and the fullest development of body and limb."[11] To his American readers, Taylor expressed a fondness for Scandinavians as a simple, rural people who were literate, though not particularly intelligent, and definitely not prepared for life in American cities.

The popularity of later works including Ole Rolvaag's *Giants in the Earth*, Willa Cather's *O Pioneers*, and Vilhelm Moberg's *The Emigrants* reinforced the viewpoint that the pioneer Scandinavians of the 1840s and 1850s encountered difficulties in their attempts to integrate into an industrialized society. For the earlier waves of immigrants, these perceptions of Scandinavia and its people as largely rural were true. In 1801, over 90 percent of Norway's inhabitants lived in rural communities, and even by 1865, when the population witnessed significant growth, more than 80 percent came from agrarian backgrounds.[12] Similarly in Sweden and Denmark, the majority of the population lived in rural areas. Over the course of the nineteenth century, the population of Sweden was essentially rural; however, like much of Europe by the end of the nineteenth century, the number of inhabitants migrating to larger towns for the purpose of work increased. Many of the people who lived within farming communities led relatively simple lives with gender roles that mirrored American patterns of life. In the Swedish province of Dalsland, for example, rural Swedes lived in an environment greatly affected by the forces of nature, century-old traditions, and socioeconomic change that made the maintenance of time-honored family life increasingly difficult.[13] When many arrived in America, the inclination of some Scandinavians was to return to these simpler ways, even within urban regions.

If Americans considered Scandinavians to be a simple, rural people, and therefore not civilized, the reasons for which they came to America further contributed to such attitudes. Prior to 1860, many Europeans still considered emigration to America to be an unreasonable goal reserved only for the most desperate, or for those financially capable of making the long voyage. For most agrarian Europeans, seasonal migrations over short distances were much more common.[14] Women left home for opportunities on farms and in urban areas as domestics and factory workers, while men migrated for manual labor in construction work to establish modern infrastructures.[15] Scandinavians who desired greater opportunities closer to home opted for short-term migration, illustrating that those in rural communities proved to be more flexible and mobile than Americans expected of a simple society. Yet, within the context of separate spheres in Victorian America, because both men and women in Scandinavia had to enter the public sphere for work, they were not aligned with the manners of the civilized classes.

Scandinavian Viewpoints on Ethnic and Racial Identity

American writers like Peyton and Taylor contributed to a growing dialogue on the perceived behaviors and physicality of Scandinavians in the early nineteenth century; however, Scandinavians conceived of their racial and ethnic features much differently. Instead of focusing on stereotypical racial characteristics, a legacy of a Nordic heritage formed the basis of understandings of a shared ethnic and cultural identity. Despite the immensity of the Scandinavian land mass that measures more than 300,000 square miles, its countries had a comparatively small population of approximately seven million people. With over four million inhabitants, the population of Sweden comprised the majority of the Scandinavian population while Swedish culture and language dominated the larger identity of Northern Europe with six of seven million people speaking Swedish as their first language.[16] This cultural dominance formed the basis of the American tendency to regard all Scandinavians as Swedes. For those who were not of Swedish origin, the dominance of Swedish identity was a point of contention. Playful competition between Scandinavians often resulted in a debate over which nation-state proved to be of the "purest" Nordic birthright. Such competition had racial undertones, yet to Scandinavians the competition was more directly connected to Scandinavian ethnicity and pride in one's nation.

The statistical and narrative information contained in *Swedish Catalogue*, published by the Royal Swedish Commission for the World's Columbian Exposition, offers a window into the divide in ethnic and racial perceptions of Nordic racial hegemony by Scandinavians and Americans. Part national propaganda, the booklet stated that more than 99 percent of the population of Sweden consisted of "native" Swedes—those being of purely Nordic background and heritage.[17] To be a native of Sweden meant that one's ethnic character remained prevalent, yet the catalogue did not focus on race to the degree that American writers focused on the topic. As the booklet argued, because the Swedish people lived on the same land for at least 4,000 years, and during this time did not assimilate with other nationalities, the ethnic origins of Swedes were "far purer than any other existing outside of Scandinavia."[18] To Swedes, ethnic hegemony was a point of pride that could be used to distinguish Swedish-ness over the otherwise uniting bonds of the Nordic race.

Not all shared in this celebration of the culture and national identity of Sweden. Many Norwegians lamented over a failed attempt to reclaim Norwegian nationalism in the political break with Denmark and many feared Swedish cultural encroachment was near. For some Norwegians and Danes, living in the cultural shadow of Sweden was far too difficult to bear. Sweden's cultural hegemony only grew stronger due to the increasing influence of a massive migration of Swedes into Norway, Denmark, and America due to deteriorating economic circumstances. Despite competitive difficulties between Scandinavians, those who originated from these three Nordic countries shared strong historical bonds, especially those between Norwegians

26 · CHAPTER 1

and Danes who shared a legacy of a centuries-long political union. As early as the 1840s, literary and political movements known as Scandinavism and Nordism gained strength throughout the Nordic countries, paralleling similar unification movements in Germany and Italy at the time. Those who emphasized nationalist ideologies sought to unite the Scandinavian countries and people of Norway, Denmark, and Sweden through a shared political, cultural, and literary heritage.

One of the most recognizable symbols of Scandinavism in America was a masculinized focus on the importance and legacy of the Viking Age. Scandinavian men used romanticized representations of the brutal seafarers to forge a masculine bond of national identity, resulting in the establishment of hundreds of Scandinavian Viking fraternal clubs and organizations across America. This shared Viking heritage between Scandinavian men appears in stanzas of the Norwegian national anthem, "Ja, vi elsker dette landet" ("Yes, We Love This Country"). The lyrics, written in 1868 by celebrated Norwegian writer Bjørnstjerne Bjørnsen, declared that in the face of hardship, Norway, Sweden, and Denmark are "three brothers [who] stand united, and shall stand like that."[19] The imagery of the three brothers remained a personification of the masculine bonds of political and cultural Scandinavism evidenced in the Scandinavian social world of Chicago.[20] Though these currents of Nordic solidarity eventually suffered a loss, they did help to maintain a tradition of cooperation and influenced attitudes about pan-Scandinavian involvement at home and among Nordic immigrants in America. As Scandinavians flooded into the cities of America prior to the turn of the century, fraternal groups referred back to these earlier political and cultural ties from the homeland, using familiar symbols and representations of the Viking Age to create a sense of shared ethnic identity and, later, to prove their rightful place in America.

Reflecting upon the period of mass migration during the mid– to late nineteenth century, Scandinavian American writers expressed their concern over the potential loss of a collective Nordic heritage. As the population of Norway, Sweden, and Denmark spread throughout the world, many Scandinavians expressed anger over the selfish decisions of Scandinavians who chose to immigrate over maintaining shared ethnic bonds. In 1901, O. N. Nelson blamed the slovenly governments and "barren and unproductive" countries of Scandinavia for the massive loss of its inhabitants. Nelson contrasted the educated and industrious Scandinavians of the mid-1840s and 1850s with those pulled by the lure of American capitalism during the latter half of the nineteenth century. Such Scandinavian "travelers, tourists, and those who ruined their financial and social conditions in the old country" emigrated to America only to meet "the sufferings and horrors" that awaited them and, as Nelson described, "the barbarity of the American nation."[21] In hindsight, such capitalist goals benefited Scandinavians whose migration patterns would coincide with the growth of an American discourse that illustrated that they were they most "fit" of all Europeans for citizenship.

Other Scandinavian Americans described the substantial loss of Nordic people not as detrimental to ethnic unity but instead as a unique opportunity for international cultural expansion of Scandinavism, especially among youth. In the 1930s, Scandinavian American scholar Florence Edith Janson saw Nordic immigration in gendered, romanticized terms, painting a picture of young, lovestruck sons and daughters who were misunderstood by their parents. Young Scandinavian men, driven by their Viking cultural heritage, sought adventure in an unknown land while young Scandinavian women followed them to America.[22] The reasons for immigration were not motivated by employment or financial need, according to Janson, but instead by the desires of young people to leave home as a rite of passage. As an immigrant herself, Janson did acknowledge the draws of the labor market, albeit incorrectly and out of assumption, by remarking that the sex ratio of young Scandinavians started to balance out after 1870 as an effect of great opportunities for female employment. She remarked, "The young and comely peasant girl had discovered that domestic service in America was both more profitable and pleasanter. She came in numbers to equal her brothers."[23] While the ratio of male to female Scandinavian immigrants was always slightly tipped in favor of males, Janson's assumption illustrates the recognition that Nordic youth were making a substantial impression in America's industrial markets, similarly embracing the ideals of ascending the social ladder through work.

Scholars like O. N. Nelson had rightful reasons for concern over the loss of Scandinavian heritage. Between the 1850s and 1890s, Scandinavians expressed an immense desire to emigrate. Using Sweden as a representative example, table 1.1 reflects the vast numbers of Swedes alone who left home for either the United States or other countries between 1851 and 1890, according to the *Swedish Catalogue*. America, as a capitalist and democratic country, held the greatest pull for Scandinavians who envisioned easy employment and greatly improved wages upon arrival, in addition to the satisfactory living conditions their friends and relatives in America boasted about in letters home. These statistics reveal why the governments of the Scandinavian countries looked upon emigration as a substantial economic and cultural loss. Comparatively, of the 136,967 Swedes who went to countries other than the United States between 1851 and 1890, as many as 124,000 made short-distance migrations

28 · CHAPTER 1

Table 1.1: Emigration from Sweden to the United States and other countries, 1851–1890

Period	United States	Other Countries	Total
1851–60	14,865	2,035	16,900
1861–70	88,731	33,716	122,447
1871–80	101,169	49,100	150,269
1881–90	324,285	52,116	376,401
Total Loss in Population	529,050	136,967	666,017

Source: The Royal Swedish Commission for the World's Columbian Exposition, *World's Columbian Exposition 1893, Swedish Catalogue, Exhibits and Statistics*, 19–20.

to neighboring countries including Norway, Denmark, Finland, Russia, and Germany. Census researchers found that out of 100 Swedes who migrated to Norway, 47 later returned, while 55 out of every 100 who left for Denmark and 75 of every hundred who settled in Germany also returned to Sweden. However, only 6 percent of Swedes who left for America prior to 1920 eventually returned home for good.[24] These statistics were indicative of a larger loss of Scandinavians who permanently left home and created a point of contention for Nordic governments looking to retain their population and heritage.

Scandinavians in Chicago during the Early Nineteenth Century

Chicago, often referred to at this time as the greatest of all the western cities, became the center of the urban Midwest by the end of the nineteenth century. The city was the product of two historical processes effectuated by the War of 1812: the spread of the market revolution and the westward movement of a diverse population across the western frontier. In the 1830s, Yankee entrepreneurs saw vast potential in the incorporated town and through land speculation established its centrality as a transportation hub by land and water. As the United States expanded its territory westward, land speculators looked for immigrants best suited to tend to the land and transform it into commercial farming enterprises. American expansionists admired Scandinavians for their low rates of crime and pauperism, the readiness with which they took to farming and to becoming Americanized, and the commendable educational and religious training they received in Scandinavia.[25] Speculators desired immigrants whom they perceived as industrious with a firm understanding of the immense economic expansion that occurred in the United States. However, considerations such as race and ethnicity would also factor into these determinations of who could best blend into American society.

In comparison to other major immigrant groups during the mid- to late 1800s, such as the Irish and Germans, expansionists determined that it would be more favorable for those of unquestioned whiteness to populate the West. Between 1840 and 1860, over four million people entered the United States, the majority from Ireland and Germany, which thoroughly alarmed many native-born Americans. Such nativists blamed such immigrants for crime, political corruption, and drunkenness. In his famous 1834 Boston sermon, "A Plea for the West," the prominent Presbyterian minister Lyman Beecher warned that Catholics sought to subdue the "religious and political destiny" of Protestant Americans by dominating their prized western frontier.[26] In an amended version of his sermon, Beecher noted the particular concern of evangelical Protestants in Illinois, who longed to see its plains "covered with an industrious, an enterprising, and an intelligent population" of farmers, mechanics, teachers, but most importantly of "working men" who instilled "a manly confidence" in the region.[27]

As early as the 1860s, land speculators in Illinois, Wisconsin, Iowa, Minnesota, Maine, Kansas, Nebraska, and the Dakotas sought to attract Scandinavian emigrants as a means of employing such enterprising working men. Speculators for these states placed advertisements in the Scandinavian foreign-language press, often employing tactics such as prepaid transportation and lodging for the potential emigrant. Tickets were available to any place in the United States from the numerous agents scattered throughout the rural districts and the large cities of Scandinavia.[28] The most important component of this strategy was the companies' policy of reaching the potential emigrant in their home. Otherwise, many rural Scandinavians might not have even known of the vast possibilities for emigration or the potential for advancement in America. In comparison to Irish and German immigrants, native-born investors hoped to see the American West built by Scandinavians whom they hoped would stay and shape its white racial destiny.

Throughout the nineteenth century, the Midwest was a primary destination for immigrants from Northern and Western Europe, especially due to its expansive amount of fertile land. A comparison of the number of Scandinavians born in Europe with the total population of each state and territory in the United States in 1880 illustrates that Illinois and Minnesota had the largest population of Swedes, Minnesota the largest number of Norwegians, and Wisconsin the largest Danish population. Most notably, the combined foreign-born Scandinavian population of all three states reflected the largest numbers of Scandinavians living in the United States.[29] Into the 1890s, the number of Scandinavians in these three midwestern states continued to grow; however, immigrants were drawn more to urban areas where their friends and families settled, which would boost the population of Midwest cities like Chicago, Minneapolis, St. Paul, and Milwaukee. The earliest Scandinavian travelers viewed these cities as mere stopping points on their way to the rich farmlands of the Midwest; however, by the 1840s, the industrial and cultural opportunities of the city drew increasing numbers of immigrants who stayed.

In the 1840s, Chicago functioned as a dividing point for a stream of diverse immigrants drawn by the promise of industry and farming, but also those driven by a desire for religious freedom. Beginning in 1836, Scandinavian settlement began with a small group of Norwegian families who established a ramshackle area known as "the Sands" north of the Chicago River where it empties into Lake Michigan. Many of these early immigrants considered this community as a temporary "squatting" enclave; they built makeshift huts and shacks but did not actually own the land on which they stood.[30] Yet, not all early Scandinavians were destitute. Touted as "Chicago's first Swede," Olof Gottfrid Lange, who arrived in September 1838, is remembered as the epitome of Nordic success. An enterprising pharmacist and businessman, Lange witnessed the fevers and epidemics bred in Chicago's swampy and unhealthy environment and brought his traveling pharmacy by "chuck wagon" to the sick. Other prominent Scandinavians like Norwegian Iver Lawson invested in property, became involved in local politics, and established a vibrant foreign-language press. In fact, between Lange's arrival in 1838 and the first known immigrant group who arrived in the fall of 1846, Swedish immigration was comprised largely of young men of middle- or upper-class backgrounds.[31] The immigrants who arrived between the 1850s and 1860s gained more of a reputation as a group who caused more social issues than they solved.

When compared to nativist viewpoints on the Irish and Catholicism, it is particularly notable that religious dissenters like the so-called "Janssonites" did not produce more of an uproar in the American press. Due to positive American perceptions of Lutheranism, the utopian experiment of Erik Jansson is remembered as a footnote within the context of the Second Great Awakening rather than an event that had the potential to threaten American social norms. Between 1846 and 1850, a group of approximately 1,500 immigrants arrived from a rural and pietistic area in central Sweden as followers of the prophet Erik Jansson. Jansson's followers came to Chicago in 1846 on their way to Henry County, Illinois, seeking to establish a utopian, communist colony at Bishop's Hill. Another notable settler, Anders Larsson, broke apart from Jansson and eventually established the middle-class community of Swede Town. In the end, Jansson's "Plymouth Rock" turned into a failed, authoritarian experiment, which culminated in Jansson's murder at the hands of another colonist.[32] Ultimately the colony and its prophet received significant attention in Scandinavia and helped to further popularize migration to America for religious dissenters despite its eventual bankruptcy in 1861. By 1870, the ranks of Lutherans swelled rapidly with newcomers from Germany and Scandinavia, though the groups faced difficulties working with each other due to regional and cultural divisions. Lutheran immigrants spoke a wide range of languages, including German, Danish, Norwegian, Swedish, and Finnish while the more conservative synods lived in tightknit rural communities reminiscent of Garrison Keillor's fictional Lake Wobegon in "Prairie Home Companion."[33] Overall, the Lutheran model that built its positive reputation on piety, education, and religious commitment was aligned with American Protestant standards, superseding the insular nature of many of its churches.

As a means of elevating Nordic whiteness, early scholars like O. N. Nelson often romanticized the early history of the Scandinavian pioneers of the 1840s and sought to bury the shaded past of their more problematic experiences of the 1850s and 1860s. This era in Chicago's history is defined by the boosterism of land speculators who took part in a massive campaign to help expand the frontier town through extravagant predictions. Speculators hoped to attract the right kind of residents, particularly white and native-born, thereby inflating the price of property within the city as a means of elevating its worth. The rising cost of property significantly increased class divisions. The "older" generation of more settled Scandinavians had the means to purchase land and were able to move into better living conditions, while greenhorns were forced to settle in squatter communities such as "the Sands" of the seventh and eighth wards. If at any time in history, Scandinavians were destined to be forever branded a social consequence of immigration by native-born Americans, the period preceding the Civil War was that time. Scandinavian immigration during the 1850s and 1860s was heavily dominated by Norwegian men. During this time period, there was a ratio of 84 women to every 100 men, which was characteristic of other European immigrant groups in Chicago's years as a young city.[34] In the absence of women, this largely male, working-class ethnic community of temporary migrants often engaged in behaviors that more refined Chicagoans looked down upon.

The prevalence of ethnic and cultural heritage exhibited in this immigrant district on the north side of the mouth of the Chicago River signified a resistance to assimilate into American society. According to the 1850 census, a little over 8,000 people occupied this north side district with one-fourth born in Germany, one-fourth from Ireland, and around four hundred Norwegians.[35]

32 · CHAPTER 1

Each immigrant group denoted its neighborhood boundaries through language, businesses, community centers, and most importantly, churches, all within an uncomfortable proximity to one another. In 1849, the separatist State Church clergyman Gustaf Unonius and other religious dissenters built the Episcopal St. Ansgarius Church as the center of the district. In spite of its Episcopal background, about half of the enclave's Swedes belonged to the church, which symbolically represented the heart of the ethnic community.[36] Conflict quickly arose between Scandinavians and the Irish who, according to Gustaf Unonius, were problematic squatters who built up "one miserable hovel by the side of another," not recognizing the similar squatting practices of Scandinavians.[37] In fact, the Sands district quite possibly gained a more notorious reputation as a morally and geographically marginal neighborhood in comparison to the Kilgubben.

The residences and businesses of the Sands provided a masculine sphere that formed the basis of Chicago's bachelor culture where civilized American men were free to frequent some of the city's most infamous saloons, gambling houses, and brothels alongside Scandinavian working men. Chicago's newspapers warned of prostitutes, pimps, and thieves who preyed upon the innocent in the Sands region, just as many of Chicago's commercial magnates sought the pleasures of this masculine world.[38] To the immigrants who lived in the Sands, the area was indeed working-class, though rich with cultural expressions and institutions not recognized by the outsider. Many even saw the area as in danger of exploitation by the rich who secretly frequented its businesses. Far from the clear, natural, orderly existence that Scandinavian culture emphasized, this early neighborhood nevertheless prompted a nostalgic reflection upon the ethnic home, as many envisioned a future of upward mobility that could propel them from such temporary surroundings.

The Cholera Epidemic of 1849 to 1854

Harvey Warren Zorbaugh's study, *The Gold Coast and the Slum*, described the north side of the city during the 1850s as an area rife with contradictions and contrasts, "not only between the old and the new, but between wealth and poverty, vice and respectability, the native and the foreign, conventional and the bohemian, luxury and toil."[39] The contrasting elements in the title of his book referred to a juxtaposition of the affluent Gold Coast and the area known to Americans as the most vile and destitute area of Chicago, where Scandinavians and other ethnic groups lived. The dichotomy of the rich and the impoverished areas of Chicago that Zorbaugh's Progressive-era study offered is crucial to understanding the city's rapid expansion as the urban center of the Midwest. Areas that were recognized as "the slum" one day could become prime real estate the next. Prior to this shift, immigrants who remained on the north side did so out of necessity and not because of sentimental ties to the neighborhood. The "slum" areas were overcrowded and cheap, yet were within walking distance to work in various sawmills, tanneries, flour mills, breweries, and the McCormick Reaper Works.

When a cholera epidemic occurred between 1849 and 1854, Americans blamed immigrants of the slum for poor living conditions, overpopulation, and unhygienic practices, rather than its proximity to the Chicago River. Unable to avoid the proximity to the river, Scandinavians were unaware that their drinking water supplied by tainted wells could prove to be deadly. The rapid spread of cholera, one of the quickest to advance of fatal epidemic diseases, came as a direct effect of an archaic water and sewage system not equipped for a booming population. In 1850, one doctor, who was seemingly unaware of the public's opinion regarding the immigrant slum, expressed surprise over the ethnic background of immigrants affected by the epidemic. When he published his findings in 1850, he identified 44 deaths among the 332 Norwegians on the north side, going on to describe the immigrants residing there as "people in moderate circumstances, who lived as comfortably as the average Americans."[40] The doctor's findings reflected a broader American assumption that Nordic immigrants occupied a higher social status than other immigrant groups outside of the context of Chicago. As late as the 1890s, medical experts held onto confused ideas that miasmas, the foul-smelling vapors that arose from unclean substances, caused disease and that epidemics emerged only out of local conditions and were not contagious.[41] Yet, the epidemic affected all classes of Chicagoans but would cause the greatest death tolls among those in closest to the Chicago River, who were also the poorest. By 1851, one out of every 36 people in Chicago died of cholera, but among Norwegians, the number reached one out of seven.[42] The disease raged every year in the summer and fall when river conditions were at their worst, coinciding with the arrival of large groups of immigrants who contracted it on the ships. The early struggles that Norwegians, Swedes, and their neighbors endured during the cholera outbreak of 1849 through 1854 instilled within the community a longing for better living conditions, as well as a desire to improve upon the urban problems unique to Chicago.

Despite this desire, many Scandinavians still lived in abject poverty made even worse by an epidemic that resulted in burials of the dead at public expense, placing a large strain on tax-paying property owners. Scandinavian newspapers reported on the effects of the epidemic that left scores of widowers and widows with no support for their children, apart from the friends and relatives who could help them.[43] The St. Ansgarius death and burial records indicated that the death of its Swedish and Norwegian congregants cost the public treasury

34 · CHAPTER 1

an estimated $6,000, while the church was accountable for placing orphans of the dead with American families.[44] In September of 1850, Swedish traveler and noted author Fredrika Bremer depicted Swede Town and the Sands as "one of the most miserable and ugly" settlements that she had yet to see in America, where it was not uncommon to see Scandinavians begging in the streets.[45] Americans who sought to offer public assistance to Scandinavians expected to see clean and respectable homes but instead saw dirty beds, unappetizing food, and immigrants dressed in filthy clothes. Yet, Gustaf Unonius pointed out that appearances were not as they seemed. A number of Scandinavians took advantage of American perceptions of Scandinavians as a comparatively industrious immigrant group. He wrote that some were sinful drunks who continued begging even after their weeks' wages were sufficient enough to feed their families because ultimately they selfishly desired to drink.[46]

Despite such meager beginnings, Scandinavian immigrants began to make positive changes in the years following the cholera epidemic; these changes affected the public's perception of their character. Unexpected social and economic improvements came through a series of police raids in the squatter areas of Swede Town, Kilkubben, and the Sands during the 1850s after Mayor John Wentworth blamed the conditions of the area for the cholera epidemic. In an official decree, Wentworth ordered demolition of the area to make way for the construction of a larger industrial and residential center reserved for the wealthy.[47] One witness to the raid recalled that eighty-one police officers drove out squatters. Afterward, a work force demolished several hundred squatter homes in one day.[48] In reference to this event, Ulf Beijbom indicated that while it was not a unique occurrence for such squatter areas to be raided and torn down during this time, the eviction order for Scandinavians was most likely carried out in a more civilized manner than Kilkubben. Police reports indicated assumptions that the Scandinavian squatters would not fight back, while the police prepared for a fight from the Irish "thugs."[49] The city bought out the remaining few who owned their properties; these few reinvested in lower-priced lots just north of the original neighborhood. Rather than viewing their relocation as a negative experience, Scandinavians with money in hand saw the removal as a beneficial opportunity for upward mobility in a new area of the city.

Upward Mobility during the 1860s and 1870s

The period of the 1860s through the 1880s illustrates the most significant shift in American perspective toward Scandinavians due to their acculturation to American ideals, economic progress, and general desire to become part of civilized society. This acceptance came in light of a wave of immigrants who arrived between 1868 and 1870 that historians refer to as the most desperate of rural Scandinavians. Prior to the 1860s, the number of Scandinavians making the voyage to America was comparatively small. During this decade, famine gripped western and northern Europe, which affected the rural populations of Norway, Sweden, and Denmark the most. During these years, emigration became a necessity for survival and culminated in a destitute group of newcomers in America searching for viable farmland or economic opportunity. In the eyes of many Americans, this group of immigrants had the potential to become a draw upon society and was not readily welcomed. Counteracting this negative response, Scandinavians in Chicago took on a more active role during this time of crisis, devising ways to assist immigrants in the process of acculturation, while also maintaining ethnic traditions.

By 1860, due to the success of the railroad, Chicago had become the fourth largest city in America, providing business and labor opportunities for commerce in grain, lumber, and later meatpacking. The "best situated" Scandinavians initiated a move from the squatter enclaves of Swede Town and the Sands into three new ethnic areas of west, south, and north Chicago. After the 1860s, new Scandinavian immigrants first settled in Swede Town and the Sands, stayed for two or three years, and moved outward to the middle-class enclaves once they grew accustomed to American values and traditions.[50] Despite a dominant cultural presence, Scandinavians constituted a smaller population of inhabitants living in Swede Town by 1868. Germans accounted for 20 percent of the 21,000 occupants of the fifteenth ward compared to only 5 percent of Swedes and 4 percent of Norwegians.[51] Germans, who had some cultural and linguistic commonalities with Scandinavians, actively competed with their European neighbors for both space and acceptance in American society. Scandinavians and Germans shared a political history, and also were connected by their Lutheranism; such pious Lutherans looked down upon Germans who built their businesses on brewing beer. Perhaps the thought that some Americans considered Germans and Scandinavians to be of a preferred racial stock of immigrants equally drove such competition.

In spite of their accommodation to American culture for matters of personal benefit, Scandinavians remained insular in their activities, rarely venturing outside of their neighborhoods other than for work. One community leader, Carl Hjalmar Lundquist, later recounted how early Swedes were particularly stubborn in their efforts to "become" American. Instead, Americans considered them as "green" immigrants who had knowledge of only their own language. Due to their stubbornness and ignorance, some Americans referred to Swedish immigrants as "the damned Swedes"[52] Despite Scandinavians' unwillingness to assimilate into American life, Americans did not regard them as necessarily foreign or backward. Their racial and ethnic character was in stark contrast to those whom some considered to be wholly unable to assimilate, such as Italian or Irish immigrants. Even if Scandinavians did not fully blend into American culture, they exhibited appropriate social behaviors and attended Christian churches, and Americans did not consider their ethnic practices to be unappealing or entirely out of step with American values. Differences in attitude between religious and secular Scandinavians with regard to cultural and ethnic issues played out in the newly established Scandinavian language press during the 1850s and 1860s.

The period following the Civil War marked an essential moment in the establishment of a prominent Scandinavian journalistic tradition in Chicago. The Scandinavian foreign-language press played a vital role in providing immigrants with the tools needed to navigate their new environment in Chicago while connecting them to events from home. The first Swedish American newspaper, *Hemlandet*, emerged out of Galesburg, Illinois, in 1855 and became the leading voice of the Augustana Synod. *Hemlandet* took a revivalist perspective in its early years, condemning worldly pleasures, cultural events, and alcohol consumption and contributed to a strong Lutheran-Republican stance among midwestern Swedes.[53] All of the early newspapers observed immigration and functioned as a voice for Scandinavians. During the 1860s, a spate of more progressive, freethinking, and theologically neutral papers like *Svenska Amerikanaren*, *Svenska Tribunen*, and *Skandinaven* began publication. This divide in the stance of the press reflected similar cultural, ethnic, political, and religious divides in the community. Regardless of ideological stance, the Scandinavian foreign-language press wielded real influence and power over the thoughts and opinions of its readers.

During the late 1860s, Scandinavians, like other nationalities in Chicago, established social assistance programs, even in neighborhoods where they were not the dominant ethnic group. Scandinavian men established a number of fraternal groups during this era in order to give assistance to new immigrants and to build a sense of masculine camaraderie. Swedes, Danes, and Norwegians established secular associations like the Svea, Nora, and Dana societies out of need but also pressure from church-oriented groups to assist the destitute immigrants of the famine years. The groups employed Viking symbols in order to cultivate an identity that reflected upon the heritage of the heroic Norse age. Such societies also appealed to a desire to promote and preserve Scandinavian heritage in a foreign land. Scandinavian secular societies brought men and women together, albeit separately, to embrace cultural traditions and emphasize the retention of language, literary, and musical traditions, and to address the need to contribute to American society. A notice in *Skandinaven* from October 1869 invited men in the community to meet for "discussing with one another how best to encourage joint action and harmony among the Nordic sister peoples in this place." Yet, often unification attempts were too good to be true and resulted in more of what he referred to as a "love-hate" relationship that was doomed to fail.[54] These earlier efforts to unify Scandinavians under one cause proved to be essential in the aftermath of one of the greatest tragedies to affect the city.

The Scandinavian Response to the Great Chicago Fire of 1871

Before one of the worst disasters in Chicago's history occurred, Scandinavians were making significant contributions to Chicago's cultural and economic future. Chicago was a destination on the minds of many Scandinavians who learned of the culture of Swede Town from newspapers like *Hemlandet*, *Skandinaven*, and *Svenska Amerikanaren* sent by relatives in Chicago. In the Swedish, Norwegian, and Danish countryside, Chicago-trained emigrant agents assisted rural immigrants on what to expect when they reached the Midwestern city, while thousands of urban intellectuals and "better-situated" people flocked to Chicago. A number of these great thinkers later built newspaper and book publishing centers, schools, hospitals, societies, libraries, and theaters during the late nineteenth century.[55] From all outward appearances, it looked as though Scandinavian settlers were turning a corner in regard to assimilating to American customs and becoming a civilized group.

Following a particularly dry summer, the city built mostly from wood was poised on the edge of disaster in early October 1871. As legend has it, the Great Chicago Fire ignited when an Irish woman's cow kicked over a lantern she had failed to bring in after her milking. The story, most likely created by a journalist to point blame at the deplorable conditions of immigrant communities like the O'Leary's, heightened ethnic tensions aimed at the Irish in Chicago as Chicagoans looked for a scapegoat to blame.[56] Ethnic tensions also simmered after such immigrant communities suffered the greatest amount of loss. By several accounts, Scandinavians were among the immigrants hardest hit by the fire. According to one observer, of the 50,000 people affected by the fire, over 10,000 were Scandinavian.[57] Assumed among the dead were several bodies located amid the smoldering debris, according to the location and missing persons reports filed by families.[58] The majority of those who lived within the area lost their homes and cultural institutions as five Swedish newspapers and a number of Swedish and Norwegian churches burned in the fire. In the aftermath of one of the biggest urban catastrophes of the time, panicked native-born Americans directed their blame at immigrants for the incident in a moment of tension that proved beneficial for Scandinavians.

Chicagoans faced the harsh reality of the need to rebuild a destroyed city but also expressed concern over the toppled social hierarchies that previously maintained civic order. As a whole, most residents of Chicago struggled to reestablish stable city structures and public relations after the fire. In the days following the fire, a clamor for postfire aid resonated across all of Chicago's social classes. Such citizens' efforts to rebuild the city illustrated the foundations of Progressivism in Chicago. Citizens with a strong vision of postfire Chicago promoted concepts of urban life and solid government rooted in social justice, welfare, and responsiveness to the everyday needs of all Chicago citizens.[59] Like later Progressive reformers, fire relief coalitions drew largely middle- and upper-class women in assisting the destitute. Reflecting the class divisions of such aid groups like the Chicago Relief and Aid Society, those offering aid tended to be more sympathetic and generous to the needs of those who were not completely dependent upon the city for aid prior to the fire.[60] Prior to the fire, Scandinavians largely fell into this category. A large portion owned properties and businesses, held reliable jobs, and were upstanding members of society. Even though reports indicated that Scandinavians were among those most affected by the fire, very few accepted or received aid between 1871 and 1873. Only 3,624 Swedes, Norwegians, and Danes received aid out of an estimated 50,000 Scandinavians citywide.[61]

Scandinavian historians of this era stereotyped their own people as having a tendency for stubbornness, especially in regard to charity. However, the real reason that so few received aid is attributed to a strong network of Scandinavian benevolent societies. Scandinavians also made a positive impression on skeptical Americans following the fire. On the north side, German immigrants became particularly vocal in the aftermath of the fire about their opposition to fireproof restrictions. Such restrictions prevented Chicagoans from rebuilding their homes out of wood by requiring expensive brick and concrete construction. While Germans vocalized their concern over the ban as a threat to their dreams of home ownership, Scandinavians acted collectively to either rebuild their homes out of the required materials in the same neighborhood or quietly moved outside the city limits so they could build homes out of materials they could afford.[62] Just as they had during the squatter raids of the 1850s, rather than fighting back against city authorities, Scandinavians followed the regulations put into place. By doing so, Scandinavians positively reflected self-restraint as an ethnic group that was willing to comply with city officials, thereby gaining favorable recognition from Americans for their actions.

After the fire, Progressive reformers directly attributed the lures of industry to the problems of a burgeoning population and overcrowding within Chicago's city limits. Progressives recognized they would be unsuccessful in attempting to do away with the lure of capitalism but instead could promote a more healthy way of city living. A group of middle-class Chicago citizens responded to this concern by using the nuclear family and household as a refuge from the "unsettling forces of city life." Sociologist Richard Sennett observed this process in the west-side suburb of Union Park, which he analyzed as an American family culture steeped in fear after the fire. Native-born Chicagoans who moved to Union Park responded to the fire's devastation by moving away from the city and sacrificing the sociability of inner-city neighborhoods for the privacy and safety of the American suburbs.[63] Instead of retreating to what was left of their insular neighborhoods, many Scandinavians connected with Chicago's native-born population to contribute to the effort of rebuilding Chicago.

Where Scandinavians demonstrated particular brilliance was in the contributions of their men to the construction industry. Scandinavian-run construction companies received recognition in American newspapers for their symbolic importance in rebuilding the industrial metropolis. After the fire, most newspaper stories sensationalized the event and used emotion to appeal to their readers; however, one story focused more analytically on the fire's causes and implications. Frederick Law Olmsted, America's most renowned landscape architect of the late nineteenth and early twentieth century, wrote an article for *The Nation* in November 1871 commenting on the satisfactory conduct of ethnic workingmen in Chicago following the fire. Given the circumstances, Olmsted admitted his expectation that laborers employed to rebuild the city would be in a state of labor unrest. Yet, this "unusual proportion" of Germans, Swedes, and Norwegians he spoke with commanded good wages, which could help them to rebuild their own homes. Furthermore, the fire created a need for additional construction workers, preferably from Scandinavia. In this leftist newspaper, Olmsted called upon Americans who placed blame on "incendiaries" for the fire, or immigrants, to take a second look at the event and the progress that certain ethnic groups like Scandinavians had accomplished.[64] During this period, the construction of iconic buildings like the Monon and Manhattan Buildings marked Chicago's entrance into the modern era as a major metropolis built by Scandinavian men with big shoulders.

In spite of the fire, the squatter settlement of Swede Town remained as the starting point for incoming Scandinavian immigrants, though the period between 1871 and the early 1900s was one of upward social mobility and exodus away from the Chicago River district. By the 1880s, a pronounced shift in the influx of immigrants coming from southern and eastern Europe contributed to great tension between "old" and "new" immigrants in Chicago vying for social standing. Middle-class Scandinavians rebuilt their homes and businesses out of brick in higher-priced lots and moved the location of ethnic restaurants, clubs, and various businesses grounded in Nordic culture to the growing north-, south-, and west-side enclaves. Another significant reason for their inner-city migration was escalating tensions with Italians, especially Sicilians, involving cultural markers of whiteness. To Scandinavians, Italian immigrants were a detriment to the progress of their community, driving down property costs because of their reputation for filth and damage to property. Non-northern European and non-Protestant groups combined with slum deterioration to speed up the process of "evacuation" for Scandinavian "greenhorns" who came into direct confrontation with "foreign folks," according to one account.[65] The growing influence of Catholicism in the Italian community, as well as tense interactions with Polish immigrants and African Americans, made getting along with diverse groups impossible. Lutheran beliefs, as well as an awareness of the value of their Nordic whiteness and interconnected social standing, were at the center of such ethnic tensions by the end of the nineteenth century.

The ethnic conflict between Scandinavians and Italians who occupied the Chicago River district resulted in violence in May 1900 when one Swedish group attempted to demonstrate social hegemony over their shared neighborhood. An article in *Skandinaven* detailed the anti-Italian rhetoric over a property dispute involving Swedish-owned buildings on Milton Avenue in an area called "Little Hell." In the dispute, Swedish business owners decried the substantial drop on property value over just two years' time when lots in the neighborhood had fallen from $120 a foot to $70. The property owners held a meeting to discuss methods to combat the Italian influx, concluding that by raising the rent for all "less desirable tenants," the group would force Italians to move away. The tone of the article was suggestive of ethnic and racial stereotypes, positing that the "Southerners" were unhygienic, that they caused property damage to the cedar sidewalks, and they opened "junk shops" that "contaminated" the neighborhood air. In retaliation, a group of Italians rented out the Swedes' own Svea Hall to hold an anti-Swedish gathering. During the tense meeting, Italians leveled angry threats against the Swedes, with one member concluding: "if our antagonists are not willing to arrange the matter peacefully, then we shall find other ways to protect our rights."[66] The tension between the two groups culminated in a series of street fights between young Swedish and Italian men. An article in *Svenska Nyheter* detailed how the Irish, despite their shared religious beliefs with Italians, joined the side of the "Lutheran Swedes."[67] In an effort to become "old stock" and even civilized like Scandinavians, the Irish knew they would have to join in their support for better material conditions if the community were to survive. In the end, the help of the Irish benefited their claims to whiteness, yet by 1903, Little Sicily replaced Swede Town due to the upward mobility and subsequent exodus of Scandinavians away from the "slum."

Chicago's Scandinavians Become "Civilized"

By the 1880s, Americans had begun to consider Scandinavians living in Chicago as a civilized class of immigrants due to their shared attitudes toward the "uncivilized" masses who threatened the social fabric of the city. In a period before popular racial classifications, Scandinavians were not yet "old stock" like Americans, but they were very close to it. Native-born Chicagoans considered Scandinavians a people who owned their property, were generally pious, occupied prominent levels of business and industry, and exhibited quaint, rather than offensive, cultural traditions. As a white, Protestant, and successful group of individuals, Scandinavians were embraced as a group Americans expected to easily assimilate to their values, traditions, and institutions. Scandinavian historians proudly reminisced about these early "civilized" immigrants, boasting that no other American city could claim as many successful Scandinavian businessmen as the Illinois metropolis.[68] Scandinavians shrewdly achieved success in the construction industry following the fire, as well as in skilled positions. Men worked as lawyers, businessmen, journalists, and other positions that required an education, which further contributed to their positive reception in Chicago. Laborers were commonplace; however, upper-class Scandinavian immigrants outshadowed those in the lower classes. In comparison to unskilled laborers, a significant number of skilled and well-paid Scandinavian men had become naturalized American citizens (37 percent of businessmen and 33 percent of professionals), further contributing to their positive image.[69] As early as the 1870s, many Scandinavians gained the means to briefly return home. A typical sight was the "swaggering" Scandinavian American man who put on the airs of a civilized American, wearing a bowler hat and Elgin watch, and exhibiting superficial city manners. These Scandinavians presented life in Chicago as the measure of a man of the world.[70] The reality, however, for new Scandinavian immigrants to Chicago was that they too would have to work from the bottom up. However, these immigrants experienced a far more beneficial path to success in comparison to other new immigrants, especially those from southern and eastern Europe.

During the peak years of 1879 and 1893, the identity of new Scandinavian immigrants shifted drastically from the rural farmer to the young, single immigrant in search of industrial work. Drawn by the promise of jobs in manufacturing and domestic service and pushed by a continued economic depression and poor conditions at home, these younger immigrants made up what became the largest group of Scandinavians to arrive in the United States. In 1879, 7,313 males and 3,686 females immigrated to the United States from Sweden alone (double the number of immigrants from the previous year), but by 1892, those figures reached 24,684 males and 17,161 females.[71] While the number of male immigrants always outnumbered females, this period saw an increase in single Scandinavian women who immigrated to America, specifically Chicago, for the purpose of work. In comparison to other European immigrants during this era, Scandinavians were the fourth largest group behind German, English, and Irish immigrants, until migration patterns shifted around the turn of the century with the heavy influx of southern and eastern Europeans. Until the early 1900s, new Scandinavian immigrants first lived in the Chicago River district "slum," which exhibited a stark ethnocentric division from other neighborhood groups. Upwardly mobile Scandinavians viewed such "greenhorns" as naturally insular, holding on to ties of language, culture, and country in deliberate ways. As one community leader reminisced, such new immigrants experienced easy acculturation to American values, exhibiting intelligent economic and business decisions and using their Nordic heritage as a complement to their ethnic identity.[72]

The 1880s marked a turning point as nearly three-quarters of Chicago's Scandinavian Americans lived in the middle-class township of Lakeview. *The Chicago Land Use Survey* estimated that Scandinavians built 43 percent of all homes in Lakeview during a period of mass movement into the area from 1880 to 1884.[73] American sociologist Harvey Warren Zorbaugh noted in *The Gold Coast and the Slum* that Scandinavian Americans were a remarkable ethnic group because they had found a way to escape the "slum" conditions other immigrants could not. Even though Lakeview exhibited a distinctively ethnic character, made up of businesses and social clubs that catered to Scandinavian clientele, Zorbaugh noted that Lakeview Township had "begun to share with the city a quite cosmopolitan character."[74] The café served as a central venue for scholarly lectures and provided a vital point of distribution for Scandinavian newspapers, while many new immigrants used the café as their temporary mailing address until they found permanent residence.[75] In addition to cafés and libraries, Scandinavians established eleven fraternal lodges in Lakeview and built more than 72 churches and over 130 secular clubs throughout the city.[76] Lakeview continued its development during the 1880s, and by 1889 the city annexed the rural suburb of Andersonville as part of an effort to modernize the city in preparation for the World's Columbian Exposition. As further means of modernization, the city opened the elevated train in 1892, which became instrumental in expanding opportunities for work for Scandinavians employed outside of Lakeview.

Such means of transportation allowed for Scandinavian women to experience the elite world of gilded-age moguls through their work as domestic servants, while retaining the cultural and ethnic values of home.

Between the 1860s and the 1880s, Scandinavians seeking home ownership migrated away from Swede Town to the suburban regions of west and south Chicago. Areas such as Humboldt Park, Hyde Park, Armour Square, and Englewood drew Scandinavians who converted farmland into bustling residential and commercial centers. During this period, a significant Scandinavian ethnic presence flourished in these enclaves as residents established fraternal lodges, benevolent and singing societies, athletic clubs, and theaters in addition to eight Swedish-language daily or weekly newspapers.[77] Scandinavian residents on the south and west sides of Chicago built new homes, improved their living conditions, and established ethnic centers, which resulted in an increase in property values over time. In these enclaves, Scandinavians occupied space along with diverse ethnic groups, including Poles, Germans, Irish, and Bohemians who could afford such high property rates. Such high prices purposefully kept out the "undesirables" who could not afford to live there and helped to maintain the high aesthetic standards that Scandinavians desired in their communities and took action to protect when standards fell below expectation.

In the 1880s, Swedes in Chicago's south-side neighborhood of Armour Square expressed similar concern for their community's health. For years Armour Square's Swedish community exhibited concern as they watched industries and the stockyards district pollute the air and water supply. Many of the area's Swedes previously endured the cholera and typhoid fever epidemics during the second half of the nineteenth century, all of which scientists linked to the conditions of the river. Aspects of Scandinavian culture that emphasized cleanliness and physical health contributed to a desire for clean living in Chicago. Such physical surroundings were nearly impossible to come by in Chicago's inner city. In this sense, the Chicago River stood as a symbol of the downfalls of urban living for Scandinavians. The waste products of Chicago's factories polluted the river, making it aesthetically unpleasant and contributed to a number of public health issues. In 1887, when civil engineers devised a plan to reverse the flow of the Chicago River away from Lake Michigan rather than directly into it, a number of Scandinavians warmly received the strategy. By the turn of the century when civil engineers successfully reversed the river, many Scandinavians already attained the means to move away from the stench of the River and downtown area.[78] Nevertheless, their emphasis on public health in Chicago drew praise from many Americans for their focus on health and the physical structure of the city they shared.

Figure 4: An undated photograph of Pauline Hegborn Nelson taken when she was a young woman. Courtesy of F. M. Johnson Archives and Special Collections, North Park University, Chicago.

Chicago's west-side enclave was similarly indicative of upwardly mobile Scandinavians who cared about their community surroundings and fostered good relations with neighboring ethnic groups. The memoirs of Pauline Nelson Hegborn, a second-generation Swedish American who lived on the west side of Chicago are indicative of a Scandinavian family who achieved success in the city as foreign-born ethnics.

Her parents immigrated to the United States as children along with their families and the two met in Chicago's suburban region as young laborers. Pauline's father became involved in building construction following the fire and her mother worked as a domestic servant in Danville, Illinois. Upon marriage, the two settled on Chicago's west side after deciding that there would be more opportunity for them in the city where they wished to raise a family. Their three daughters were born during the 1880s and 1890s and the family lived together in a modest brick home the family owned.[79]

Although Pauline was a child at the time, she observed the diversity of her neighborhood, noting that Irish, German, Swedish, and Norwegian immigrants all coexisted within the same city space. Yet, even through the eyes of child, it was clear that ethnic divisions remained, especially in regard to the Irish families who shared the neighborhood. Interactions between Irish and Scandinavians were "congenial"; however, the patrol wagon visited one of their neighbors, an Irish family by the name of O'Leary, at least once a week.[80] The Nelsons faced their fair share of struggles during this time, much like any other immigrant group, yet they made intelligent financial decisions and did not rely upon others for help. Nelson recalled that her family, as well as many people within the neighborhood, took in boarders when times were tough.[81] This common practice contributed to a variety of other tactics used by Scandinavians to achieve financial independence. In the next century, more of Chicago's Scandinavians came to realize the goals of home ownership and social mobility.

By the 1890s, the Scandinavian foreign-born population of Chicago had grown to almost 72,000 people (43,032 Swedes, 21,835 Norwegians, and 7,087 Danes) or 6 percent of Chicago's entire population. Distance separated the three groups, though ethnic affiliations and cultural practices interconnected them.[82] To its earliest settlers, Chicago was a dirty and barren environment and not the kind of place where a family would want to establish a home separated from the farms and fields of the Midwest. During the earliest waves of nineteenth-century immigration from northern Europe, Chicago's native-born population viewed Scandinavians with disdain as a potential draw upon the new city, just like any other immigrant at the time. Between the 1840s and the 1880s, Chicago's Scandinavians proved their worth as citizens through labor, property ownership and care, and positive behaviors that connected to an identity as good, Republican Lutherans. A number of early historians argued that, by the 1880s, Scandinavians in Chicago had become assimilated and fully Americanized; however, this was not the case.[83] Instead, by examining both Scandinavian and American perspectives, it is clear that Scandinavians exhibited a proclivity for public relations but also for the bonds of whiteness that tied the groups together. Into the twentieth century a growing number of Scandinavians remained in Chicago and built communities in the image of Nordic villages and towns centered upon cultural institutions viewed as appropriate and civilized—not offensive—by Americans.

On the eve of the World's Columbian Exposition of 1893, Scandinavians were decidedly in a more favorable position than when travelers first encountered them in the young city during the 1840s. Between the 1860s and the 1880s, many of the first settlers migrated away from the early "slum" of downtown, financed the construction of homes and businesses, and maintained an aesthetic of ethnic traditions and community-centered commerce. Scandinavians were always racially white, but now they occupied the same racial status as "civilized" Americans and were worthy of American citizenship. The World's Columbian

Exposition began during the same era that witnessed the emergence of Victorian anthropology, scientific racism, Social Darwinism, and other forms of race "science." As the next chapter discusses, such racist discourse positioned Scandinavians at the apex of an imagined racial hierarchy as the Nordic race. The basis of such discourse underlined the displays of the Exposition and set the stage for a much broader discussion on European immigrants, racial "fitness," and the privileges granted by way of whiteness. This new discussion on race and ethnicity displayed at the exposition reached millions of fairgoers, who after the fair began to reconsider racial fitness and citizenship in an era of shifting immigration patterns. During the 1890s and into the 1900s, anthropological and scientific findings on the races of Europe, which linked behaviors to racial features, reached the public through the press. This dialogue, coupled with a shift in gendered societal roles for men and women, resulted in a beneficial treatment of Nordics in Chicago and throughout America. By the twentieth century, "science" granted such fortunate individuals with blonde hair, blue eyes, and Nordic racial "stock" a new measure of white privilege.

CHAPTER 2

Vikings and Dumb Blondes

The Construction of American Discourse on Nordic and Scandinavian Whiteness

The late nineteenth and early twentieth century marked an important period in the "fracturing of whiteness" by anthropologists, sociologists, and pseudoscientists as a means of denoting cultural and physical difference between white races in America.[1] The racial hierarchy constructed by these writers created distinct, unmovable categories of race, though differences in interpretation and terminology led to confusion and messiness, especially in the press and in American culture. Americans and European ethnics understood these racial categories in completely different ways based on what bestowed their group with the greatest structural advantage, especially when addressing the apex of the hierarchy: the so-called "Nordic" race. The popular slapstick film series of the 1910s, *Sweedie, The Swedish Maid*, provides significant evidence of the complicated nature of whiteness.

The character of Sweedie was a product of discourse on whiteness and gender roles in Chicago during the early twentieth century and formed the basis of a lasting stereotype of Scandinavian ethnic identity. In the early days of silent film, productions distinguished between Nordicism, which connoted race in a biological sense, and Scandinavianism, which included ethnic and cultural differences such as language, cultural norms, gender roles, and class. According to film historian Arne Lunde, Nordic characters were mythical, essential, and "natural," yet portrayals of Scandinavian hyper-whiteness in film were far different from portrayals of Scandinavians in American life.[2] The *Sweedie* film series, produced by the Essanay Studio, included twenty-nine comedic short films between 1914

Figure 5: Wallace Beery dressed in drag for *Sweedie's Hero*, 1915. Courtesy of Wikimedia Commons.

Figure 6: Artist W. H. Southwick's 1914 rendition of Wallace Beery that reflects his most famous role as Sweedie. Courtesy of Wikimedia Commons.

and 1916 and featured American actor Wallace Beery. According to the established hierarchy of race, Nordic men and women now occupied a category of race privilege, yet American and immigrant audiences saw something much different in the *Sweedie* films shown at Chicago's movie palaces. While such film representations helped their cause, Scandinavians were still immigrants and therefore had to appropriate American codes of whiteness in order to achieve acceptance.

The most significant element of the films was that a male actor dressed in drag—an intentional gag meant to defeminize Swedish women specifically and domestic servants generally—played the title character. Domestics constituted the classic "women adrift" that most middle-class Progressives feared. While they did not occupy a homogeneous group, women living "adrift" were mostly young, single, independent wage earners who lived apart from their families and acted out of their assigned place in society.[3] The American approach of addressing the problem of women living "adrift" was to ridicule, stereotype, and place blame on the choices of particular immigrant women for living outside of social norms. To American audiences, Sweedie was a caricature of the typical Scandinavian domestic servant of the early twentieth century: she was stupid, physically repugnant, and hardworking to a fault. She resisted Americanization in dress and manner, acting in childish and impulsive ways that one might interpret as a threat to the patriarchal order or as dangerous.[4] What is more significant, however, is the manner in which her character upended the narrative on the intelligent white man par excellence of the Nordic race and contributed to confusion over this cultural hierarchy.[5]

The practice of stereotyping European immigrants was a means by which Americans came to terms with the massive waves of immigration during the early twentieth century. Even before Essanay Studios popularized Sweedie, the stereotypical "Swedish" maid was engrained in American culture. Such jokes even began to make national headlines.[6] The *New York Times* featured one such farce where the residents of Englewood, New Jersey, were treated to a match between the Women's Club and a rival team of eighteen "girls" comprised of well-known local amateur baseball players. Receiving the biggest laugh, however, was a player dressed in a yellow wig tied up with a green ribbon. According to the article, "a big Swedish maid with flaxen locks," played by a man with a big mustache was said to have "brazenly smoked cigars" in an effort to play

Figure 7: Actor Wallace Beery in his portrayal of "Sweedie the Swedish Maid," brazenly smoking a cigar. Courtesy of Wikimedia Commons.

50 • CHAPTER 2

up the gag for the crowd. Such common jokes of the day made use of robust masculinity to play upon the absurdity of cultural norms and cross-dressing.[7]

The Sweedie films used similar gaffs as a means of emphasizing stereotypes of both race and gender. In *Sweedie Learns to Swim*, Beery wore a bathing costume in order to emphasize his muscular arms and legs, further masculinizing the character. When his bathing companion, a woman also dressed in drag, tries to lure Sweedie into the waves, she swats "him" away and braves it alone, taking short, ridiculous jumps into the surf. While Sweedie played upon American cultural stereotypes formed around the "dumb blonde" persona of the "Swedish" maid, the fact that "her" physicality did not mirror this persona is indicative of the expressed confusion over whiteness during the early twentieth century. The beautiful and later sexualized portrayals of the essentialized Nordic woman in American film and culture quickly overshadowed the mannish, brunette, and bulky difference of Sweedie's character. American portrayals of Scandinavian men and women as clumsy, rural, and childish worked in their favor and helped to further elevate their race. Rather than "dangerous" or "deviant" like other European immigrants, to Americans Scandinavians were innocuous while their whiteness helped to elevate their social status.

Scandinavians, Whiteness, and Gender in American Culture

Between the 1850s and the 1890s, physical anthropologists, race "scientists," and sociologists created a discourse on the desired traits of immigrants from Northern and Western Europe. Newspaper editors and popular culture references expounded upon this hierarchy of race and convinced Americans that certain physical markers, especially blonde hair and blue eyes, could help identify all Scandinavians. Their perceived racial features distinguished Nordics from all other immigrant groups, which many used to their advantage to elevate their racial status.[8] In 1893, the nation's leading "race" scholars put their findings on display at the World's Columbian Exposition, which became an event of immense cultural importance to America as it neared the turn of the century. Between May and October 1893, Chicago's Exposition hosted 27 million international visitors who learned about the cultures, values, and institutions of the world on display at the fair.[9] At the time, Americans operated under theoretical perspectives on race, such as social Darwinism, which posited that only the "strong" will survive, and the strong should allow the "weak" to die off. The language of empire and civilization drove middle-class notions of a racial hierarchy where fitness equated wealth, power, and success. On display at the fair, American scholars offered a variety of displays that both embraced and expanded upon such racial thinking to more directly identify an ideal physicality of race.

From 1893 on, Nordic whiteness took on a marked importance within the American and Scandinavian discourse on race. The World's Columbian Exposition exposed its visitors to a variety of ideas on race and whiteness through displays intended to draw in viewers. At Norway's pavilion, modeled after a stave church from the twelfth century, visitors viewed ethnographic exhibits focused on the "best" elements of Norwegian culture as viewed by white fairgoers. In their most notable display, a group of Norwegians sailed a replica Viking ship, appropriately named *Viking*, across the Atlantic Ocean, down the Hudson River and Erie Canal, and across the Great Lakes to Chicago.[10] The stunt, which, within the context of the fair, marked a feat of modern technological advancement, served a larger figurative importance for Norwegians, and Scandinavians at large. The Viking journey was so notable at the time that the *New York Times* reported to its national audience that the ship became the "gem of the Exposition" even though its presence challenged the exposition's "Columbian" focus.[11] The *Viking*'s sailing symbolized the Vikings' "discovery" of America, and Scandinavian newspapers used the forum of the Exposition to position Nordics as more American than Americans. American readers may have taken offensive with this argument if, for example, it was an Italian community making the same argument for Columbus. This, however, was not the case. Instead, the "homemaking myth" illustrated the role Scandinavians and Scandinavian Americans played in furthering the narrative of white privilege on their own behalf.[12]

In the years following the fair, Americans made use of stereotypical assumptions of race as a means of distinguishing Nordic immigrants from the other "races" of Europe. This process was further complicated by a wave of studies published around the turn of the century, most notably William Ripley's *The Races of Europe* and Joseph Deniker's *The Races of Man*. Ripley and Deniker set the standard for signifying difference among the white races of Europe and guided subsequent race commentating and nativist rhetoric built around dealing with the "new" immigrant classes. Both studies elevated Nordics to the top of an imagined racial pyramid and set a precedent for Nordicism and arguments for white supremacy, and they also gave rise to a new set of racial assumptions reflected in the highly problematic studies of Madison Grant and Lothrop Stoddard during the 1910s. American and Scandinavian American newspapers reported on the positive and negative stereotypes created around Scandinavian ethnicity and Nordic physicality. The result of this combination of rhetoric on white privilege, racial fitness, and journalistic reporting was highly beneficial to those who occupied the Nordic race. Such discourse established a location of structural privilege as Nordic people, considered part of the "civilized" middle class in Chicago, now were the whitest of the white races as informed by Americans and Scandinavians. However, this constructed discourse also led to a host of negative, class-based stereotypes associated with the assumed behaviors and manners of Scandinavian immigrants. For many Americans, such assumptions pigeonholed Scandinavian immigrants into the role of Vikings and dumb blondes.

Aside from the scholarly discussion of the invention of ethnic identity, historical studies of immigrant groups from an urban perspective pay attention to language, religion, culture, and homeland traditions in defining a group's collective ethnic identity.[13] Yet, this emphasis shifts within the historiography written by Norwegian and Swedish scholars, especially in regard to methodology, to focus on the dynamics of the collective group rather than the native-born American perspective.[14] The focus of this chapter instead emphasizes the importance of a multiplicity of viewpoints. For Scandinavians, the World's Columbian Exposition served as both a showcase of homeland products as well as a chance to display the true nature of Scandinavian culture as a collective identity shared across continents. To Chicago's Scandinavian Americans, this was a tangible persona linked to traditions of home rather than a superficial whiteness.

In the years after the fair, American perceptions of the "typical" Scandinavian continued to focus more on Nordic physical and behavioral traits rather than a richer ethnocentric identity. Scandinavian American scholars began to devote their energies to excessive venerations of their ancestors and the homeland while also mirroring the language of race scholars of the day as a means of claiming that Nordic whiteness was impeccable.[15] Despite the best efforts of Chicago's Scandinavians to depict their community as one of intelligent, hardworking individuals eager to prove themselves within a new country, Chicago's citizens interpreted their race and ethnicity by relying upon existing misconceptions of European immigrants as a whole. While these interpretations were not always positive, a unique process took place in which the perceived physical traits and behaviors of an immigrant group informed American beliefs on racial and ethnic identity, rather than the hegemonic group members constructing their own beliefs on Nordic whiteness.

The significance of this process of the construction of Nordic whiteness lies in the fact that Americans came away with relatively positive reflections on an immigrant group from a worldview that did not always present immigrant groups in the most positive light. By investigating this process and its results, this chapter further explores the process of social construction that resulted in a gendered and racialized Nordic whiteness between the 1870s and the 1910s in America. Such prescriptive literature formed the basis of understandings of white privilege and acceptance into the "Nordic race" that remain firmly entrenched in American society today.

Race, Class, and Work in Domestic Service during the 1870s and 1880s

As Reconstruction came to its failed conclusion in the South, the Gilded Age, with its pompous obsession with capitalism and the fruits of financial success, shaped American attitudes regarding race, power, and civilization in the North. The second industrial revolution was in full swing, drawing a new cadre of able-bodied immigrants throughout the world, hoping to fulfill the promise of the American dream that rewarded hard work with success. An economic crisis during the 1870s propelled Europeans to come to America; the downfall of the Scandinavian export market led to the largest influx of immigrants to date. Between 1878 and 1879, the number of Swedish emigrants alone more than doubled from 5,390 to 11,001, and by 1888, emigration to America reached 54,698 Swedes in one year.[16] Aside from sheer numbers, these new Scandinavian immigrants were a more diverse group than those who had come before them in many ways. The two most important differences between the generations of immigrants were age and their reasons for emigration to America. These immigrants, largely young, unmarried men and women, traveled to Chicago to join family and friends who arrived in previous waves. Most notable was the striking number of young women who arrived at this time. The arrival of Swedish immigrants effectively tipped the ratio of females to males in the age group 15–29 years to 136 females to 100 males—a vast departure from the male-dominated ratios pre-1880s.[17] For Norwegians, men continued to outnumber women as they had in previous waves; however, this group was younger than previous groups. By the turn of the century, more than 70 percent of all men and 62 percent of all women who left Norway for America were between the ages of 15 and 30, and nearly 80 percent of those men and women were single.[18] This group of young, unmarried Scandinavians were the first to come into regular contact with their Chicago neighbors through employment and through media exposure. Further interaction between Americans and Scandinavians in Chicago began to form the basis of class-based, concrete opinions regarding Scandinavian culture and Nordic whiteness.

During the 1880s, the arrival of even greater numbers of Scandinavians in the United States further drove intellectual and casual discourse on their worth as new immigrants. Between 1881 and 1890, according to the *United States Census*, 88,132 Danes, 11,370 Norwegians, and 29,632 Swedes immigrated to the United States, totaling 129,134 Scandinavians during the span of nine years alone (13 percent of the total immigrant population of America).[19] The city of Chicago witnessed a 118.6 percent increase in population, boosted almost entirely by the peak migration waves of several immigrant groups, including Germans, Irish, Swedes, and to a lesser extent, Norwegians and Danes. The Swedish-born population in Chicago increased by roughly 233 percent to more than 43,000. By 1890, the Swedes of Chicago represented 10 percent of the city's immigrant population, making Swedes the third-largest ethnic group behind the Germans and Irish.[20] One of the greatest draws for Scandinavians, particularly Swedish women, was that of domestic service, in which Americans conceived of their worth in racialized and gendered terms.

Advertisements in newspapers such as the *Chicago Daily Tribune* and the *Chicago Daily News* illustrated a growing preference among potential employers throughout the 1880s. Advertisements for work reflected a desire to employ a certain type of worker at the most prestigious addresses in the city, including the robber baron mansions of Prairie Avenue and the North Shore. These workers needed to have the ability to cook, sew and mend, and do general housework; but, preferably, they needed to fulfill the preferred qualifications as a "competent" and "young" girl of Swedish, Norwegian, or Danish descent. Agencies such as G. Duske in downtown Chicago published special requests for "good German and Scandinavian girls for private families, hotels, and boarding houses" alongside classified ads. By the turn of the century, one-fourth of Chicago's domestic servants were of Swedish origin, while three-quarters of Norwegian-born women working outside of the home were servants.[21]

During the late nineteenth century, Irish, German, Scandinavian, and Polish women performed the bulk of domestic work. On the national level, Swedish women were among the ethnic groups represented in household labor, along with the Irish, Germans, and Norwegians. Scandinavian women were the most popular ethnic group employed as domestic servants across America; 62 percent of Swedish-born women and 46 percent of Norwegian-born women took domestic positions in 1900.[22] A selection of state labor studies indicated that employers preferred American-born domestics as their first choice, followed by Scandinavians as their second choice.[23] Yet, the question remains: why would American employers actively recruit recent immigrants from Sweden, Norway, and Denmark to work in their homes when many of them did not have a firm grasp of the English language or American domestic customs? Reasons for such decisions lay in the media's portrayal of Nordic women as both hardworking and easy to control but who also reflected racial whiteness that would make the mansions of Chicago more appealing to elite guests.

A distinctive set of stereotypes and cultural images constructed by American newspapers fueled the desire to employ Scandinavians expressed by Chicago's elite employers. Racial theories on human progress such as Social Darwinism and Andrew Carnegie's "Gospel of Wealth" further shaped the ideologies of Chicago's social elite during the Gilded Age. Borrowing language from Charles Darwin's seminal 1859 work, *On the Origin of Species*, Social Darwinists like William Graham Sumner saw evolution as a natural process that occurred in human society just as it did in nature, where only the "strong" survive. Society should leave men—who could not provide for their family because a predisposition for vice, extravagance, idleness, or imprudence impeded their labor—to "die off" to make way for stronger races.[24] Chicago's newspapers and other American works used the language of Social Darwinism to portray Scandinavians, particularly women, as a component of the "strong" white races. In the late nineteenth and early twentieth centuries, American and Scandinavian American writers like O. N. Nelson, Kendric Babcock, John Commons, and Henry Pratt Fairchild considered rural Scandinavians to originate from especially strong racial stock. Steeped in romantic associations of rural life and virtue, they argued that Scandinavians' rural connections from home worked to their benefit in America. Economist John Commons predicted that Scandinavians would not become a financial draw upon the American government like some "new" immigrants would because of their rural heritage.[25] Because Scandinavians were "strong" and able-bodied for work, they were more readily accepted into white American society.

The rural persona for Scandinavian women translated into white privilege in similar ways, though it was also trivialized to reflect American gender norms. In 1886, a *Chicago Daily Tribune* article portrayed the seemingly simplistic lives of rural Scandinavian women against the backdrop of a striking Nordic landscape as a means of placing emphasis on their natural, bucolic femininity. The article's author noted the "dreary existence of some Norwegian women" who worked as dairy maids during the early summer months of May and June. The nature of their jobs required them to stay with the cattle in valleys and high in the mountains and the women were said to have led lonely lives "with only fortnightly visits at the most from their relatives or lovers."[26] Such romanticized and even sexualized depictions of Scandinavian mountain maidens shaped the American perceptions used to identify Scandinavians from other European immigrants. In addition to the emphasis on their rural backgrounds, Chicago's newspapers also portrayed Scandinavian women as quiet and loyal and rarely capable of a disagreement. Middle- and upper-class female employers viewed such traits as especially favorable for domestic service and assumed they would not have problems maintaining dominance over Scandinavian maids in their homes.

In reality, a significant portion of Scandinavian women were already accustomed to urban life and appropriate social interactions after gaining work experience as domestics in Scandinavian cities. Once in America, many Scandinavian servants worked as live-in help, which provided them with continual interactions with their American employers and enabled them to learn English quickly, unlike other domestics who lived apart from the families for which they worked. During the Gilded Age, the most prestigious homes in America were the ones in which employers staffed their homes with live-in help. For such elite Americans, only the strongest workers would suffice. Scandinavian domestics still executed similar tasks as other ethnic groups, yet American employers rewarded them with comparatively higher wages and greater esteem. One Swedish scholar found that in 1913 the wages of Scandinavian domestics were considered "excellent"; the newly arrived woman could make $4 a week but could quickly receive a raise of $3 a week for commensurate growth in language and work ability.[27] The typical experience of domestic workers was not so appealing. In 1901, a Chicago newswoman went undercover as a live-in servant and reported in the *Chicago Daily Tribune* on how the lady of the house expected her to work fifteen hours a day for which she made only $2.75 a week plus room and board as an American. Her wage was a dollar and a half less than the national average, and similar work conditions compelled some of Chicago's domestic workers to form the Working Women's Association of America during the same year.[28] One could argue that Scandinavian scholars like E. H. Thörnberg emphasized the positive experiences of domestic servants in Chicago as a means of elevating Scandinavian ethnicity, though the fact that even Americans were paid less than Scandinavians points to a deeper process of racial construction at work.

Firsthand accounts of Scandinavian domestic servants in turn-of-the-century Chicago offer further exploration into the reasons that American employers gave preferential treatment to workers of Nordic descent. Stina Hirsch, whose family worked as Swedish domestics in some of the most opulent homes of the North Shore suburbs of Chicago, recalled that the positive treatment her relatives received from their employers caused other ethnic groups to view them with disdain. Their exposure to the good life of the Gilded Age elite influenced their values, habits, styles, and behaviors and they acquired consumer desires "they could hardly afford." Other European immigrants accused Scandinavian domestics of acting in snobbish ways, yet Hirsch admitted that these were the qualities "that seemed to distinguish live-in Swedish domestics from any other group of immigrants" and on the North Shore, "everywhere were Swedish women, much sought after and well paid."[29] These workers exuded a quiet confidence and sought to learn American cultural norms, but, altogether, employers rewarded them for their whiteness as they adopted the civilized values of work and racial strength elite Americans valued.

When Scandinavian women first began to work as domestic servants in the homes of Chicago's elite, their community rallied in support of their sisters in service and viewed their work as both safe and beneficial to their future endeavors. Yet, for domestic servants of all nationalities, there was an unavoidable social stigma attached to domestic service within American culture—the women who worked as servants were taken care of by their employers for the most part, but above all, were servants to others.[30] As many employers saw the economic discrepancies of their workers as an opportunity to treat their help however they saw fit, many Scandinavians began to view the labor of domestic servants as above "their girls." In an article published in the Swedish-language newspaper, *Svenska Nyheter*, one journalist created a comparison of two positions available to Swedish women: maid or "factory girl." They used this comparison to stress the importance of domestic work for women who sought security and pushed for them to avoid the various problems that factory girls encountered. However, the author also emphasized the difficulty of work within domestic service and hinted that Scandinavian women had more opportunities than other immigrant women.[31]

As Scandinavian women illustrated pride in their positions as domestics, their employers spoke to other elite women of their success, which was echoed by the Scandinavian American and Chicago press. One American advertiser illustrated the popularity of Scandinavian women in domestic work as part of an emerging American cultural norm. The producers of Sapolio scouring soap employed extensive marketing of their products during the consumer revolution of the 1870s and 1880s and capitalized on the new ethic of hygiene celebrated by the Victorian class. Their famous slogan used to sell Hand Sapolio, a popular soap, emphasized the importance of personal hygiene and cleanliness in the home and argued that consumers "can't be healthy, or pretty, or even good unless [they] are clean." In an advertisement that appeared in both *Skandinaven* and in Chicago's mainstream newspapers, the producers of Sapolio Scouring Soap claimed that "American families learn that Norwegian girls are tidier, cleanlier, and faster than the Irish and German girls" by using their product.[32] Racial connotations and the cult of true womanhood implicit in Sapolio's advertisements were not lost on its consumers. The soap company's advertisements regularly featured images that played upon the elements revered in the Victorian domestic sphere, such as babies and children, while making the argument for the connection of whiteness and civilized behavior with cleanliness. By employing Scandinavian women as domestic servants, America's elite could pride themselves on promulgating the benefits of whiteness and civilization.

Not all characterizations of Nordic whiteness and Scandinavian domestic servants made during the late nineteenth century were positive at face value, yet still resulted in structural privilege. The cultural stereotype of the loyal, quiet, and hardworking demeanor of Scandinavian domestic workers contrasted with another that depicted Scandinavian immigrants as slow, dimwitted, and gullible. In 1891, a *Chicago Daily Tribune* article argued that Swedish women were not slow and that "they have been working for freedom [even] if they don't say much." The article epitomized the stereotype of the Nordic immigrant who was not loud or boisterous like those Americans read about in the newspapers who defended themselves against capitalist employers during the labor wars of the 1880s. Swedish women were eager to attain greater equal rights without causing a scene or drawing attention to themselves. A Scandinavian woman interviewed in the article corroborated this image by explaining that women in her community "go to the colleges, they practice the professions . . . but they didn't get their rights by too much talking."[33] Historian Joy Lintelman stated that American public opinion of Scandinavians prior to the turn of the century tended to focus on their "slow" nature as a coping mechanism in dealing with linguistic and cultural difference.[34] Scandinavian language and social practices created an initial barrier between immigrants in search of employment and American employers who could not understand their speech patterns and initially considered them unintelligent. Surprisingly, there were also benefits to this unfortunate stereotype. The emerging perception that Scandinavians were dumb meant that, as an ethnic group, they were harmless rather than *dangerous* as the media portrayed some of the darker races of Europe.

Scandinavian writers also contributed to the stereotype of Scandinavian through class-based jokes made at the expense of lower-class and rural compatriots. One common joke featured a Scandinavian servant standing in the kitchen next to a cooked pig, holding an apple in her mouth and curled paper in her ears because she did not translate the recipe properly.[35] The impetus behind this commonly shared joke in Scandinavia intended to depict "backward" rural laborers as dim-witted or frivolous, and the humor was different from an American perspective. Instead, rural Scandinavians were of strong racial stock, though still the center of ridicule because of their immigrant, foreign status. Even before the *Sweedie* films portrayed the dim-witted Swedish maid to Chicago's audiences, American magazines and newspapers constructed the stereotype of the Scandinavian "dumb blonde." In one such jab at the lack of intelligence among Scandinavian domestics, the popular satirical magazine, *Puck*, published a joke similar to Scandinavian humor:

FORTUNE TELLER: I can read that there is to be a wreck in your home, and it will be caused by a blonde woman.

PATRON: Oh, that has already occurred. Our new Swedish maid let the dumb-waiter fall and broke all the dishes.[36]

According to this joke, Scandinavian domestic workers struggled in the American household to acclimate themselves to popular customs, especially in homes with more modernized technological features than that of Scandinavia. Furthermore, use of "dumbwaiter" alongside "Swedish" maid was a play on words intended to depict the servant in comparative fashion. The influence of the dim-witted persona of Scandinavian women and men was especially strong in the upper Midwest, where the infamous Ole and Lena jokes began to circulate. Such folk humor represented the strong Scandinavian influence in places like Chicago as a product of the immigrant experience. Ole and Lena jokes employ the fractured English of the recent Scandinavian immigrant and Scandinavians used to make fun of themselves but also illustrate the oddities of American cultural differences. One example referenced a variance in social practice that seemed strange in comparison to Scandinavian culture:

Ole says Americans are funny: First they put sugar in a glass to make it sveet, a tvist of lemon to make it sour, gin to make it varm dem up, and ice to cool it off. Den dey say, "Here's to you," and den dey drink it demselves."[37]

Scandinavians and Scandinavian Americans participated in the process of assigning physical and cultural attributes to their own ethnic group in comedic ways, constructing an innocuous persona of the "typical" Nordic immigrant. Even if Scandinavians were "dumb blondes," this image was one that ultimately capitalized on racial whiteness. In the years leading up to the World's Columbian Exposition in 1893, Scandinavians in Chicago and abroad began work on displays that projected the characteristics and benefits of the Nordic race to an international audience.

Nordic Whiteness on Display at the World's Columbian Exposition of 1893

The opening of the World's Columbian Exposition in May 1893 marked the most significant American cultural event of the late nineteenth century. Chicago architect Daniel Burnham designed the fair to symbolize the progression

60 · CHAPTER 2

of America as a civilized, modern nation in the same vein as ancient Greece and Rome and built the White City in the Beaux-Arts style to represent a white utopia. The fairgrounds covered more than 600 acres along the shores of Lake Michigan; the "Great Buildings," with a facade made from temporary wood and steel frames covered with staff, appeared to be constructed out of marble and were called "the White City." The displays housed at the White City projected the latest technological might, consumer ideals, and civilized culture and white racial progress of America to an international audience.

The World's Columbian Exposition exhibited great influence over its 27 million visitors. It reinforced their beliefs, encouraged a newfound American patriotism, and suggested new ways of viewing American civilization in a time of social and political unrest. The event produced a reading list of guidebooks, newspaper and journalist accounts, photographic view books, and a host of other written reactions to the fair's emphasis on education rather than entertainment. In particular, the White City received its most notable attention as an appropriation of European aesthetics in an American context. The White City inspired Wellesley English professor Katharine Lee Bates to write the poem that became "America the Beautiful," which recounted the "alabaster" city with its gleaming white buildings, modern inventions, and all that represented the benefits of white civilization in America. Yet, underlining the fair's message of progress was a "utopian construct built upon racist assumptions."[38]

Much like the facade of whiteness the Great Buildings of the fair represented, the fair's millions of visitors were introduced to evolutionary, Victorian ideas about race presented in a utopian context and displayed in exhibits described as "ostensibly amusing."[39] In the years leading up to the fair, a notable scholarship authored by cultural and physical anthropologists, physicians, botanists, and other pseudoscientists of race established ties between the language, literature, and history of world peoples and their prehistoric past. During the eighteenth century, Swedish physician and botanist Carl Linnaeus pioneered biological definitions of the human race in his 1767 book, *Systemic Naturae.* In his study, he labeled five varieties of human species who possessed physiognomic characteristics that varied by culture and place: The Americanus, the Europeanus, the Asiaticus, the Afer or Africanus, and the Monstrosus. Linnaeus defined all species by skin, hair, and eye color and cultural tendencies that delineated one race from the next. The Americanus, for example, had red skin; black, straight, thick hair; was "righteous, stubborn, zealous, and free"; was regulated by customs; and "painted himself with red lines," otherwise definitive of the "savage" native American in Linnaeus's descriptors. By contrast, the Europeanus race had white, "sanguine," or "browny" skin; "abundant, long hair and blue eyes";

was "gentle, acute, and inventive"; and was "regulated by customs," but in more civilized ways than the native American.[40] The scientific racial classification system constructed by Linnaeus created the basis of most human racial hierarchies and informed notable nineteenth-century theories authored by Charles Darwin and Herbert Spencer, as well as exhibits on display at the World's Columbian Exposition.

The exhibits featured in the Great Buildings of the White City emphasized that racial progress since primitive times occurred through the evolutionary theory of polygenism, or the idea that the human races are of different origins, rather than monogenism, which posits a singular origin of humanity. The polygenic focus of the anthropological exhibits at the fair served a twofold purpose: to further solidify the association of white progress with the categories of "European races" and to exhibit colonial progress since the era of Columbus. Robert Rydell wrote that the fair did not merely reflect American racial attitudes of the late nineteenth century, it "grounded them on ethnological bedrock" by such established scientists as Otis T. Mason, curator of the Smithsonian's Bureau of American Ethnology. Recognizing that the fair was intended to educate the masses, Mason admitted that the displays did not represent all of mankind, yet saw the exhibition as "one vast anthropological revelation" that represented all of the world's peoples in pictures or displays of foreign governments and concessionaires.[41] Such displays were deliberate in content and location; exhibits of foreign governments the fair commissioners decided were of undeveloped, uncivilized racial stock were relegated to the Midway Plaisance, away from the millennial advancement that the White City represented. When the fair's commissioners sent out invitations to foreign governments to build ethnocentric displays at the fair, some of the first countries to enthusiastically respond were also those deemed backward or of darker racial composition, including Japan and China, who were relegated to the Midway Plaisance away from the prioritized white, European countries' displays. Many white American fairgoers moved along a path that took them past the anthropologic displays of scientists on the hierarchy of human races and through the displays of European nations, while deliberately navigating them away from the uncivilized Midway Plaisance. Therefore, it is fitting that the fair's visitors formed viewpoints on white privilege and European ethnocentrism that informed their opinions and self-identification as white.

In contrast to the foreign displays relegated to the "darker" Midway Plaisance, the displays of the Swedish, Danish, and Norwegian pavilions in the White City represented the utopian world of racial progress that the World's Columbian Exposition espoused. Scandinavian dignitaries understood the importance of the occasion to portray their home countries in the best possible manner that appealed to international audiences and elevated the racial status of their people in America. The fair's planners designated a series of days of the exhibition for participating nations to hold cultural celebrations as a means of demonstrating the most positive elements of their country's traditions to the American public. The festivities of "Sweden's Day" brought the "importance of the Swedish people to the city's notice" as 10,000 Swedish Americans paraded alongside the great halls of the White City.[42] In the calendar of the exposition, delegates of separate states and countries received just one day of the exposition to highlight their culture in ways that appealed to a broad, general audience. Sweden's representation in the fair during "Sweden's Day" illustrated a deliberate, concerted effort of the country's delegates to communicate to an international audience that Scandinavian culture was refined and an important component of the growing Midwest.[43] The pomp and circumstance of the event could be seen throughout Lakeview in the months leading up to the world's fair. Scandinavians celebrated their triumphs while also taking into careful consideration the ways the fair's delegates could formulate a lasting impression of Chicago's Scandinavians as a

Figure 8: The Swedish Government Building at the World's Columbian Exposition built to reflect old-world Swedish architectural style. Courtesy of the Library of Congress.

cultured and distinguished ethnic group. Most importantly, Scandinavians used this opportunity to mark their entrance into larger American society through acculturation. Through their assigned ethnic "day" and cultural pavilions, Scandinavians emphasized traditions of home purposely aligned with the values of civility that white Americans prized the most.

Quite possibly the boldest and most deliberate display of Nordic whiteness at the World's Columbian Exposition was that of the celebration of Leif Erikson and the replica Viking ship previously mentioned. Norway's delegation used the two symbols as a means of emphasizing to American fairgoers that the Vikings were the first European "discoverers" of North America. In his aptly titled book, *America Not Discovered by Columbus*, Scandinavian American writer Rasmus Anderson created the "homemaking myth" in 1874 by arguing that Norsemen were the "true discoverers" of America, not other white Europeans. If Scandinavians were of older racial stock than any other ethnic group who claimed sovereign status for colonizing North America, they were due a special status in America.[44] The irony of the true history of the Vikings was lost on Anderson, as well as most of the first Scandinavian American historians of the late nineteenth century.

The first historical descriptions of Vikings transcribed in English heroicized the brute masculinity involved in marauding and pillaging in a glossy, nineteenth-century version of the "typical" blonde, blue-eyed Nordic. The symbol of the Viking in popular memory embodied a race of tall, "wild" men whom O. N. Nelson styled as "strong and robust, having white bodies, yellow hair, broad shoulders, wiry muscles, florid complexions, and fierce blue eyes that during excitement gleamed with fire and passion."[45] The cultural symbol of the Viking also represented strong individuality and a love for freedom to Scandinavian men who adopted the identity as a means of connecting ethnic tradition to an imagined masculine image. Vikings represented the epitome of the evolved man according to Nelson and Anderson. Despite the sordid past of the Viking age, Nelson interpreted the racial features of Vikings as that of the stereotypical features of Scandinavian men in the 1890s as a means of further benefiting Nordics in America.

Given a different context or racial climate, the Scandinavian celebration of Leif Erikson as the true "discoverer" of America could easily have backfired and detrimentally affected the position of Nordics in America, but instead it worked in their favor. In the months leading up to the World's Columbian Exposition, a group of prominent Norwegian Americans in Chicago organized a celebration meant to contrast with the city's commemoration of Columbus Day in October 1892. In an effort to educate the American public, but also venerate Leif Erikson's "discovery," the group arranged a panel of prestigious speakers who best represented successful Scandinavians living in America. A journalist from the *Chicago Tribune* described the event as civilized, intellectually stimulating, and thoughtfully argued. Though distracted by "pretty girls with red frocks," the pageantry impressed the journalist. The audience displayed the era's ideals of racial purity, with "beautiful mothers and fathers" with Nordic racial features there to recount the heroic traditions of Erik the Red.[46]

The reporter's infatuation with the Nordic whiteness and privilege of the prominent Scandinavian Americans in attendance furthered the importance of the event's message to Americans. In the "large company of sons and daughters of the land of Vikings," the reporter shared the words of the speakers, including Norwegian American attorney A. J. Elvig, historian John Fisk of Harvard University, and the editor of *Skandinaven* P. A. Conradi, all of whom impressed the American journalist. Fisk's lecture focused on the historical origins of Scandinavians in America and their racial legacy of whiteness by noting for the audience that the first white child born in America had a Norwegian mother. Fisk argued that word of the Norseman's journey and birth of a white child in what would become the new world later influenced Columbus through records he located in Rome prior to his infamous journey. Conradi called upon the audience to reflect upon Columbus's theft of credit for "discovery" of the new world and to teach their children that "the sturdy sons of Norway should [receive] the honor" and "reward" for claiming North America. The reporter concluded by stating that, editorially, the speakers proved the group's position and that Eriksen should be given his due in history books as the true "discoverer" of America 400 years before Columbus.[47] The position argued that the Leif Erikson celebration, which was widely reported to the *Tribune*'s readers, had the potential to affect their consideration of Scandinavians' social and racial position in America.

Many of the representative countries in attendance at the World's Columbian Exposition that were invited to construct pavilions as a means of displaying their cultural artifacts published guidebooks for distribution to the viewing public. The guidebooks offered an organized map of the tables, posters, and displays of the pavilion but, most importantly, fueled propaganda on their country's representative demographics that the public would view in the best light. Some of the delegations were comprised of almost entirely native countrymen, who traveled to the event to present goods and products on behalf of their country, rather than representatives of local leadership. The Royal Swedish Commission, for example, sent Swedish delegates who could advertise the cultural benefits of Sweden and Scandinavia from an international perspective, while local Swedish Americans consulted on matters of local concern.[48] Delegates artfully planned the exhibit in an effort to display the rural quaintness of Sweden's countryside.

Architects of the display modeled the Swedish pavilion after a typical Swedish barn for a twofold purpose: to illustrate Swedish culture in accurate terms and to connect Swedishness to a common American idea that rural people were of strong racial stock.

Reflecting upon romantic American associations of rural life and virtue, the delegation made careful distinctions between products that would best represent Scandinavians in positive terms and representative ideologies on Scandinavian culture that Americans commonly stereotyped. The agricultural department displayed a selection of typical Swedish fare, including displays of Swedish fish products, including caviar and pickled herring, as well as various types of Swedish cheeses, or Herrgårdsost, along with cheese-making machines.[49] In the manufacturing department, the Swedish Ladies' Delegation displayed Swedish-style handiworks such as embroidered table décor, curtains, wall hangings, and rugs that combined old-world charm with a modern sense of design. However, the section of the Swedish pavilion that focused statistical data on education, public works, sport and leisure, and works of literature was the most popular among fairgoers.[50] A display focused on physical development, training, and conditioning that illustrated the extent to which Swedish education centered on the connections between mental and physical fitness left the most lasting impression on American observers.

Statistics on the physical attributes of the "typical" Nordic individual at the Swedish pavilion shaped turn-of-the-century discourse on American perceptions of Nordic whiteness. The *Swedish Catalogue* of the fair attributed Sweden's healthy climate and reasonable social conditions to the excellent overall health of Nordic people. In comparison to Britain, the country Americans most commonly associated with strong racial stock, Swedish researchers found that out of 1,000 children born between 1871 and 1880, 775 boys and 798 girls in Sweden survived their fifth birthday, compared to only 734 boys and 763 girls in England.[51] In addition to healthy youth, researchers corroborated the findings of contemporary anthropologic discussions of the late nineteenth century regarding positive physical characteristics that Americans associated with Scandinavians. "The Swedes are acknowledged to be one of the tallest nations of the world," exclaimed one researcher, who used statistical findings to connect physical stature to region of origin and age. As noted in compulsory military examinations, the average height of Swedish men was no less than 172 centimeters (5'8") between the ages of twenty to twenty-one, though researchers explained that the statistics were not definitive of absolute height. Instead, a more accurate measurement taken of Nordic men between the ages of twenty-two and twenty-three illustrated a more accurate stature because, according to one researcher, "in this northern climate, the men are not fully developed" until their early twenties.[52] This documented eagerness of researchers to place an emphasis on the tall stature of Swedish men exhibited a desire to portray Nordic masculinity in a way that highlighted their virility as a race and played upon assumptions of Nordic racial features.

Methods of sport and an emphasis on the athleticism of Scandinavian athletes on display at the World's Columbian Exposition further emphasized the virility of the Nordic race. Pehr Henrik Ling founded the "Swedish system" of gymnastics, exercises, and maneuvers in the early nineteenth century that combined his academic training in anatomy and physiology with physical fitness. The Ling method of gymnastics associated physical strength with mental agility and stressed that a person could become more intelligent through better exercise. His method, the *Swedish Catalogue* noted, revived "the ancestral spirit in the Swedish people" through sport, which ultimately linked to racial fitness. Exercise drew out the "great qualities, the strength, the courage and the will" that defined "the Scandinavian race," according to the catalogue.[53] Athletics, particularly the Ling method, were of great importance to the preservation of the white races and a beneficial element that Scandinavians could contribute to American society. Several of Chicago's Scandinavian American high schools and colleges, including North Park College on Chicago's north side, placed an emphasis on the Ling method, connecting the importance of the intellectual growth of Scandinavian youth to physical fitness. At the turn of the twentieth century, many American schools soon began to adopt the Ling method in their regular physical fitness curriculum.[54]

Scandinavians were also remarkably intelligent, even without formal gymnastic training, according to the *Swedish Catalogue*, because of their racial fitness. As the Swedish Commission's report explained, "at the commencement of the century a person who could not read was rarely met with, and nowadays the whole nation may be said to be able to read, with hardly a single exception."[55] The report found the Scandinavian countries of Denmark, Norway, and Sweden to have remarkable rates of national literacy: 99.5 out of 100 Scandinavians could read and write by the 1890s. In comparison to a "random" selection of countries' literacy rates that included mostly "new" immigrant countries, researchers found that only 21 out of 100 Russians, 58 out of 100 Italians, 61 out of 100 Hungarians, and 78 out of 100 Americans were literate.[56] Not only were Scandinavians overwhelmingly literate, they were even more literate (and thus more intelligent) than Americans, once again returning to the framework that poised Nordics above Americans in racial stock.

The Swedish Commission and the Swedish Ladies' Committee used the forum of the Exposition to emphasize the Scandinavian dedication to equal rights in education regardless of sex, class, or age. The *Swedish Catalogue* detailed how, in the later years of primary schooling, students focused their studies more intensively on Scandinavian geography, zoology, botany, hygiene, cookery, geometry, and drawing. A significant portion of the school week was to be dedicated to health and wellness as teachers drilled students of all ages in Ling's gymnastics, facilitating the growth of several voluntary gymnastics clubs across Scandinavia.[57] While Scandinavian youth earned the same education regardless of sex and class, the Committee's viewpoints reflected similarities to the cult of true domesticity in America during the nineteenth century. Women deserved the right to higher education, but that right was not to interfere with a commitment to their roles as women. The Committee noted in the catalogue that once Scandinavian women completed primary school, their families often sent their daughters to special cookery and housekeeping schools. However, the committee failed to report that the majority of Swedish families in the late nineteenth century would not have been able to afford to send their daughters to formalized domestic training post–primary school. In these elite training academies, young women spent an average of six to twelve months focused on the basic skills necessary in keeping their own homes or, more importantly, the homes of other families.[58] After completing a curriculum in the domestic sciences, graduates could find employment in some of the more elite households of Europe and America as professional, proper maids and cooks, according to the catalogue. The Swedish Ladies' Committee's report misled readers to believe that most of their country's young women received formal training in the domestic arts, most likely as a means of further illustrating the positive behaviors of Scandinavians in anticipation of American readers.

Another display at the Swedish pavilion that American viewers used to inform characteristics of Nordic whiteness featured public baths. Due to the harsh winter conditions of the north, nude public bathing had grown in popularity by the late nineteenth century. Despite the fact that Swedes were far less prudish than Americans in regard to nudity, the display focused on the importance of public hygiene as the need for these baths rather than Scandinavian cultural difference. Because Scandinavians prided themselves on cleanliness and public health, such public baths were integral to a rural population that did not yet have access to modern conveniences. Scandinavians had different ideas surrounding modesty and the human body than their American neighbors, but for the sake of propagandist display, the Commission pointed out separations along lines of class and sex in Sweden's public baths. The larger baths generally provided separate divisions for men and women with additional divisions provided by way of higher fees. The public made use of the warm baths, which were either hot air or vapor, while the upper classes could bathe with members of their own class in larger swimming pools and receive scrubbing and massage from bath-attendants.[59] The practice of "social bathing" on display at the Swedish pavilion was so popular in Sweden that Saturday was declared "tub-day" by northerners, which the commission explained was "very Swedish" by practice and commonly known as an important element of Scandinavian culture.[60] Comparatively, prudish Americans found the thought of strangers, or even family members, bathing together publicly to be inappropriate and a symbol of a more sexually expressive culture, regardless of the fact that many other Europeans saw public bathing as a common, habitual practice.

Perhaps even bolder on the part of the Royal Swedish Commission was their acknowledgment of a national problem of alcohol consumption, particularly among Swedish men. The reason the commission chose to illustrate this notable social problem points to a likely willingness to connect with American Progressives involved in the temperance movement in the states. Sweden saw a vast improvement in the problem of annual consumption of alcohol by the late nineteenth century due to a powerful temperance movement of their own. In the early nineteenth century, when Swedes "had not the best of names," statistics estimated that each inhabitant consumed no less than *10 gallons* of alcoholic beverages a year.[61] The Swedish Commission was keenly aware of how the public might have perceived these figures and made a point of displaying Scandinavia's general commitment to the integrity of moral character for both men and women.

In Denmark, Sweden, and Norway during the 1880s and 1890s, there was a noted commitment to philanthropic work focused specifically on "preventative philanthropy." Scandinavian Progressives used this term to distinguish the commitment of men's and women's reform groups who worked to protect children from the dangers of society. Such organizations focused on the values of piety, morality, and temperance to build outlets for self-help, charity, nursing and medical care, and mission service. In particular, many of the Lutheran-based organizations sought to combat the problems connected to alcohol consumption, a noted social problem for Scandinavians regardless of age, class position, or sex. Likewise, the Women's Committee noted in their catalogue that, "as a rule, the Swedish woman is temperate, though sad exceptions exist."[62] While fewer women than men suffered from alcoholism, the Committee saw the importance of honest publishing as a word of caution but also as a showing of outward commitment to the Progressive cause.

The displays found at the Women's Pavilion at the Exposition further educated the public on social differences that existed between Swedish men and women as a means of portraying appropriate feminine behavior. Among the most conspicuous features in the character of the Nordic woman, "self-sacrifice, presence of mind and prudence, ability and acuteness, together with a passionate sense of revenge" defined the nature of Swedish women, according to the Swedish Ladies' Committee.[63] On one hand, Scandinavians defined Nordic women by their domestic capabilities, as "the emblem of her house-wifely authority were the keys, handed over to the bride, and often remaining with the house-wife in her grave," even in ancient times.[64] Yet, in contrast, many of the traditions, laws, and rituals of Swedish society illustrated a pattern of relative independence among Swedish women, both single and married, including legislation that prohibited women entering into marriage by force and prevented spousal abuse. Due to an unbalanced sex ratio in the Northern provinces during the nineteenth century, legislation allowed for consideration of sons and daughters as equitable heirs to their parents' estates.[65] The delegation recalled stories of foreigners who visited Sweden during the early nineteenth century who expressed their admiration for the Swedish woman in her performance of such "manly pursuits" and the "spirit and intrepidity she evinced."[66]

Over the course of the late nineteenth century, Swedish women received additional legislative gains, including the right to possess property, the right to separate property owned in common with her husband, and the revocation of the requirement to attain consent of her nearest kinsman for marriage purposes. Alongside the comparatively progressive legislation on behalf of women in Sweden was the identification of the "woman problem" introduced by the Fredrika Bremer Association in Sweden. The association's goal was to promote "a sound and steady development of reforms in the condition of women, morally and intellectually as well as socially and economically."[67] This display at the Women's Pavilion of progressive social practices of gender parity shared by Scandinavians illustrated a desire to portray Nordic women as characteristically strong with few negative associations.

Delegates from the three Scandinavian countries represented at the World's Columbian Exposition intended that the information contained in their reports would help educate the fairgoing general public on the positive contributions of Scandinavians from an international perspective. Moreover, Scandinavian delegates purposefully documented the best elements of Nordic whiteness that would elevate the race, especially amid growing concern over racial fitness and the imagined racial hierarchy established in the years following the fair. Overall, Scandinavians hoped that Americans would recognize them as moral and intelligent citizens capable of blending into their society and becoming American.

70 · CHAPTER 2

The goal for many Scandinavians living in Chicago and other American cities was to assimilate without forfeiting ethnic and cultural traditions. Because of the privilege granted by their Nordic whiteness, this goal was accomplishable in contrast to southern or eastern European groups who were not nearly as white as Nordics. In the years following the World's Columbian Exposition, journalistic reporting on Nordic whiteness coupled with the emergence of new racial ideologies, as well as a discourse on gender, culture, and society, further heightened the social position of Scandinavians living in America.

In these same years, a grouping of Scandinavian American intellectuals, newspaper editors, and historians took to the task of elevating the social and racial status of Scandinavians well above that of the "new" immigrant groups. Scholars such as O. N. Nelson continued to perpetuate the "homemaking myth" by rewriting the history of Scandinavians in the most positive of terms. Admittedly, Scandinavian American writers of the late nineteenth century contributed minimally to a larger body of nativist literature. However, their most significant contribution to the narrative came through their claims to a special racial status. By identifying Scandinavian Americans as members of a courageous, masculine, adventurous, freedom-loving "race," "nation," or "people" who shared racial stock with other northwestern Europeans, filiopietistic writers made sense to those who also understood whiteness as part of a larger hierarchy of race.[68]

Nelson was one of the first filiopietistic writers to support a Pan-Scandinavian framework within historiography of Nordics in *The History of Scandinavians*, which further underlined the importance of Nordic whiteness from an American perspective. According to Nelson, Nordics were part of the "Caucasian" race because of their close ties with members of the civilized Teutonic subspecies, namely the English, Germans, and the Dutch. Membership in this shared racial subspecies spelled destiny because of political affiliation.[69] Scandinavians spoke of their racial identity in very different ways than Americans did. Before the twentieth century, Scandinavians often used the terms "Scandinavian" and "Nordic" interchangeably regardless of discussions of race or ethnicity, with "Nordic" most often used to discuss alliances across nationalities. Scandinavians were not as deliberately focused on proving the worth of their whiteness outside of an American context. Therefore, Scandinavian writers spoke more of shared ethnic traditions that linked individual nationalities.

Nelson noted that while Danes, Norwegians, Swedes, Germans, Dutchmen, and Englishmen all shared a common mythology and superstitions, he singled out Danes, Norwegians, and Swedes as having the closest ethnic group connection based on the common language they spoke.[70] When Nelson did analyze racial features, he did so along country lines. Physically, he stated, "the diverse influences of Denmark, Norway, and Sweden have developed different characteristics of the people in the respective countries." Descendants of the northern part of Sweden typically had a very fair complexion as they were the "purest descendants of the Goths" while Norwegians and those residing in Danish Jutland could be "as dark as Frenchmen," according to Nelson.[71] Nelson's distinctions between racial features and ethnic traditions for the Scandinavian groups resonated with scholarly communities in America at the turn of the century, but most likely were not as popular among readers outside of academia.

Nelson's impressions of the behavioral characteristics of Scandinavians articulated the parameters of Scandinavian whiteness adopted in America over time. He admitted that the Scandinavians, with all their virtues, were not without their faults. Behaviorally, they tended to be narrow-minded, clannish within cities like Chicago, and given to making social and political demands. Overall as a group, they were "sober, earnest, industrious, and frugal."[72] As a man of Scandinavian origin, Nelson expounded on the masculine traits of others within his ethnic group, broadly stereotyping Swedish men as proud, somewhat haughty, and well-dressed gentlemen who complied rigorously with current rules of etiquette and who drank the most expensive wine. The "bows, bobs, courtesies, and hat-liftings" of Swedish men set them apart from other Scandinavians by distinguishing age, condition, and class distinction.[73] Nelson admitted that Swedish men tended to be jealous of Norwegian men and vice versa, despite similar behavioral traits, while he considered Danes as pacifists who rarely engaged in political or social extremes. Nelson argued that from the perspective of other Scandinavians (and Europeans as a whole), Swedes were often called the "Frenchmen of the North" for their snobby air and distinctive refined tastes.

In comparison to Swedes and Danes, Nelson found that Norwegians were far less ceremonious and held very little class distinction among them. If a Norwegian happened upon a stranger, he or she would be treated, according to Nelson, with a certain kind of cold courtesy described more as a casualty of shyness than rudeness, much like the ways some described Germans. Above all, Norwegians were "independent, somewhat haughty, radical, progressive, and extreme."[74] In spite of all of his stereotypical characterizations, Nelson emphasized that he based his findings on his own observations as a person born in Sweden. Yet, many of these stereotypes would not translate to American views of Scandinavians. Instead, Americans used the press and other indicators of social mores to shape their perceptions of Nordic whiteness.

The most influential works on racial and anthropological discourse of the late nineteenth century were William Z. Ripley's *The Race of Europe* and Joseph

Deniker's *The Races of Man*, both of which supported polygenism in linking race with innate human physical features. Influenced by the work of the French eugenicist Georges Vacher de Lapouge, who used typologies to classify humans into a hierarchy of three races, American economist William Ripley infamously constructed a map of Europe according to the cephalic index of its people. Ripley rigidly defined racial features like skull shape, stature, pigmentation, eye and hair color, and nasal form by identifying photographs of prototypical European human subjects. In opposition to Ripley's positions on race, French anthropologist Joseph Deniker wrote *The Races of Man* to contend that Europe was comprised of ten races he saw more as "ethnic groups" than the ambiguous concept of "race," while ideologies and terminology of both traditions sometimes overlapped. The two books informed the racial ideologies of American white supremacists, nativists, and eugenicists like Madison Grant who used Deniker's term *Nordic* to define the apex of an imagined pyramid of race as a means of exterminating the "unfit." From the turn of the twentieth century on, both academic and more generalized writings on race reflected upon this imagined hierarchy of race as a means of elevating the Nordic race and the privilege of people who fell under its category.

Nordic Whiteness, Beauty Culture, and Femininity in the Early Twentieth Century

In the early 1900s, the American press replaced the ideal corseted Victorian woman of yesteryear with a more vivacious, public representation of femininity. Historian Lois Banner noted this shift in popularity from the "voluptuous woman" to Charles Dana Gibson's iconic Gibson girl as one that posed a successful challenge to European hegemony over popular standards of beauty. During the antebellum era, the "frail, pale, willowy woman enshrined in the lithographs of fashion magazines" was the norm, but following the Civil War, a "buxom, hearty, and heavy model of beauty" superseded the former ideal.[75] Banner attributed this shift to the influence of a popular burlesque troupe known as the British Blondes. Led by an audacious British showgirl, Lydia Thompson, the troupe's comic plays entertained working- and middle-class Americans by making fun of (or "burlesquing") the operas and social habits of the upper classes.[76] During these comedic performances, the shapely troupe of women would play men's roles in tights—a great departure from the bustles, hoops, and frills that kept the female body of the Victorian era hidden. What the American media found most fascinating about the British Blondes, however, was their blonde hair. Banner attributed this fascination to the small proportion of blonde-haired people in the United States in the 1860s; over the course of the 1890s, this fascination would grow with the advent of a flourishing beauty industry that offered women the chance to improve upon or completely transform their physical appearance.

As demonstrated at the World's Columbian Exposition, a popular health movement and new spirit of athleticism prevailed in the 1890s, shifting the standards of feminine and masculine physicality. While the lithe, natural beauty of the Gibson girl replaced the voluptuous, corseted woman of the postbellum, conversely, the athletic, muscular man on campus replaced the dandy gentleman of the bachelor classes. According to Charles Dana Gibson's illustrations of the Gibson girl, which first appeared in *Life* magazine in 1890, the new ideal in feminine beauty emphasized a slimmer figure attained through athleticism, and idealized a dedication to comfort in clothing. Like many important cultural models, the Gibson girl appeared to represent a number of styles to different groups of women. The blouses and skirts she wore for athletic activities appealed to female reformers like Charlotte Perkins Gilman, who wrote that the Gibson girl was "braver, stronger, more healthful and skillful and able and free, more human in all ways."[77] The working classes also claimed the Gibson girl as one of their own. The mystery of Gibson's original model for the figure haunted journalists. As Banner revealed, Gibson would not comply with the demands of journalists to know whom his vision encompassed, and therefore, reporters were even more determined to find the original model among the working classes in order to "demonstrate that the wealthy were not the sole possessors of beauty, that beauty, in the end, was democratic."[78] Regardless of whom Gibson truly intended as his prototypical "girl," his illustrations mirrored the young, athletically minded Scandinavian women who became a topic of discussion in Chicago during the late nineteenth and early twentieth centuries.

In the earliest days of the developing cosmetics industry, women were largely responsible for the creation and organization of an emerging beauty culture to a remarkable extent. Both Kathy Peiss and Nan Enstad emphasized the importance of immigrant and working-class women as entrepreneurs in this feminine culture who played a central role in redefining mainstream ideals of beauty and femininity into the twentieth century.[79] By this time, it was becoming acceptable for women of all classes to venture outside of the home for public entertainment and leisure. As their visibility within the public sphere grew, it transformed the ways that women viewed themselves and others within it. For women of different racial or ethnic backgrounds, the notion of using cosmetic products to enhance or reshape their outward appearance to meet American standards of beauty meant the promise of whiteness. While this was true for many groups of women, the media placed those with the lightest features at the forefront as the models of beauty, according to popular cosmetic trends. One example of this trend introduced to female consumers in the early twentieth century was bleaching agents intended for cosmetic use.

Previously, producers warned women who made use of hydrogen peroxide and bleach as household cleaning products of their potential for altering the color of fabrics. Influenced by trends adopted by the modern American women, but also as a response to prevailing racial theories, Sears Roebuck introduced a new product in 1896 to female consumers in the pages of its catalog: a liquid, hydrogen peroxide–based cosmetic product that promised to transform even the deepest tresses into flaxen locks.[80] Next to the advertisements for hair bleach, the company promoted its blonde wigs and hairpieces made from real hair and charged at a premium due to the lack of availability of true blonde hair in the United States. Women with darker skin tones could also choose to lighten their skin with a variety of products. These products had a dual purpose for immigrant and working-class women; for them, cosmetics and paints marked distinctions between social classes in a time when whiteness meant the promise of acculturation and acceptance.[81]

One Scandinavian retailer in Chicago recognized the demand for products that would change the skin tone of women who desired to have features that were more Nordic. In an advertisement, Elén Maria Nordic offered women a return to the days of "creamy, flawless complexions enjoyed by the world re-nowned beauties in the court of King Gustav III of Sweden."[82] By using these tissue creams, cleansing oils, and astringents, women in Chicago could highlight the same admired features as their Scandinavian neighbors. For women who used these products to bleach their hair and skin, the choice to manipulate their appearance in such as drastic way to conform to a new ideal of femininity was significant. Over time, the invention of these cosmetic products and subsequent physical manipulation would explode into a contemporary feminist debate regarding female identity and character. Yet, at the beginning of the twentieth century, it was a much simpler process that reflected a desire for physical change to evoke the ever-increasingly popular standard of Nordic racial features. During the following decade, Chicago's newspapers expanded upon this concept of shifting ideals of beauty and masculinity to emphasize a standard that closely resembled the features of Scandinavian whiteness.

Chicago and New York at the turn of the century witnessed the birth of the urban celebrity—a social darling of the media whose only real accomplishments included marrying well and remaining visible in the public spotlight. These urban celebrities preceded the famed ingénues of film or the cabaret girls and performers of the Ziegfeld follies and comprised the standard media fodder of the day. Female readers were able to follow the everyday activities of their favorite social debutantes through the gossip columns of their newspapers, which often focused on large events such as weddings or romantic scandals. One such section in the *Chicago Tribune* featured "Gossip from Gotham" for its readers who sought to follow the urban celebrities of New York, which the popular press epitomized for its glamour and cosmopolitanism. In February 1898, the *Chicago Tribune* reported the courtship of Nellie Neustretter by railroad mogul William K. Vanderbilt, equating Neustretter's "beautiful face and wondrous eyes" with her Swedish ancestry. Described as a "rather tall" and "dizzy" blonde of twenty-eight or twenty-nine, Neustretter was the "luckiest woman in Paris" swept off her feet by the robber baron who was "smitten with her beauty."[83] In the press, her Swedish heritage contributed to her dizzy or dumb blonde persona. She was a beautiful, Nordic woman wooed by the likes of an American millionaire.

In a media scandal closer to home, the *Tribune* reported in April 1903 of the "romantic marriage" of Miss Lotten Lillieberg, which it described as "a cultivated woman of the highest type of Swedish beauty" and "highly connected in Sweden," to Judge Arthur Henry Chetlain of the Cook County Superior Court. The couple, who met when Lillieberg worked as a "companion" to Chetlain's mother, secretly married and kept the family in the dark until the newspapers reported the marriage in the society columns.[84] While it is unclear as to why the couple kept their marriage a secret, the reporter's use of "companion" insinuated that Chetlain employed Lillieberg as a domestic or caregiver for his mother. Despite "the connection" that Lillieberg may have had in Sweden, the marriage of a working girl to a high-standing public official could have potentially led to undesired gossip for the Chetlain family. Society columns that reported on the public lives of women of Scandinavian descent contained an underlying discourse focused on their physical attributes, notably their Nordic whiteness, as a factor in their societal positions. American women who read Chicago's gossip columns received a clear message that while class status was a vital component in ascending the social ladder, physical beauty could also help you "marry up." As one *Chicago Tribune* article joked, Chicago's legal age at marriage needed to be lower, "especially for Swedish women."[85] The press gave special attention to Nordic women rather than men due to emerging images of racial superiority but also because of the tendency of the media to focus on the changing roles for women marking the end of separate spheres.

Women in America had taken part in beauty pageants ever since Phineas T. Barnum held the first public display of women's faces and figures before a panel of judges in 1854. Significantly, Barnum originally used the concept of the beauty pageant as a display of female beauty to be a showpiece of Swedish songstress Jenny Lind. Barnum praised Lind as a "mantle of moral respectability," according to Lois Banner; yet he held an equal fascination with the regular newspaper accounts of noted beauties.[86] Despite the lavish prizes Barnum offered to the winners of his public pageants, potential contestants were difficult to come by during the Victorian era, which prized female presence in the home and dissuaded women from the public stage. Instead, Barnum found much more success with the concept of the photographic beauty pageant; women who feared association with those of disreputable social standing were much more inclined to participate in media promotional devices that portrayed them as society beauties. It was not until the World's Columbian Exposition that the public beauty pageant would gain credibility as a morally acceptable activity for young female participants. At the Exposition, alongside the buildings that housed statues of classical female goddesses, Sweden and Norway placed female participants on the public stage as a symbol of proud cultural heritage in America and at home. One featured display, the Congress of Beauty, presented young women from various representative countries dressed in the folk costumes of their native lands, and it quickly became one of the most widely visited exhibitions at the fair.[87] Despite the fact that the Congress of Beauty was not a typical beauty pageant in the style of Barnum, the display nevertheless made a crucial impact as commentators realized the popularity of public displays of the female form following the fair.

Between the 1850s and the 1890s, newspapers across the country regularly held photographic beauty contests, which became a media staple long into the 1920s. This era of the Gibson girl reflected an American fascination with the publicly displayed female figure and with the creation of this media darling came a new form of pageantry: the beauty contest. While the American public was slow to adopt the beauty pageant as a standard in entertainment, Europeans were the first to accept the notion of female beauty on display. Nevertheless, many of Chicago's newspapers reported the minute details of such cosmopolitan beauty pageants, especially those focused on international beauties. One such contest held by a popular French magazine highlighted the virtues of its various international beauties. A feature in the *Chicago Tribune* paid particularly close attention to the Norwegian and Danish contestants. The paper described one Norwegian woman with a French name, Hugues Le Roux, as a "blonde beauty" who nevertheless lacked a sense of style the author mistook as representative of all Norwegian women. In spite of this fashion faux pas, the author found Le Roux to be equal in feminine beauty to her Scandinavian competitor Adolphe Brisson—a Danish girl who showed a great sense of poise,

Figure 9: Doris Manz, daughter of Gustav Manz, a notable jeweler and goldsmith who designed for Tiffany & Co. Manz was the daughter of German immigrant parents. Because of her whiteness, artist Neysa McMein asked Manz to pose for one of her covers for *McCall's* as "The Scandinavian Beauty" that captures the diverse types of American beauty. Courtesy of Gustav Manz Blog.

influencing the author to describe the young woman as "more interesting" than a "grown American woman."[88] To the press, it was Brisson's foreignness, her distinct feminine qualities as a Scandinavian woman that made her stand apart from the physicality of most American women of the day. This comparison of American and Scandinavian virtues would become part of a larger process in creating stereotypical images of Nordic women identified by their assumed physical features.

In June 1908, the Chicago Swedish Society's Central Association for the Old People's Home held a local beauty contest that resulted in a confusing outcome. The pageant held at the Society's annual picnic sought to decide upon the "prettiest Swedish girl in Chicago." Upon announcement of the contest, the picnic's attendance doubled to over 6,000 attendees eager to see the city's prettiest girls on display. After the contest, the judges announced six finalists; however, the pageant would end in a deadlock as the judges could not agree upon a winner. The head judge joked, "We will bring beauty experts to our next picnic, and with their aid will make the award."[89] Just as the local Swedish community insinuated that Swedish women were, indeed, the most beautiful in the city, Chicago's newspapers continued to find beauty in all Nordic women. In another report about a national beauty contest, one author posited that Chicago's Scandinavians might possibly be the most beautiful women in the world. Chicago, which the author considered the most cosmopolitan of all American cities, was unique for its array of diverse ethnic women, yet Chicago's Scandinavians exuded a certain type of natural beauty not found elsewhere. To him, Chicago's spirit and climate made these "Scandinavian beauties" more radiant that "any bloom along the fiords of the North sea."[90]

In March 1912, another Chicago beauty pageant asked the public to be the judge in determining "Chicago's most beautiful working girls." The contest counted Miss Goldie Johnson, a Swedish saleswoman in Marshall Field's candle shade section as one of its contestants. In an interesting illustration, the *Chicago Tribune* asserted that Johnson did not have typical Swedish features, but instead had a "mass of light brown hair, big brown eyes emphasized by finely penciled brows, [and] a pretty mouth." Nevertheless, the author drew attention to Johnson's Nordic complexion as one "that would make any beauty parlor famous."[91] Nordic whiteness was clearly becoming a sought-after physical characteristic for women, and even men, who desired a certain way of life.

Chicagoans and Scandinavians would continue to form gendered opinions and stereotypes regarding feminine traits and features considered beautiful into the new era. As the city's newspapers and periodicals reflected such public discourse—both positive and negative—Chicago's Scandinavians played a significant role in driving the conversation in ways they wanted to portray their community and its people. As this chapter illustrates, there was a significant process undertaken by Scandinavians and their neighbors that came to define social perceptions of racial and ethnic identity around the turn of the century. This process was one negotiated by both groups; however, for Scandinavians, the process of identity formation turned in their favor as Chicagoans noted their preference of Scandinavian immigrants over other groups based on their perceptions of physical and behavioral characteristics. The culmination of these thematic discussions would continue to influence the lives of Chicago's Scandinavians well beyond this era and into contemporary American history. As the next chapter explores, the ongoing discussion of white privilege granted to Nordics positively translated into the workplace as well.

CHAPTER 3

The "Swedish Maid"

"Strong" Nordic Workers in an Elite American World

During the early twentieth century, several Scandinavian writers recorded impressions of travel to the United States for the purposes of documenting the differences between the two cultures. In 1912, Swedish author Johan Person dedicated a chapter of his travel narrative to "Our Serving Sister[s]"—domestic servants whom he believed were the ethnic pride of Sweden. According to Person, by the 1910s Chicago's middle-class employers viewed Scandinavia as "nation[s] of servants—domestic, happy, willing to work, friendly and beautiful servant girls."[1] Not only were Scandinavian women an asset to families who were lucky enough to employ them, stated Person, but they were also good citizens in the eyes of their community, stating that "the Swedish American newspapers count them as their best subscribers, the Swedish American churches as their best members, and Swedish Americans in general, we believe, as their "best girls."[2] Person's identification of the qualities Americans looked for in their domestic staff was not just an illusion of national conceit, nor was it an exaggeration of American stereotypes that favored Nordic physicality. Middle-class Americans, especially women who followed the mantra of true domesticity, employed Scandinavian women in their homes because they required less work to "civilize." To Chicago's most privileged classes, Scandinavian women possessed the racial and ethnic qualities they wished to represent outwardly as American consumers.

The U.S. *Report of the Immigration Commission* supported Person's observation that American employers sought Scandinavian women as domestic servants

80 · CHAPTER 3

first before considering any other ethnic group. Next to native-born servants, American employers exhibited a notable preference for employing Scandinavians in their homes because they had a reputation for being "honest, diligent, and hardworking, willing to learn and they were seldom complaining," as one employer responded to the survey.[3] In response to demand, a stream of young, single Scandinavian women arrived in Chicago between the 1890s and the 1910s looking for employment as servants. In Norway, Denmark, and Sweden, relatives often gave money to these women to make the journey to America.[4] By 1900, domestic service was the most popular choice of employment for Scandinavian women in America. According to Ulf Beijbom, over 61 percent of Swedish-born women worked as maids or other domestic staff in Chicago, Irishwomen were second at 54 percent, and Hungarians and Norwegians were third at 46 percent.[5] Work as a domestic servant provided many benefits to Scandinavian women, including a living wage and job security, while many employers encouraged them to learn English. Scandinavian live-in servants often encountered better material conditions than newly arrived men and therefore had the capacity to contribute more to their families and the community through their earnings.

For Scandinavian women living in Chicago between 1890 and 1910, the job of "Swedish maid" offered vast social benefits. Immigrant women could acculturate to American customs, live in one of the homes of Chicago's affluent North Shore region, and eventually move up in social status by earning good wages. Many of the Nordic women who worked as domestics in Chicago during the early twentieth century reflected on their time in only positive ways, such as Stina Hirsch, whose family worked as domestics in the mansions of Chicago's elite North Shore region. She recalled that the experiences of her family members as domestics influenced their values, habits, styles, and behaviors. Hirsch admitted that these qualities "seemed to distinguish live-in Swedish domestics from any other group of immigrants," and that on Chicago's North Shore "everywhere were Swedish women, much sought after and well paid."[6] Yet, when one contrasts the experiences of Scandinavian domestics with other groups of women who worked in service during this same period, the stark division of positive and negative outcomes raises a paradox.

The "Swedish Maid": Diligent Worker or Sluggish Buffoon?

The standard historical narrative on domestic service does not commonly focus on the position of one involving honest wages, excellent living conditions, and an overall desire on the part of the worker to remain employed in the line of work.

Instead, the history of domestic service in America lends itself to a focus more on the negative aspects of the position, and rightfully so. David Katzman referred to the position as "the last pre-modern occupation" as a means of stressing the incompatibility of live-in service with modern values. Living conditions and wages for domestic servants were equal to or better than female factory operatives, yet all classes looked down upon the work of the maid.[7] Since the colonial era, when a class stratification emerged in the southern colonies, elite plantation mistresses typically reserved the role of domestic servant for slaves. In fact, according to David Roediger, terminology was key in determining distinctions of both race and class in connection with the menial job. During the mid–nineteenth century, it was insulting to refer to a white woman as a servant in the south because the terms "servant" and "slave" were often interchangeable. In the north, employers called free blacks "domestic servants" and white women "help," which led to a point of contention among those who worked as "help," namely Irish women.[8] Largely, women employed as domestic servants did so out of necessity for economic survival rather than out of a desire to work in another woman's home.

Women's place within the home was one of the most important determinants of class during the nineteenth century. Middle- and upper-class husbands afforded their wives the benefit of remaining in the private sphere, which created a stark class divide with women whose economic survival required their work. As more upper-class women took part in activities that required their absence from domestic duties, they found the need for additional help within the home.[9] Popular thought on the races best fit for domestic service shifted throughout the nineteenth century in association with the different waves of immigrants who arrived. By the late nineteenth century, the "Bridget" or female Irish servant began to fall out of preference among employers who instead were inclined to hire groups they considered "essentially servile," This differed by region. For example, an 1871 issue of *Harper's Bazaar* encouraged middle-class Americans in places like San Francisco to consider hiring Chinese servants because of their instinct to be a "machine" of servitude, while other employers employed newly arrived immigrants from northwestern Europe.[10] As Amy Kaplan argued, "manifest domesticity" informed the employment decisions of a large portion of the middle and upper classes who shared in the logic of the American empire. An innate desire to both conquer and domesticate the foreign, and therefore control the threat of foreignness within the borders of the home and the nation, was key in such domestic mistresses' decisions, even if was not overtly expressed.[11] American domestic employers desired an employee whom they could control, even if it did lead to a contentious, gendered battle between immigrant and native-born women.

82 · CHAPTER 3

If middle-class and elite American women favored hegemonic control in their domestic arrangement with servants, perception was key to their employment decisions. One of the reasons that employers desired Scandinavian women as domestic servants was due in part to the negative associations with Irish servants. Nineteenth-century artists and writers devoted their energies to highlighting the negative aspects of Irish servants' crude qualities, savage disposition, and a physique not aligned with Victorian femininity.[12] By the late nineteenth century, while some American women continued to employ Irish workers, they preferred to employ servants from Scandinavia because they perceived them to be less of a problem. This practice escalated in the years following the World's Columbian Exposition as a noted preference for "Swedish maids" coincided with the emergence of the new hierarchy of race constructed at the turn of the century. The elite of the North Shore suburbs went to great lengths in the years after the fair to employ individuals of Nordic and Alpine descent because of the perception of whiteness, and therefore civilization, built into the social consciousness of the day.

During the early twentieth century, however, the "Swedish maid" became the subject of cultural jokes in America, not because of their racial status, but because of their status as working-class immigrants. Even though Scandinavians occupied the highest echelon of the hierarchy of race as Nordics, they still retained their immigrant status until they moved up the ladder of social class or became American citizens. Therefore, negative stereotypes and assumptions attached to the "Swedish maid" came about not out of contention over whiteness, but rather because of the servile nature of their jobs. Many self-avowed Progressives considered their employment of immigrant workers in their home to be the ultimate self-sacrifice in social assistance. Because of the sacrifice of their private sphere, these mistresses of the home could command the hardest workers and, because of their class status, they were free to treat their help as they pleased. American employers also desired employees who would best display their homes as part of the business elite of Chicago. As their homes reflected the qualities civilized Americans held dearest, including cleanliness, integrity, and modern opulence, so too did these qualities reflect in the people who maintained the home's beauty. American employers prioritized stereotypical Nordic features in advertisements aimed at attaining workers who reflected the employer's affluence. Some employers even displayed signs of envy and disdain toward their workers who posed a threat to their position in the hierarchy of race. Insults aimed at the intelligence of their workers illustrates the process of "othering" their workers by way of class difference; even if their workers were whiter than they were, they were still immigrants.

Scandinavian domestics who endured harsh treatment and even those treated appropriately by their employers commanded more pay for their work and used their savings to eventually elevate their class status. The Scandinavian American press spoke highly of women who worked in domestic service out of pride, but also out of a desire to separate Nordics from the negative assumptions of native-born Americans. The press reminded its community that Scandinavians were not "essentially servile" like other immigrant groups, but that they were exceptional because of their Nordic racial status.[13] Many Scandinavians made use of such assumptions regarding their lower-class status to elevate their social position in America. Most American employers required their domestic workers to have a basic understanding of English and of the functions of an American household. By accepting these standards, Scandinavian domestics accelerated the process of acculturation and acceptance into civilized society.[14] The benefits their patience provided them, especially higher pay, made the impertinent behaviors of their employers temporarily bearable.

Mass Immigration and Demographics of Chicago's Scandinavian Communities

Between 1879 and 1893, the pull of American industry brought the largest influx of Scandinavian immigrants to Chicago during a dire time of crop failures, overpopulation, and unemployment at home. The group—largely comprised of young, single men and women between the ages of 15 and 29—came to Chicago in hopes of supporting their families back home.[15] Edith Janson reflected on her own decision to leave Sweden for Chicago as one motivated by a desire to help her parents. Prompted by her best friend to come to Chicago to work as a domestic servant, Janson later recalled her confidence in her earning potential as a young Scandinavian woman.[16] In addition to the high interest rate Scandinavians received for American dollars earned, many conceived of the American labor market as highly valued and revered by its workers. One *Svenska Tribunen* editorial reflected this viewpoint, noting, "[the worker in Sweden] knows that the American worker is more respected socially, even if the requirements for good work are higher than here, and he submits to these strict demands, because it increases his self-respect."[17] At the time, the labor market of Scandinavia was in flux, struggling to come to terms with modern, industry-driven international commerce while workers felt the pressures to transition from ill-prepared employers. An examination of the age and sex of workers illustrates that Chicago's Scandinavians had excellent prospects for furnishing the city with young laborers. Ulf Beijbom noted that the willingness of young Scandinavian men to

84 · CHAPTER 3

accept almost any kind of employment may have outweighed the fact that they arrived without any real vocational training for the industrial and constructional work that predominated the labor market.[18] In 1890, the percentage of those who worked in unskilled, manual positions largely originated from Germany, Ireland, Sweden, Norway, and Denmark, particularly among female immigrants (see table 3.1).

Scandinavians worked largely in unskilled, manual labor in 1890 but, according to filiopietistic writers like O. N. Nelson, they expressed a great sense of pride in their positions and demonstrated a willingness to learn quickly and adhere to their employer's demands better than other groups may have. The continued waves of immigrants coming from Scandinavia watered down the statistical numbers of those credited for their work in skilled, professional positions. By 1890, only 1 out of 1,017 Scandinavians worked in a job that required previous education or skill—1 out of 5,914 was a clergyman, 1 out of 5,089 a musician, 1 out of 7,236 a physician or surgeon, and 1 out of 3,074 a teacher—while the remainder of immigrants were largely farmers, merchants, or servants.[19]

As further waves of immigrants continued to arrive in Chicago by the early twentieth century, those who had previously arrived and worked as unskilled laborers had begun to transition upward on the social ladder. A substantial number of Scandinavians who arrived before 1890 acquired skills on the job, learned English, and moved into better paying positions. An influx of immigrants from southern and eastern Europe likewise created a demographic shift in the working classes. When considering the vast numbers of young, Scandinavian immigrants who arrived between 1890 and 1900, the discrepancy of manual laborers is even more significant. In 1879, 7,313 males and 3,686 fe-

Table 3.1: Percentage of manual workers of selected groups in the labor force, Chicago, 1890

Country of Origin	Male	Female
Native White	53.56	55.59
Great Britain	72.40	71.73
Germany	85.85	90.48
Ireland	86.24	91.17
Sweden and Norway	90.39	95.10
Denmark	86.02	91.44

Source: U.S. Census Bureau, *The Eleventh Census of the United States: 1890* (Washington, D.C.: Government Printing Office, 1890–1896), 650–651.

males immigrated to the United States from Sweden alone, which was twice the number of immigrants from the previous year, but by 1892, the number of new immigrants rose to 24,684 males and 17,161 females.[20] Even though this ratio favored men, there was a substantial increase in young, single women arriving in America from Scandinavia for the purpose of work. In 1900, Scandinavians still gravitated to manual labor, but in contrast to those employed as unskilled workers in 1890, the number of Scandinavian, Irish, and German manual laborers had fallen (see table 3.2).

Despite an influx of new immigrants, the number of Scandinavian men working in unskilled labor dropped by approximately 12 percent while, even more drastically, Scandinavian women in unskilled positions dropped by nearly 15 percent. One might attribute these figures to marriage, which likely took some women out of the labor market. For example, in 1900 only 70 percent of German women worked in manual positions compared to 90 percent in 1890, while even more drastically, 91 percent of Irish women worked in 1890 compared to only 61 percent by 1900. Comparatively, many Scandinavian women chose financial and personal independence over marriage. Traditionally, American social conventions did not allow women to marry while employed, especially those who worked in domestic service. Because the personal decisions of workers often came down to marriage or the individuality that their jobs afforded them, many women delayed marriage or chose to remain single altogether.

In an effort to understand the problems of immigrant congestion in large cities throughout America, the Dillingham Commission conducted a comprehensive study of immigrant groups represented in America's seven largest cities

Table 3.2: Percentage of manual workers of selected groups in the labor force, Chicago, 1900

Country of Origin	Male	Female
Native White	43.16	39.18
British	56.07	45.53
Germans	69.03	70.03
Irish	71.67	61.72
Scandinavian	78.02	80.54
Poles	90.67	87.66
Italians	83.99	80.03

Source: U.S. Census Bureau, *The Twelfth Census of the United States: 1900* (Washington, D.C.: Government Printing Office, 1900–1907), 516–523.

86 · CHAPTER 3

in 1900. The study created a snapshot of urban immigrant communities, exhibiting the living and working conditions of the largest immigrant groups in each city. In its study of Chicago, researchers identified the Townsend street district and the community of Lake View as the two most predominant Scandinavian neighborhoods in the city according to demographics. The Townsend district, which researchers described as a neighborhood in flux, was mostly Swedish; first- or second-generation Swedes occupied 85 out of 161 households.[21] The Commission observed loyalty among Swedes who lived in the Townsend District, many of whom lived in the neighborhood for more than ten years. The district exhibited a comparatively balanced sex ratio of men to women (327 men to 332 women) who were relatively older than those who resided in Lake View to the north (50 percent of men and 45 percent of women were between the ages of 30 to 44 years of age).[22] The Townsend district also exhibited a generational divide between older, foreign-born individuals and their American-born children who worked or were in school.[23]

Historians previously concluded that once Scandinavian women married, they did not work outside the home due to old-country gender norms, which dictated that their place after marriage was the home.[24] Yet, in analyzing the demographics of Scandinavian women who worked between 1890 and 1900 in Chicago, the number of those who worked after marriage appears to have been higher than previously assumed. Table 3.3 shows that the number of Swedish wives who worked outside the home residing in the Townsend District appears

Table 3.3: Wives at work, by general nativity and race of head of family in the Townsend District, 1890

Nativity/Race	Total Number of Wives Reported	Total Number of Wives at Work (%)	Average Annual Earnings
Bohemian	143	27 (18.9%)	$137
German	122	10 (8.2%)	$151
Hebrew (Russian)	90	7 (7.8%)	(No answer)
Hebrew (Other)	29	0	(Not applicable)
Irish	78	3 (3.8%)	(No answer)
Italian, North	53	7 (13.2%)	(No answer)
Italian, South	218	41 (18.8%)	$127
Lithuanian	117	3 (2.6%)	(No answer)
Magyar	20	0	(Not applicable)
Polish	338	23 (6.8%)	$153
Serbian	7	0	(Not applicable)
Slovak	64	3 (4.7%)	(No answer)
Swedish	111	23 (20.7%)	$205

Source: U.S. Immigration Commission, *Reports of the Immigration Commission: Immigrants in Cities; A Study of the Population of Selected Districts in New York, Chicago, Philadelphia, Boston, Cleveland, Buffalo, and Milwaukee*, vol. 26 (Washington, D.C.: Government Printing Office, 1911), 324.

The "Swedish Maid" • 87

to have been small (20.7 percent). However, considering the trivial survey response rate (only 33 percent of the 332 women responded), one could assume that their numbers were higher, especially compared to other northern and western European women.

As the survey illustrates, Swedish wives reported average annual earnings of $205, which was nearly $50 higher than the earnings of all other immigrant groups represented in the district. Of the Swedish women who did work within this district, married or single, a command of English may have made a vast difference in earnings. The Commission's study of the Townsend district found that out of 117 Scandinavian males and 139 females surveyed, 91.5 percent of the men and 82 percent of the women spoke English. This was a far higher percentage than any of the other groups surveyed; an overwhelming number of individuals were also literate.[25] The Commission report noted that Swedes, Germans, and the Irish were the highest immigrant wage earners in Chicago, while Swedes earned the highest wages among foreign-born individuals. Additionally, the children of Scandinavian immigrants benefited from education and the work ethic assumed of them, and they were able to command far more in average yearly wages than their foreign-born predecessors. Scandinavian Americans who reported their wages to the Immigration Commission averaged annual earnings of $327, with the majority earning $400 to $500 a year, compared to foreign-born Scandinavians who only brought in $221.[26] The report concluded that Scandinavians exhibited a particular eagerness for adaptation to American society, especially given their English-language acquisition and growing skills in the workforce. Their high rates of literacy, combined with an eagerness to join the ranks of civilized Americans greatly benefited the ways in which others perceived their work ethic.

Norwegians and, in smaller numbers, Danes who lived in the tenth, eleventh, and fourteenth wards in the West Town community of Chicago also exhibited a strong desire to acculturate to American customs in order to receive the benefits provided by reliable work in the public sphere. However, in the private inner workings of the Norwegian community, the Lutheran church, lodge halls, and other religious and secular meetinghouses illustrated a desire to remain ethnic. A member of the community, Olaf Ray, noted that the working-class Scandinavians who patronized the community's saloons rarely spoke English. Instead, according to Ray, even by the turn of the century, "nothing but Norwegian and Danish could be heard, and occasionally Swedish as the Swedes began settling among us."[27] In their work lives, especially those where American managers supervised them, Norwegians and Danes spoke English or prioritized its acquisition. The community voice, *Skandinaven*, understood the importance of English acquisition, especially for Scandinavian American children and stressed this

88 · CHAPTER 3

point in an editorial published in 1900. In spite of a temperate bend that encouraged Scandinavian American children to "read instead of drinking beer and brandy," the newspaper's editor noted the vital importance of further education in America. In a message aimed at Scandinavian youth employed as common laborers and domestic servants, the editor encouraged readers to attend night school at Northwestern High School as a means of becoming "acquainted with conditions in America." The explicit goal was for Scandinavian youth to use their knowledge to "rise above the level of hewers of wood and drawers of water for others" and eventually join the American middle class.[28]

In comparison to the more residential Townsend District or the working-class neighborhood of West Town, Lake View was the middle-class, commercial center of Scandinavian life in Chicago. Annexed to Chicago in June 1889, the farming community grew to accommodate the growing ethnic population and became known for its shops, restaurants, and meeting places that catered to Chicago's Scandinavian population. By the 1900s, Swedes were the dominant ethnic group in Lake View constituting 54 percent and 57 percent of the population of enumeration districts 763 and 765, respectively, in the twenty-fifth ward.[29] In contrast to the Townsend District, Lake View's residents were relatively younger while a significant component of its men occupied skilled positions. Children under the age of 15 comprised nearly 40 percent of the community's population while the majority of the adult population was between the ages of 20 and 40. According

Table 3.4: Occupational structure in 1900 of adult Scandinavian men and women in enumeration districts 762 and 765 (older than 15 years)

Men			Women		
Occupation	Number	%	Occupation	Number	%
High officials	6	1.2	Entrepreneurs	6	1.2
Large entrepreneurs	7	1.4	Domestic servants	22	4.4
Low officials/clerks	47	9.5	Laundresses	12	2.4
Small entrepreneurs	42	8.5	Saleswomen	11	2.2
Artisans	149	30.0	Needle workers	43	8.6
Skilled workers	84	16.9	Clerical workers	14	2.8
Unskilled workers	44	8.9	Factory workers	2	0.4
Service workers	66	13.3	Nurses	6	1.2
No answer given	51	10.3	Boarding	2	0.4
			Teachers	5	1.0
			Service workers	5	1.0
			No answer given	373	74.5
Total	496	100	Total	501	100

Source: U.S. Census Bureau, The Twelfth Census of the United States: 1900; Matovic, "Embracing a Middle-Class Life," in *Peasant Maids—City Women*, 269.

to the U.S. Census of 1900, adult Scandinavian men who resided in Lake View largely worked in skilled positions or as artisans while adult women who worked found positions as either needle workers or domestic servants (see table 3.4).

One question that arises from these findings points to the high percentage of women who did not respond to the census question of occupation. Scholars have found that census reports on the sexual division of labor are often misleading. Married and widowed women had invisible employment inside and outside the home as small-scale entrepreneurs running a bakery, a boarding house, or a laundry. Because responders did not consider these positions—which were an extension of the domestic sphere—to be "work," they did not report their occupations to the census enumerator.[30] Another misleading census result stems from the number of women who reportedly worked as domestic servants. Significant numbers of women who previously called Lake View their home worked as live-in domestics with families, thereby creating a preponderance of young, Scandinavian women living in areas outside of Lake View. Otherwise, Lake View was far more ethnically Scandinavian than census records illustrated. What remains clear about the census results, however, was that a younger generation of Scandinavians living in Lake View in 1900 held mostly skilled, respected occupations in comparison to other ethnic groups living in Chicago. Furthermore, Lake View grew into an insular community defined by its Nordic whiteness for young families looking to raise their children in the ethnic traditions and familiarities of home.

By the 1900s, Lake View was abuzz with activity, as new immigrants moved into the neighborhood and business owners capitalized on the needs of their Scandinavian neighbors in keeping the traditions of the old country alive. Compared to the larger urban centers of Sweden, the commercial district of Lake View was more accessible to the recent immigrant and was comprised of popular meeting places, Scandinavian restaurants, dance halls, and theaters where patrons could engage in the language and culture of home.[31] The centrality of religion was likewise evident. Four of the community's churches were established between the 1880s and 1890s, including the Elim Swedish Methodist Episcopal, the Trinity Lutheran Church, the Lake View Mission Covenant, and the Swedish Evangelical Mission Covenant Church of America. Both the church and primary schools in Lake View were instrumental in preserving the culture and tradition of home.

A majority of the primary and Sunday schools taught lessons in the languages of home and English. Over time, this dual immersion would become a problem for Swedish children of the first and second generations because daily life in Lake View often included use of a jumbled form of the combined languages.[32]

Figure 10: Stanley and Milton Swanson, Swedish American children circa 1912. Courtesy of the author.

The use of Norwegian, Swedish, or Danish also divided generations of older community members and new immigrants from second-generation youth born in America. Eventually, Lake View's businesses became a point of contention regarding ethnic polarization. The Dalkullan bookstore sold only books written in Swedish; shops and restaurants like Belmont Hall, the Viking Temple, and, later, the Temperance Café Idrott fostered an insular culture that excluded patrons who did not speak Swedish. In many ways, social expectations in Lake View were backward compared to other communities throughout Chicago. The older generation, despite the benefits of skilled work and societal acceptance, consistently took offense to the actions of mostly younger Scandinavians, who wished to assimilate into American life.

One insular practice that peaked anthropologic enthusiasm was the endogamous marriage patterns of many Scandinavians. According to the Census of 1900, the Nordic population of Chicago maintained significant white racial potency: 92 percent of Swedish-born individuals married Swedes, 86.5 percent of Danes married Danes, and 86.9 percent of Norwegians married Norwegians.[33] If intermarriage with other ethnic groups took place, the partners often came from other Scandinavian countries or from Germany, or they were native-born Americans.[34] While it was not a conscious decision for immigrants to marry in order to maintain Nordic whiteness, it was a concept revered by eugenicists during the early twentieth century. Young Scandinavian men and women also followed a unique division of sex in marriage patterns and economics by often delaying marriage until financially secure. In 1900, the average age at first marriage for members of the Trinity Lutheran Church in Lake View was 28 for men and 24 for women compared to the average ages of 25 for American men and 22 for American women.[35] In Scandinavia, especially among the poorer classes, women tended to marry much younger. Once in America, many Scandinavian women consciously postponed courtship and marriage. When they did marry, couples often practiced family planning as a means of limiting family size. Despite the prevalence of endogamous marriage practices and the desire of many Scandinavian parents to teach their children about their ethnicity, Scandinavian American youth expressed a desire to be American rather than Scandinavian. This is one of a number of reasons young Scandinavian American women sought work as domestic servants during the late nineteenth and early twentieth century in Chicago. Both generations of women knew the possibilities the occupation offered for social mobility as women and as immigrants and many were willing to accept less-than-hospitable circumstances if their situation eventually led to acceptance as racial and cultural equals by Americans.

American Demand for the "Swedish Maid"

From a historical perspective, there is a clear synonymous association between Scandinavians and the job of domestic servant. By the late nineteenth century, one in five Chicago households employed domestic servants, who made up 60 percent of the city's wage-earning women. This was the leading occupation of women in Chicago at that time.[36] What was once considered a working-class position suited for older women who wished to supplement their family wages became popular among younger, immigrant women during the 1870s and 1880s. This shift coincided with the largest wave of Scandinavian immigration during the nineteenth century, comprised of young men and women who flocked to America with the promise of good employment and a place to live. In Scandinavia, such positions entailed endless manual labor with no promise of upward mobility or a share of the farm if domestics worked for their families. The draw of a higher social status and independence expressed in the letters of friends and family already in the United States played a significant factor in the decision of many young women to emigrate.

92 · CHAPTER 3

In their letters, friends and relatives emphasized the opportunities that Midwestern cities like Chicago offered Scandinavian women. In 1871, one young Swedish domestic explained in a letter to her sister that a Scandinavian domestic in Chicago "can support herself and her husband rather well on her earning, without his earning anything," concluding that she and her husband got along on her wages alone.[37] Despite Wibäck's insinuation that Scandinavian men did not have to work, the division of labor by sex was relatively equal for men and women. Books by Scandinavian travelers in America played another role in the decision to emigrate for many women who hoped to secure employment as domestics. Isidor Kjellberg, a popular Swedish author, painted an idyllic portrait of work as a domestic servant in the home of Chicago's elite in the 1890s, where Scandinavian workers exhibited both social and economic freedom. Kjellberg explained that Scandinavian domestics worked "from 6 in the morning until 7 in the evening. Every Sunday and Thursday afternoon she is free; there is never a question of 'earnest money.'"[38] Payment in "earnest" was a practice in which employers promised their workers a certain salary for their labor, only for the workers to receive far less money when they completed their work. Instead, Scandinavian workers and their employers settled upon fair wages for a decent day's work. As the experiences of Scandinavian domestic workers illustrate, elite employers favored their work ethic, appearance, and attention to detail and sought to fill their homes with the finest "Swedish maids" money could buy.

In 1889, prior to the opening of the World's Columbian Exposition in Chicago, a group of wealthy Chicagoans pondered the potential of a residential escape far from the bustling downtown business district. The idea of moving away from the confines of city, which was dirty and filled with immigrants, appealed to residents of Chicago's posh Prairie Avenue district. Earlier in the 1850s, German immigrants who found success in the transportation industry went about constructing the planned community of New Trier Township. The idyllic village of New Trier, modeled after Trier, Germany, encompassed a new vision of progress and growth of Chicago's North Shore suburban region.[39] Chicago's elite saw the North Shore as an opportunity to build a utopian Chicago modeled on the richest and homogenously white communities of the East Coast. One of the group's leaders was Joseph Sears, a financier with money to spare, who purchased the 223 acres of land between Wilmette and Winnetka in preparation for what he referred to as a "pioneer experiment in planned living." To Sears, such planned living entailed palatial mansions with modern conveniences like plumbing and heat; paved streets and walkways; and recreational parks, but most importantly, his perfect residential society of Kenilworth maintained a "homogenous character."[40]

Figure 11: Joseph Sears, founder of Kenilworth, an idyllic suburban region north of Chicago. Courtesy of the Joseph Sears Family Papers, Photographic Collection, Kenilworth Historical Society.

In order to ensure the community's homogeneity, land deeds contained rigid restrictions to preserve the racial and class-based character of the town Sears envisioned. Village restrictions required high-quality home construction, consistent maintenance and upkeep of large lots, and massive premiums to guarantee that only the rich could reside in the town. The most important element in preserving the town's whiteness was the requirement that limited land deeds only to Caucasians.[41] Increasing numbers of affluent Chicagoans migrated north of the city to Kenilworth and the surrounding suburbs of Wilmette, Glencoe, Highland Park, Lake Forest, and Evanston in order to adopt Sears's mantra of planned living and homogeneity. Builders set back large estates away from roads and surrounded mansions with coach houses, garages, and stables to keep the family unit and its staff in close proximity.[42] Kenilworth drew the attention of many prominent visitors to the World's Columbian Exposition of 1893, including the fair's famed architect, Daniel Burnham, who designed Sears's home and another residence. Another Chicago architect, Franklin Burnham, designed Kenilworth's railroad station and a number of its homes, and George W. Maher, a contemporary of Frank Lloyd Wright, brought his distinctive Prairie style to the small, affluent village. After the Exposition, Chicagoans began to refer to Kenilworth and the North Shore as "the tuxedo of Chicago," understood as the playground of the very wealthy.[43] Within a matter of several years, Kenilworth and its neighboring communities grew to become one of the most affluent areas in all of the United States with property values matching and even exceeding the most elite addresses of the East Coast. With such mansions came the need for a well-trained and attractive labor force who could live up to the expectations of the privileged families who employed them.

North Shore employers sought to staff their homes with the most efficient workers with high moral character but also desired servants whose physical features would match the opulence of their homes. While Chicago's robber barons toiled in the world of business, their wives maintained their homes and employed the very best workers to do the domestic duties they did not wish to take on. A significant number of North Shore's elite wives actively sought Scandinavian domestic workers by issuing advertisements and by visiting employment agencies. Advertisements for domestic positions appeared in both American and foreign-language newspapers, including all of the major titles of the Scandinavian American press. In an era before fair labor practice laws, potential employers used direct, even discriminatory, language to place ads that favored certain physical and behavioral qualities desired in a servant. Some advertisements made clear the expectations and moral standards of potential employers, such as one advertisement placed by a female employer in *Svenska Tribunen* who desired to find a "Christian Swedish young or middle-age girl for housekeeper."[44] To these mistresses of the home, their help reflected upon their moral character, and therefore these elite women desired domestics who would mirror their piety, purity, and domesticity to their guests.

Advertisements in English-language newspapers like the *Chicago Tribune* often demanded competence as the most vital quality desired of potential employees and were specific as to which groups they would—and would not—employ. One wealthy family with a Michigan Avenue address called for "a competent German, Swedish, or Norwegian girl for general housework in an American family" and made it very clear that "no Irish need call."[45] In this advertisement as well as others, the desire for competence was often a thin veil for establishing a racial and ethnic social hierarchy in Chicago and other cities. Other employers specifically noted that they wanted only Scandinavian women who fit within a certain age range to work in their homes; one potential employer requested, in a help-wanted advertisement, a "Swedish maid, not over 30 years," for general housework and cooking in their home.[46] According to many similar advertisements that requested younger help, it was clear that competence and youth were at a premium in the eyes of potential employers who desired workers who made their homes more attractive and could do their jobs well. As time went on, Scandinavian women would prove themselves as especially talented cooks and attentive servants for Chicago's elite, while Chicago's newspapers continued to illustrate this preference for Nordics in service jobs.

Chicago's newspapers published an array of requests by middle-class employers who specifically sought Scandinavian, German, or Polish women to perform daily cooking, cleaning, and childcare chores, and to display their prosperity. Prior to the turn-of-the-century social construction of race, advertisements used coded language like "strong" instead of more deliberate racialized language like "Nordic" or "Alpine" to refer to the context of preferred workers. American families stated their desire for Scandinavian and German servants who were not necessarily physically "strong," but displayed strong racial stock. Their workers were women whom they entrusted with their most private of social spheres, who educated and cared for their children, and who cooked their family meals, and therefore needed to be of good, strong character. Because of this, German and Scandinavian women were hired more often than Italian and Jewish women in Chicago households because of considerations of race that were not deliberate but nevertheless employed. From the perspective of northern Europeans, especially those from rural origins, factories did not provide an appropriate workplace for young women, whereas domestic service offered more security, independence, and ideal preparation for married domestic life. Differing cultural norms and a distaste for menial labor were the main reasons why Italian and Jewish women shied away from domestic service and sought industrial work.[47]

The World of the "Swedish Maid"

Scandinavian women seeking employment advertised their services in the "situations wanted" section of Chicago's newspapers and illustrated self-awareness of their preferential status by specifically noting their ethnic background. Several advertisements were frank about the employee wanting to take on only "light housework" in a small American family, while one Swedish girl emphasized her desire to work for a "first-rate" family in a "large North Shore home" in the *Chicago Tribune*.[48] Others used the language of American employers to note their "strength," like one "green" Swedish girl who described herself as "strong and willing" and in need of a "good home more than wages."[49] Scandinavian women employed this key term, as well as "capable" and "competent," within advertisements to signal to potential employers that they would make good servants and would not follow some of the more negative stereotypes that preceded them. Into the twentieth century, Scandinavian women became even more specific as to the types of tasks they would—and would not—take on in potential employment. Many specified that they were in search of second jobs that required light housework and that would not require laundry duties or other such arduous tasks. In return, American employers would be ensured maids with a knowledge of English and excellent references, according to the potential employee.[50]

Scandinavian men as well as women acknowledged an understanding of preference for their ethnic group in service-related positions. What differed, however, were the demographic elements they provided to would-be employers due to gendered divisions of labor. In one advertisement, a Norwegian man named J. Anderson sought work as a chauffeur and skilled mechanic; he specified that he was 28, single, and could work in the city or country. Another man described himself as a "middle-aged married Swede" and desired work as a coachman in a rural environment away from downtown.[51] Advertisements often provided the age and marital status of male job seekers and played upon American stereotypes of Scandinavian male identity as simple farmers, noting desires to return to the countryside. Such requests to return to the countryside illustrated positive masculine images of Scandinavian pioneers whom the elite admired for their spirit and rugged individualism. For Scandinavians in service work, the practice of seeking better employment when dissatisfied with their current positions was one that carried over from home. In this process of horizontal mobility, Scandinavians attempted to advance their skills, often bettering their bargaining position for the next job, with the goal of becoming a live-in servant in a millionaire's home.[52] For Scandinavian men operating in a world of American gender divisions that stressed the male importance of the attainment of wealth, their goal indicated a desire for acceptance and upward mobility in Chicago.

Upon entering into Chicago's workforce, Scandinavian men and women learned that employers could exploit their labor just as easily as any other ethnic group and would therefore need to advocate for themselves or risk falling into unfortunate situations. As Chicago's industries grew, so did untrustworthy employment agencies that stationed agents at Union Station waiting to descend upon the droves of immigrants arriving on trains from New York. Agents approached Scandinavian men and women using their native language and appeared to have the best interest of their neighbors in mind. Such employment offices understood the premium placed on the work of young Scandinavian men and women and opened scores of offices in Lake View, some of which were operated out of homes where business transactions took place across a kitchen table. Agents were pervasive in their efforts to exploit new immigrants, not only waiting at Union Station but also walking the streets of Lake View, combing through rooming houses, restaurants, churches, and immigrant aid societies in the neighborhood.[53] When these employment "agencies" nabbed a potential client, they required registration fees whether or not the applicant was able to pay; if he was unable, the agency garnished their first month's wages. The work of "strong" Scandinavians was in great demand, yet many found themselves struggling from the outset to rise out of a cycle of poverty.

In response to the problems created by exploitative agencies, good-hearted community members worked to establish free employment agencies that would serve the needs of Scandinavians looking for work and help them enter a safe workplace. One such advocate, Othelia Myhrman, combined her efforts with the Swedish National Union to create an employment agency to aid newly arrived Scandinavian women who sought positions as domestic servants. After her arrival in Chicago in 1874, Myhrman worked as a domestic, which inspired her ambitions to help others. After a series of bad employment choices, she settled into a comfortable position when a fellow Scandinavian domestic suggested her employer to Myhrman. Newspapers such as *Svenska Nyheter*, *Svenska Kuriren*, and *Skandinaven* reported on the positive efforts of such agencies, as well as the number of employees who made use of their services, which often totaled several hundred a month. In May of 1903 alone, the free employment bureau of the Swedish National Association placed 225 men and 120 women in open positions throughout Chicago, which was the largest number employed through the efforts of the bureau.[54] The efforts of Swedish national agencies and word of mouth helped to protect would-be domestics from exploitative work practices, which other ethnic groups may not have enjoyed.

The Norwegian National League Employment Office witnessed similar numbers of successful employment transactions and noted its success in employing women as domestics. The office reported that demand was actually greater than the number of applicants as North Shore residents clamored for Scandinavian help in their homes to the point that their agents could not keep up with requests. One *Skandinaven* article specified that the average pay for domestics employed through the office ranged from $4.00 to $5.00 a week and offered the additional incentive—that this residence would not require its domestics to do the arduous task of laundry—in an effort to pull more available help to their agency.[55] Other Scandinavian employment offices in Lake View and the Townsend District witnessed similar demands, finding that Scandinavian men and women were able to locate reliable domestic work almost as quickly as they placed their advertisements.

98 · CHAPTER 3

Once men and women were able to locate secure positions, their experiences varied greatly, yet the location of their employers were a determinant of their outcome. Based on the size of the family and their home as well as their wealth, employers kept a staff that ranged from three servants all the way up to twenty. Between the 1890s and World War I, many Chicagoans considered the number of servants employed as indicative of wealth and family status within society. Stina Hirsch's mother, who worked as a servant for the Armour family of meatpacking fame, recalled that their Lake Forest home regularly employed a staff of eleven, divided by sex with the female servants living in the main house and the males residing in the coach house.[56] The spacious interior of the family's home maintained a typical Victorian style with spaces divided between leisure and work. On the servants' side of the home stood a number of rooms devoted to labor beyond the sight of the family, including sewing, ironing, floral arranging, and silver polishing, which adjoined a spacious laundry room. Conversely, the family's living quarters were dedicated to indoor leisure, including living and sitting rooms, a library, dining areas, dens, studies, music rooms, billiard and other playrooms, sunrooms, a terrace, and vast bedrooms with separate baths for adults and children.[57] The divisions of the home and its opulence symbolized a tradition addressed by sociologist Robert Coles who wrote that the North Shore families largely represented that of the old stock of Americans who inherited their wealth and therefore continued to view society as one comprised of separate spheres.[58] However, with the massive influx of good help in their homes over time, affluent North Shore wives were able to enjoy both spheres—the leisure of home life and the benefits of travel and volunteer work within North Shore and Chicago society.

The experiences of work in the North Shore homes varied from family to family, yet Scandinavian domestics could expect a generally positive experience based on the accounts of various workers. Like the founders of Kenilworth, many families expected their staff to maintain an outward appearance of professionalism and efficiency. The Sears family, however, went beyond to guarantee the satisfaction of their staff, which was largely Scandinavian. In the Sears's home, servants could expect to take on a majority of the housework; Dorothy Sears's diaries and letters illustrated that her daily schedule was representative of a life that affluence could afford her. According to her diary, from August until October of 1905, the Sears family enjoyed a vast European tour, and Dorothy returned to recording the events of daily life, which often lamented of "awful fit[s] of laziness," "playing with the baby until bedtime," voice lessons, trips downtown, and shopping.[59] Like many other elite families of Chicago, the Sears family sent their children away to boarding preparation schools on the East Coast when they reached school age, and therefore, the servants were required to care for the only young children. As Sears's diary and various accounts illustrate, many families that employed Scandinavian domestics were accommodating and offered them many chances to assimilate into modern American society.

The availability of dual-language cookbooks and the questions posed to advice columns in Chicago's newspapers during the late nineteenth century indicated that there was a desire among North Shore families for their "Swedish maids" to learn English. One advice-seeker asked *Chicago Tribune* columnist Marion Harland: "I have a Swedish maid who is anxious to learn English. Can you suggest some books [with] interesting yet simple words that I could get for her from the public library?"[60] Harland advised the writer to converse with her servant, rather than force her to read books, illustrating her suspicion of some of the more selfish desires of female employers. Many employers forced their workers to assimilate by learning English, while others desired the satisfaction of berating their help in a language they both understood. Nevertheless, the reader's question indicated a half-hearted desire to educate servants in American customs and traditions.

One popular cookbook written by Carl Grimsköld, *Swedish-American Book of Cookery and Adviser for Swedish Servants in America*, became a best seller after employers purchased the book in order to help servants learn English. The book, designed for the "newly arrived Swedish servant girl" contained advice, menus, and recipes in double-columned pages with Swedish on the left and English on the right. In the Introduction, the author explained in Swedish that he hoped that his book would rid its reader "of difficult problems which are associated with the greenhorn's position as a result of being unfamiliar with local language and habits."[61] The author simultaneously wrote an introduction in English intended for the mistress of the house to read in "modeling a kitchen mechanic," emphasizing self-control, consideration, and patience. Playfully, Grimsköld wrote a "recipe" for the employer to follow in which he advised them to mix equal parts of discipline and charity together, "let it simmer well, and let it be taken daily (in extreme cases in hourly doses), and be kept always on hand. Then the domestic wheels will run quite smoothly."[62] Grimsköld's attention to the position of both the servant and the mistress of the house acknowledged the difficulties of both employer and worker in finding common ground. Such advice books and columns illustrated a desire among employers to amicably work with their help and educate them in American ways so they could assimilate into society. The end goal of the process was to have a "strong," assimilated domestic staff whose physical attributes made their homes appear even more opulent.

By the twentieth century, Scandinavian domestics perpetuated a continuous draw of workers into service positions in the homes of Chicago's North Shore elite through letters home that expressed the higher wages and good treatment they received in comparison to other ethnic workers. Immigration historians often attribute the positive content of such correspondence to the loneliness and isolation that domestics often felt; however, the details of many letters suggested a largely positive experience.[63] Typically, Scandinavian domestics were paid comparatively well and received Thursday and Sunday afternoons off with a set curfew of 10 p.m.; employers found that their workers were more efficient in their jobs when they were given time off, especially to engage in acceptable activities such as church attendance. By the 1900s, this leisure time became so common that on Thursdays, as young Scandinavian women flocked to the trains exiting the North Shore for the city, conductors announced stops in Swedish and Norwegian for "Torsdagsflickor," or "Thursday girls," which they called Scandinavian domestics.[64] While one could speculate as to the validity of the positive experiences encompassed in their employment, further evidence from the employers' perspective suggests that Scandinavian domestics were indeed preferred in the homes of Chicago's elite.

One series of letters between a member of one of Chicago's oldest families, Walter Franklin Newberry, and the family's former domestic servant, Hannah Mathison, illustrated that the Newberrys considered Mathison as a member of their family. Throughout the summer of 1893, Mathison, who worked a number of years for the Newberry family, earned enough money in her position to travel home to Norway to tend to her ailing mother; upon her departure, however, Mr. Newberry wrote to her pleading for her return. In her reply, she recounted her gratitude to the family for a wealth of different benefits, including her acquisition of English.[65] Furthermore, Mathison's replies suggested a genuine connection with the family that went well beyond a typical work arrangement, as she concluded each letter with "love to you all" and a plea for Newberry to "kiss little Walter, Hannah . . . and grandma Newberry" in her absence.[66] One could argue that Mathison's correspondences with her former employers were indicative of an incredibly unique work experience. However, Mathison's positive recollections of her work as a domestic are reminiscent of a large portion of experiences recorded by Scandinavian domestics of their work.

As increasing numbers of Scandinavian women found positions in the homes of Chicago's elite, the Scandinavian and American press showed an interest in their experiences. From both perspectives, journalists wanted to know why Scandinavian women fared better in domestic service than other ethnic groups. In 1891, the well-known editor of *Svenska Tribunen*, C. F. Peterson, wrote "The

Servant Girl," in an effort to bring attention to the diligent work of Swedish maids. Peterson remarked that Swedish women were in high demand by Chicago employers due to their perceived worth in society. Because of their value, the domestic "underwent beautification under the influence of her enviable profession . . . she appears in elegant clothing, learns the language under the tutelage of the lady of the house and soon begins appearing as a lady of society."[67] While Peterson's assessment of employers' intentions to make Swedish maids into ladies of society was an overstatement, a notable shift in manners and behaviors often occurred where Scandinavian women became more knowledgeable of proper society etiquette and current fashion trends.

In comparison to other positions available to immigrant women, such as shopgirl, seamstress, factory worker, waitress, or shop assistant, which required "10 to 12 hours of daily effort" and hard labor, Peterson remarked that the first objective of the Scandinavian domestic was becoming a "real lady" through her work. Achieving this objective was entirely possible according to the author, who pointed out that Scandinavian domestics could expect to learn English, as well as how to become an "American girl" by way of their female employers.[68] The clear intention of most employers was assimilation, or at least acculturation of their domestics to American norms. The process of transforming Swedish maids into American girls was made easier by way of their racial whiteness in comparison to other immigrant groups. Furthermore, Peterson and other Scandinavian writers illustrated that this was an acceptable and even welcomed process, noting the benefits of acculturation for young women in the community.

By the 1910s, Lake View witnessed a generational shift as a large number of Scandinavian American youth were growing into adulthood. As typical of second-generation immigrant groups, many of Lake View's youth had dreams of leaving the old neighborhood, attaining jobs or going to school, and everything else that signified the process of becoming American. Young Scandinavian American women expressed their desires to attain types of employment that were different from their mothers' generation. In an article published in June 1903, the editor of *Svenska Nyheter* reflected upon these desires, which in his opinion were driven mostly by youthful goals for independence and leisure. The choice of the second generation to become a maid or a "factory girl" offered many benefits and drawbacks in both positions. As the editor explained, "if the girl works in a factory, she is able to live at home, or together with some other girl, or alone, wherever she wants. . . . If she takes a position as a maid, she has a safe place in which to live, and she need not worry about the food question."[69] The editor understood that during young adulthood, "the desire is strong for pleasure," and that the monotony of both positions could prevent youth from participating in nighttime leisure.[70] The editor concluded that while factory work provided a tempting allure of independence, the maid's work was much healthier and provided far more security for a young working woman. Nevertheless, young Scandinavian Americans continued to pursue positions that offered both independence and a chance to earn higher wages and gain further credibility in the American workforce.

The domestic virtues and cultural potential of integrating Scandinavian women into American society found equal praise in the American press. One article printed in the *New York Herald* commended Scandinavians for using positions like domestic service as a stepping-stone to further opportunities. Rather than some unfortunate immigrants who exhibited no ambitions for upward social mobility, the author argued that young men and women from Scandinavia "set out with hopes and determination to make their fortunes and gain such positions in life as they can rightfully claim by virtue of their ability, honesty and industriousness."[71] When *Svenska Tribunen* reprinted the article in Swedish, the editor pointed out that Scandinavian domestics could expect top dollar for their labor, earning "fifty to seventy five, even one hundred kroner per month, after she becomes accustomed to American ways." The benefits of assimilation were great, and according to community newspapers like *Svenska Tribunen*, giving into the process could mean pay equal to that of skilled men. Opportunities for worker and employee would only multiply, according to one editor, who wrote, "In twenty years has there been such a demand for Swedish workers." America had become the capital of produced consumer products, which led to an overall boost in prosperity for an increasing number of white, middle-class citizens who could now hire domestic help.[72]

National women's publications such as *Harper's Bazaar* noted a growing trend among society women not only for hiring Scandinavian domestics, but also for doing everything in their will to keep their help. In a 1908 article, a reader from Hartford, Connecticut, gave explicit instructions on how she kept her Swedish domestic happily employed for three years. While her method of domestic management included a reasonable amount of worker autonomy, the author stressed that she did not want to give readers the impression that her house was "ruled by the maid." Acknowledging that she prioritized the comfort and well-being of her domestic, the author emphasized to the magazine's elite readership that, as employers, they needed to maintain hegemony within the household. If employers maintained this balance and offered "a little tact and consideration" to valuable domestics, the result could produce "careful, neat, and most willing service" rather than a hostile environment in her kitchen.[73] The author's com-

The "Swedish Maid" • 103

mon sense advice could apply to all domestic workers; however, her emphasis on ways to maintain a healthy relationship with one's Swedish maid illustrated the commodity of their labor.

Studies written by American women, including Lucy Maynard Salmon's *Domestic Service* and Lillian Pettengill's *Toilers of the Home*, illustrated an American curiosity with the true experiences of foreign domestics and took varied approaches to the discussion. In *Domestic Service*, Salmon took surveys of domestic employers across America and found that her respondents admitted that they often chose their servants based on their physical appearance. In one survey, "Mrs. V" applied to an employment bureau for domestic help but refused six applicants because they were not "pretty" or "refined," eventually finding a Scandinavian woman who met her standards.[74] American women who intended to fill their homes with proper domestic help practiced a significant measure of vanity, but also strategy, in finding workers who exhibited outwardly attractive features, most often focusing on fair complexions.

Lillian Pettengill found this to be the case when she was an American college student posing undercover as an immigrant girl for the sake of exposing feminine snobbery toward domestic help at the turn of the century. In her first encounter with a potential employer, Pettengill commented that one of the first remarks made was in reference to her feminine appearance. Remembering her embarrassment, Pettengill noted, "After she considered me from top to toe, she remarked with much enthusiasm and for all the world as if I were a prize cow up for sale, 'You are a nice *looking* girl; yes, a *very* nice looking girl.'"[75] Pettengill's study similarly illustrated an underlying discourse on perceptions toward European ethnic groups. One employer was skeptical about her intentions, not that she was an American posing as an immigrant, but that she was potentially a "rough Irish girl" instead of a German, as she was posing under the alias "Eliza."[76] By the 1910s, the "Swedish maid" was becoming a popular character in American culture used to characterize the benefits and drawbacks of immigrant workers. By this time, as the ranks of Scandinavian immigrant women grew to staggering numbers, competition for good domestic positions grew scarce. Though surprisingly, as competition grew, many Scandinavian women began to criticize the positions they had become synonymous with, like Inge Lund whose investigation of domestic service painted a negative image of the popular job.

Lund, whose 1917 work exposed the drawbacks of domestic work for Swedes, took a similar approach to Lillian Pettengill's study by posing as a newly arrived Swedish immigrant. Her muckraking study, *En Piga i U.S.A (A Maid in the U.S.A.)*, recounted Lund's experiences in New York, where she navigated between two different personas: the newly arrived greenhorn and the seasoned, literate immigrant who had worked in the United States for years. One important element in finding suitable employment that Lund overlooked, however, was the importance of solid references, even for Swedish maids whose reputations preceded them. In an interview for a domestic position, when asked by the lady of the house about her experiences with domestic work in Sweden as well as the United States, Lund lied and responded that she had been a Swedish maid for a long time. After getting tripped up because she had such a firm grasp of English but lacked the necessary references, Lund realized she was caught in her own lie by her potential employer. At that moment, the employer leaned forward and yelled, "Tell me the truth!" to which Lund replied she was stunned by the woman's harsh treatment of her.[77]

Lund's investigative report is theoretically shallow when one considers those in domestic service who encountered real problems including adultery and sexual harassment. One Swedish maid, Caroline Hansen, recalled her first job in a large home next to the Lake Forest Country Club on the North Shore as highly unfavorable when she was forced to witness her employer's dalliances while her husband was away. "The lady was not very nice," she explained, and every time her husband had to travel out of town for work, "she had somebody else come in. I wasn't used to that. I thought it was terrible."[78] As an inexperienced Swedish maid, Hansen also encountered problems with sexual harassment. In one job, she reluctantly recalled one instance when she had to defend herself "against the advances of a hired man" and another time from one of her employer's sons. In remembering these instances, Hansen illustrated both her intelligence and common sense, as she remarked, "I may have been green, but I wasn't that dumb."[79] Her experiences reflect upon the American cultural assumption of the Swedish maid as dim-witted and lacking in self-awareness, illustrating the persistence of negative, classist associations with the position.

Disappearance of the "Swedish Maid"

By the 1920s, the number of Scandinavian women in America who pursued domestic work had begun to dwindle. Following WWI, a notable shift in preference occurred among Americans who started to hire African American women for work as domestic servants because they felt they could exert better control over them. Changes in the national economy and labor market coupled with new opportunities for white women in skilled positions and the effects of the great migration vastly altered the labor market for domestic work.[80] Scandinavian women also gained a reputation for exhibiting a superficial sense of self-worth that their employers fostered. Domestic work also became cyclical for many women. Inge Lund used this pattern as the basis for her study, seeking out temporary places to stay in settlement homes and "safe" hotels between the times she settled with a family. The cycle would begin once again when Lund became dissatisfied with her employment because the mistress of the home grew increasingly demanding.

Most importantly, those who worked as domestics for a number of years used the skills they attained in order to move up the ranks of employment. Largely, Scandinavian women gained vital work experience, but most of all, acquired social skills and confidence needed to attain positions that could afford them more independence. As this shift occurred, a second-generation of Scandinavian Americans came of age that had similar goals in getting ahead in society. Quite possibly, the most alluring position available to young women, especially those of the second generation, was that of the "shopgirl." Like domestic work, the job surrounded women with the allure of the finest consumer goods available to Chicago's consumers.

Chicago was the birthplace of some of the world's most famous department stores, including Marshall Fields and Montgomery Ward—stores established as a direct effect of the industrial boom of the 1890s to cater to the needs of a growing elite class connected to the boom. Modeled after the traditions of fine gentlemen's shops in London and New York, the emerging moguls behind these department stores saw an immense opportunity to capitalize on the emerging tradition of female consumerism. The differences between these small shops and major department stores were vast, as moguls like Marshall Fields helped to build an empire of major stores that catered to the female buyer's needs; most famously, Marshall Fields's mantra to "give the lady what she wants" proved to be the impetus needed for such grandiose success.[81] Department stores, Susan Porter Benson asserted, were the agencies of a class-based culture, which carried "the gospel of good taste, gentility, and propriety to those who could afford its wares." Yet the contrast of such a culture came with the women whom they hired to sell to bourgeois matrons.[82] The job of the shopgirl, therefore, became one that was quite selective in both practice and range, just like domestic service.

As Benson pointed out, classist attitudes created a limited supply of middle-class women willing to stand behind a counter, and department stores were not equipped with the amount of income such women could earn elsewhere. Therefore, the economic decisions of its managers forced department stores to employ working-class women. In what Benson dubbed "the Cinderella of occupations," employers looked to transform their working-class shopgirls into genteel saleswomen by introducing them to the latest styles and fashion and encouraging them to emulate the ladylike behaviors of their customers.[83] In many of the more industrialized areas of the country, women in stores were less likely to be foreign-born than women in other occupations. However, in Chicago, immigrants from the British Isles, Scandinavia, and Germany were always well represented among saleswomen in department stores.[84] The world of commerce readily accepted those of northern and western European ancestry as the experiences of one young Scandinavian American illustrate.

During the summer of 1902, like many Chicago teenagers who had recently graduated high school, Pauline Hegborn Nelson expressed her excitement in her journal over the potential employment opportunities the city offered. That August, Hegborn would apply for and receive a job working as a shopgirl at Montgomery Wards located at Michigan Avenue and Madison Street—the heart of Chicago's commercial district. Hegborn's mother wanted her to become a domestic servant like herself; however, Pauline expressed that she wanted an "American" job. In comparison to the arduous tasks of her mother's generation, Hegborn described her job as one "she enjoyed every minute of," regardless of the relatively low wages she received for her work in comparison to other positions.

At work, Hegborn excelled in her position as a shopgirl and described Montgomery Ward as "a nice place to work" where the "bosses and crew ladies and all the help were a very nice type of people" that she admired.[85] She took great pride in her required work uniform, which consisted of a long, black skirt, shirtwaist, and hair bows made of black velvet—an image modeled after Chicago's elite female consumer. Quite possibly, the only negative encounter Hegborn recalled of her time at Wards was her daily trek past Browning Kings Men's store. In the mornings, the male employees of the store would stand in the

Figure 12: A photograph taken of Pauline Hegborn Nelson, fourth from the right, and her coworkers at Montgomery Ward's circa 1900. Courtesy of F. M. Johnson Archives and Special Collections, North Park University, Chicago.

doorway watching the shopgirls on their way to Wards. The young men called out to the women, trying to persuade them into a date for the evening, which Hegborn described as "unbecoming" in their efforts to attract female attention.[86] Like many other women in the 1900s, Hegborn later resigned from her beloved position at Montgomery Ward upon marriage. In comparison to a job she took later in life at a local grocery, Montgomery Ward's work culture allowed her to "try on" the experience of occupying another class temporarily.

Other opportunities for young Scandinavian American men and women illustrated an emphasis on educational advancement and the professionalization of work. The Augustana Hospital of the City of Chicago opened its training school for nurses in 1913 as a unique opportunity for young Swedish women who were active members of the Lutheran Church to become certified nurses. This highly selective training program offered the opportunity for women within the community to earn a significant amount of money and respect for their skills. During the school term of two years, the school required its female students to live in the home provided by the Hospital, submit to a period of probation, and take both day and evening classes and unpaid work within the wards of the hospital until graduation.[87]

The application process was markedly tedious and designed to narrow the ranks of applicants down to Swedish or Swedish American women who were familiar with American customs, could speak excellent English, and were upstanding members of the Lutheran church. As the handbook for nurses specified, the general requirements for admission included the following specifications: "Good health and physique, good moral character, age no less than twenty-one and not more than thirty five years, love and aptitude for the work, and . . . an academy or high-school education."[88] Just like the requirements of good domestic servants of the past, the expectations for Scandinavian American women remained in place—a nice appearance, youth, and enthusiasm for work continued to drive the ethnic and racial standard. Regardless of such intense conditions, the training school for nurses retained an average of eighty students a year with twenty-one graduating from the school in 1913. Upon successful completion of the nursing program, graduates of the Augustana Hospital training school for nurses found themselves in high demand, and many were able to attain positions as hospital and training school superintendents, assistants, surgical nurses, visiting social service nurse, and nurses in private families.[89] Training programs like those offered at Augustana Hospital illustrate the efforts of the community to educate their youth and give them opportunities their parents may not have had.

The experience of work for Chicago's Scandinavians played a significant part in building American cultural constructions of Nordic whiteness, especially in regard to assumptions regarding the work ethic and physicality of "Swedish" maids. Many Scandinavians found that because of their employers' preferential treatment at work, the public provided them with a notable amount of leeway when it came to social norms. The pull of American culture was strong, and as the next chapter will demonstrate, not all Scandinavians were interested in partaking in the socially acceptable forms of leisure that their communities offered. Just like any other ethnic group in Chicago, Scandinavians found themselves involved in public scandals, negative social commentary, and crime, regardless of the otherwise positive associations and assumptions of their group. What varied, however, was the response of Chicagoans and Scandinavians to news stories and events that painted Nordic men and women as deviant, immoral, and even suspect.

CHAPTER 4

Scandinavians Behaving Badly

Vice, Representation, and Reform
in Early Twentieth-Century Chicago

In 1910, at the height of a citywide panic over white slavery and vice in Chicago, public prosecutor Clifford Roe warned of the dangers of female individualism in a city "filled" with potential white slavers. While his warnings to lone Chicago females were stern, his case studies and arguments read like many of the other white slavery narratives published between 1900 and 1912, when the city shut down its red light district. In Roe's writings, Chicago's single immigrant women were always helpless victims in a cruel urban world. In one of his case studies, Roe published the testimony of one young Swedish woman who arrived in Chicago in October 1910, only to quickly "fall" into a life of forced prostitution, according to Roe. Roe's case study became one of the first to document the underside of Scandinavian immigrant life and illustrated a unique dichotomy of representation of seemingly exceptional Nordics. After all, "in morality and intelligence," as Herbert Casson put it in *Munsey's Magazine* in 1906, Scandinavians were virtually American.[1]

Upon her arrival from a small town in Sweden, a young man invited the twenty-year-old on a date in a park near her uncle's home where she was staying. The woman accepted the advance of the young man, only to be subjected to the man's forced "relations" with her, as Roe wrote. While she was able to fight him off, she lost her cousin's watch in the squabble—a small indiscretion that inevitably led to her subsequent downfall. According to her police statement, she was afraid to return to her uncle's house after losing the watch and, instead, walked the streets all evening with only $1.50 in her pocket—just enough to rent a room at 24th and State Streets from "a colored man." The next day, the same man approached her in the same neighborhood and suggested a room where she could stay the night, and make five dollars by having "relations" with him. The next day, the young woman met "Mrs. D," described in the police report as a "colored woman" who took her to a house on Dearborn Street, unaware that the house was a well-known brothel.

All signs pointed to the clandestine nature of the establishment and the black woman's intentions: she asked the young Swede if she liked to make money, she "powdered her up," and took her to some of the local saloons to "hustle" men to return to the brothel. This pattern continued for two weeks until "Mrs. D" saw in the newspapers that the young woman's uncle had reported her as missing and returned her out of fear of prosecution.[2] This reported case of white slavery was similar to other stories of young, immigrant women, lured away from their families by temptations of wealth, promises of love, or dangers of desperation. White slavery narratives of this period, written by pastors and other social purity advocates, always victimized certain racial categories of women, especially those classified as "Nordic," linking them to American "girls," who were also always victimized.

While the woman's own police statement admitted to several indiscretions on her part, the message she expressed in the courtroom painted a much different picture. In this version, she was an innocent victim lured into white slavery by a "colored" woman looking to make money in a racially divided world where her virtues and fair features as a Nordic woman could gather a premium in this sexual underworld. Despite his previous knowledge of the woman's police statement, Roe sensationalized the story she told in the courtroom and perpetuated the image of the woman as a victim of drugging and forced submission to the wiles of a "dangerous negress." Rather than a desperate woman, afraid to return to her uncle's home after losing a watch, she was now even worse off—now, she was a "thin, frail young woman," aided by a physician into the courtroom, whose only folly was taking a drink of lemonade at a dance that a young man named John had given her. In this new piece of testimony, the woman reported feeling dizzy upon drinking the lemonade, only to regain consciousness in a bed "in an entirely strange room." When Roe inquired in court as to why the young woman did not fight against her kidnapper, she replied that the "girls" were "pushed into submission" by whippings and beatings by the "negress" and customers until "their spirits are broken" and "are forced into a life from which they cannot escape." These new details, which the young woman had not previously provided in her statement to police, provided important context in a case of supposed white slavery.[3]

In 1933, upon comparison of Roe's reflections on the court proceedings and the Swedish woman's actual police statement, sociologist Walter Reckless noted a significant contrast between the "facts" presented in the case and the literary details added by Roe to draw public sympathy for the young woman. Remembering the 1910s, when the sensationalism of white slave traffic overshadowed the realities of female autonomy, Reckless nevertheless argued that the massive gap between truth and fiction were highly problematic when reflecting on the actual historical problem. According to the process of the case, Reckless reported that a friend of the girl's uncle appealed to Roe for help after the case reached a standstill eleven days after her disappearance. Rather than escaping the brothel and running to the police station, an investigator found the Swedish woman in a rear room of a saloon at 30th and State Streets. Within the case file, even the investigator emphasized that he was "attracted by the fact that a colored woman was accompanied by a very [white] pretty girl." The next day, police arrested both women and upon review of the case, the Swedish Council suggested to the United States Immigration Bureau that the young immigrant woman be deported. While Reckless admitted that the outcome of the case was uncertain, he hinted that the young woman acknowledged her indiscretions and refused to prosecute the men she accused during her trial.[4]

The ideological gap between Clifford Roe's and Walter Reckless's studies illustrate a vital division between perceptions of female sexuality during the white slavery "panic" of the late nineteenth century and the more realistic accounts of what actually occurred acknowledged in the findings of Chicago's Vice Commission. This gap is significant when considering the uniqueness of the case Reckless presented. Finding any public discussion of Scandinavians acting outside of the social roles Americans prescribed them is comparatively difficult when considering the wealth of cases focused on other immigrant groups in Chicago. Historians have begun to analyze this gap in our understandings of the context of morality and private spheres in relation to the white slavery panic of the early twentieth century; the topic remains an understudied, yet vital, element in the Scandinavian immigrant experience.[5]

Chicago: City of Sin and White Slavery

By the turn of the century, many citizens and newcomers regarded Chicago as one of the most lawless cities in the United States, rife with crime, corruption, and sexual danger that threatened young immigrants who arrived within its borders looking for job opportunities and independence. One of the biggest public debates of this era focused on the threat of "white slavery"—a term that appeared with great frequency at the turn of the century to refer to an extreme form of prostitution in which a woman was often exploited through some form of physical coercion, typically involving kidnapping. Between 1900 and 1910, the city came under media scrutiny when reform-minded individuals warned of "white slavers" responsible for the abduction of young, innocent European women. From an American perspective, immigrant women living "adrift" were not autonomous but, rather, victims poised to become a cautionary tale of male sexual exploitation. Conversely, Scandinavians used the barrier of language to create an insular discussion of the dangers of Chicago's city spaces from an ethnic perspective. Newspaper editors admitted to the particular vulnerability of Nordic women, whose imagined racial whiteness could attain top dollar in the American underworld of vice. Yet, Scandinavians were aware of the dangers their youth faced and held them accountable for the ramifications of their decisions, regardless of sex. Over the course of the 1910s and into the 1920s, stereotypes of the "women adrift" began to shift, as the assertive behavior of young independent wage earners eventually forced reformers, sociologists, and the media to acknowledge the active role they took in shaping their own lives.[6] While Americans feared the downfall of "women adrift," Scandinavians expressed a more progressive viewpoint on the dangers of vice and threats to female virtue. Instead, Scandinavians gave their youth agency in their own lives and often held them accountable for the ramifications of their decisions, regardless of sex, social, or marital status.

Recent works also tend to omit discussion of the connections of men and crime, viewpoints of the community toward crime, and proposed solutions to prevent their youth from becoming wrapped up in criminal activities.[7] From this omission, one could conclude that such documentation simply does not exist and that Americans viewed Scandinavians as pious, responsible people in comparison to other ethnic groups, who therefore did not elicit public concern. A wealth of primary source documentation, however, suggests the prevalence of an open dialogue in the Scandinavian press as to the dangers their young women and men faced. While the community discussed these dangers with noted concern, the tone of these conversations usually pointed to the actions of the perpetrators. Scandinavians were responsible for their own actions and community leaders expected those involved in vice to shoulder the blame for shaming the good name of Lutheran piousness, and subsequently Nordic exceptionalism.

The adults within the community gave Scandinavian youth the internal responsibilities of appropriate behavior, grounded first in the culture of home and continued in Chicago. Scandinavians used the ethnic press to build an insular discourse on the dangers of Chicago's city spaces while counseling their youth to act in ways that would bring the community pride and not shame. Community members actively put measures into place to steer their youth away from dangerous situations, largely focusing on the establishment of settlement homes as a haven for youth living adrift. Nevertheless, some Scandinavians found trouble within the city, which their newspapers widely reported in an effort to show support for their accused youth, while also expressing a disdain for their behaviors.

At the same time, Chicago's newspapers also took note of such social problems, but often viewed any connections between Scandinavians and city crime as isolated events that were not representative of the larger group. This chapter begins to analyze the significance of this forgotten "dark" side of Scandinavian Chicago, which included episodes of public drunkenness, sexual crime and prostitution, and illegitimacy. In bringing this history to light, this dialogue opens further ideological connections between a city coming to terms with modernity and shifting ideals of sexual morality framed by race. Rather than viewing immigrants as victims of their own circumstance, the focus of this chapter employs a feminist approach to explore the progressive viewpoints of Scandinavians toward female agency. Investigating such tragic histories from the viewpoint of historical actors, casual observers, sociologists and social workers, and the ethnic press offers a more complete picture of Scandinavians' encounter with vice outside of the framework of victimization.

Scandinavian Impropriety in Chicago

From the earliest days of settlement in Chicago, newcomers established stereotypes for all immigrant groups arriving in the city during an era of massive industrialization. For instance, Americans often depicted the Irish as rough drunkards who were prone to public fighting, while some viewed Italians as insular and sneaky, not allowing outsiders into their community establishments. Chicagoans created stereotyped perceptions of various immigrant groups as a method of coping with overwhelming diversity and crowding within neighborhoods, and Scandinavians received negative attention. One of the most common stereotypes focused on the drunken workingman who spent his evenings on a barstool at his favorite local tavern. The same was true of Scandinavian saloons, especially those run by Swedes, which were located within insular neighborhoods. In comparison to Swedes, Danes and Norwegians tended to operate saloons on the fringe of their neighborhoods and designed their taverns to appeal to a larger ethnic patronage. Despite a large component of teetotalers within the Lutheran church, some of the Lutheran-minded groups like the

Swedish and Norwegian singing societies met at bars. The argument went that the saloons were more spacious than meeting halls and could accommodate large numbers of people, while also being centrally located. In almost every way, the family-run saloon served as the center of the community for socializing and leisure but, in some instances, served as an unfortunate catalyst for crime.

When embarrassing public scandals arose, like that of the dismissal of the superintendent of the morgue of the Cook County Poor House for drunkenness in July 1891, Scandinavian newspapers first took a position of support on behalf of their accused compatriot. As one article, "Victimized Countryman," explained: a few days prior to the incident, superintendent Dr. Wimermark left for Minneapolis to attend the United Scandinavian Singers gathering and left another man, Mr. Pyne, in charge. In Dr. Wimermark's absence, the president of the board of trustees visited the Poor House and left explicit instructions with Pyne that he would have the right to discharge any personnel charged with drunkenness. This might seem like an odd set of instructions given to a man left in charge of a morgue; however, the president of the board knew that a number of workers were Scandinavian men who were stereotypically prone to drunkenness. The article charged both Mr. Pyne and the president of the board with discrimination against Scandinavian workers who, the editor argued, were falsely accused of negligence and drunkenness.[8] Stories like this one were common in the pages of Scandinavian newspapers, which often claimed false accusations of drunkenness and vice against their fellow countrymen.

In an effort to boost the image of their fellow citizens, newspapers published periodic tallies comparing the crime rates of Scandinavians to that of other immigrant groups. In January 1884, the most widely circulated Scandinavian newspaper, *Skandinaven*, made a notable announcement. According to the paper, during the previous year, there were "only six hundred and eighty-three Swedes arrested, four hundred and thirty-six Norwegians, and no Danes," compared to "five thousand, four hundred and eight Irish, and over twenty thousand American-born"—a figure that the editor called a "favorable indication for the Scandinavians."[9] Despite the fact that the Scandinavian newspapers used mostly Norwegian or Swedish language, articles such as this reflected upon figures reported in the larger, English-speaking publications. Six years later, in December 1891, *Skandinaven* claimed that over the course of the year, there were fewer Scandinavians accused of crimes than ever before, indicating, "Scandinavians are law-abiding" as the few cases that came before the courts were for "minor offences."[10] While Scandinavian newspapers played a major role in calming the fears of the community, these publications conversely sensationalized the actions of Scandinavians involved in crimes of passion as a means of defense.

Studies have shown that the actions and attitudes surrounding problems of vice were present in other urban areas with a large Scandinavian population. Joy Lintelman's case study of the 1907 records of the Minneapolis City Workhouse indicated that the inmates were a largely homogenous population whose sentences pointed to factors related to class rather than race or ethnicity. In 1878, the Minneapolis City Council established the workhouse as a means of channeling the free labor of prisoners jailed in the city into public improvements. Of the overall ethnic population of Minneapolis, 8.78 percent were Swedish and 5.44 percent were Norwegian and, in comparison to those documented at the workhouse, the Irish illustrated the greatest disproportion of those jailed. However, Scandinavians constituted nearly 20 percent of the workhouse population and were charged with public drunkenness, vagrancy, larceny, and disorderly conduct.[11] At the Minneapolis City Workhouse, the majority of Swedish inmates were single (76 percent) and mostly men; however, there were also twelve Swedish women sentenced to the workhouse and they comprised 5.4 percent of the female workhouse population. In contrast to the large component of single men, the majority of Swedish female inmates were married and younger. Drunkenness was the most common crime, followed by prostitution, which accounted for 20 percent of the women arrested.[12] Lintelman's study represents a microcosm of larger issues pertaining to Scandinavians involved in crime in urban areas other than Chicago. It is clear that Scandinavians committed crimes just as other ethnic groups did, despite the racialized assumption that they did not.

The news stories that emerged in Chicago's newspapers were ones that involved Scandinavian women engaged in shameful crimes that had the potential to tarnish the reputation of their communities. At the turn of the century, Scandinavian newspapers took particular care in defending the good name of female workers whom the American press feared would "fall" into dire circumstances. Joanne Meyerowitz found a disproportionate amount of Swedish and Norwegian women lived adrift compared to the ethnic distribution of Chicago. Out of the 6.3 percent of Swedes and 4.8 percent of Norwegians who comprised Chicago's total foreign-born population, 14.2 percent of Swedish and 14 percent of Norwegian women lived adrift in 1880, according to the Women Adrift Samples of the Federal Census of 1880.[13] Studies show that new immigrant women such as Italians and eastern European Jews built strong family and kin networks while Swedish and Norwegian women had more options when it came to living arrangements.[14] Although domestic servants did not constitute women living adrift, Scandinavians and Americans grew concerned over their tenuous position in society. Domestics occupied a gray area in regard to the attitudes expressed by those outside of their circumstances, especially native-born Americans. A good portion of Scandinavian domestics lived with their employers or with family, though they were still a matter of concern because they were single, workingwomen and therefore judged as being naive to the dangers of cities like Chicago. Given these attitudes, some considered the work of domestic service to be relatively safer than factory or shop work.

Yet, all young Nordic workingwomen, regardless of their positions, were not able to escape the judgment of an older guard of men in the community who judged them for their seemingly frivolous and irresponsible behaviors. In an 1872 letter to *Skandinaven*'s editor, a Norwegian man named Kund Larigelando expressed his outrage over the vanity of young Norwegian women who dressed like "American girls." Larigelando warned that the influence of American culture damaged every sense of Norwegian propriety for these women and when they could not afford to do so, they simply "sold their virtue." "After all," he exclaimed, "that is why the houses of shame exist."[15] Larigelando's public shaming of young Norwegian women who were trying out new customs as a means of becoming American was indicative of a generational divide but also of gendered, patriarchal structures intended to keep women in their assigned place. To Larigelando, if young Norwegian women stayed in the home and did not act selfishly through their desires to work, these problems would not exist. The tastes that workingwomen acquired were the problem, which he ostentatiously assumed led to prostitution.

In response to his claims, three "industrious shop girls" appealed to the editor of *Skandinaven* to publish their plea in defense of the reputation of young working Norwegian women in Chicago. It was insinuations like his, the women claimed, that created lasting negative stereotypes and could potentially affect future employment and public opinion. "We have come to the United States of America, where we get our good, honest pay either as servants or shopgirls until we get better positions," the women pleaded. In order to succeed within American society, the young Norwegians argued that work for wages outside of the home was crucial for higher education or marriage, and, therefore, women's work was imperative to the community. The pay was "always enough to keep [them] dressed respectable" and in conclusion, the women retorted "we do not wish to have our reputation spoiled by a person like K.L . . . we have always been respected by the Americans and we intend to remain so."[16] From their plea for the rights to work, these young women clearly expressed their desires to earn their own money while still adhering to the American social order, which encouraged women to marry, preferably at a young age.

The following summer, a similar debate arose between *Nya Verlden*, the paper consumed by middle-class, liberal Swedes and the more "modern" *Svenska*

Amerikanaren, over the respectability of Swedish women who worked as maids. In the first charge, *Nya Verden*'s editor expressed his offense over the frivolity of maids he described as "much finer ladies with clothing much more expensive than their mistresses." The editor eyed these women with suspicion because they earned only "four to five dollars a week."[17] He concluded that these women earned their extra income in ways that were not appropriate to mention in a respected community newspaper. In response, the editor of *Svenska Amerikanaren* argued that Chicago's Swedish maids were good, hardworking young ladies by and large. He pointed out that domestic work promised "steady employment, good pay, excellent treatment and lighter duties" and therefore, if women who worked as maids wanted to spend their hard-earned money on personal items, they had earned the right to do so.[18] It was not his right to question whether they were earning extra money to buy fine goods, frivolous or not.

In 1903, the editor of *Svenska Nyheter* spoke out about these negative assumptions of older Scandinavians in an effort to rationalize changing social mores and to argue that work in domestic service was "safer" by comparison. In this new industrial world, "the desire to go out in the evening is strong" and young Scandinavian workingwomen should be given leeway to have fun with peers after a hard day's work. Furthermore, the editor argued that community members needed to step back and offer young workingwomen a certain level of agency in their decisions, thereby placing the responsibility of whatever dangers they may encounter on them. After all, he retorted, long nights out on the town could result in consequences "far beyond the pale face and the weary body." The responsibilities of Scandinavian youth were far different from that of his generation and they understood that young women longed to become American. In this changing world, there were no chaperones, no "thoughtful lady of the manor to place restraint on her activities," especially in regard to domestic servants. While their actions could potentially have consequences "detrimental to the girl mentally, morally, and physically," from the perspective of this editor, let girls be girls.[19] Not all Scandinavians shared the newspaper's opinion; however, even youth from Chicago's most upstanding Nordic families started to have a greater sense of autonomy.

Many young workingwomen took this responsibility to heart, like Pauline Hegborn, a Swedish American teenager who wrote in her journal of going to movies or theaters, visiting restaurants and coffee shops, and touring various city museums like the Art Institute of Chicago. As she explained, "It was not unusual for a group to get together and go to a picnic on a Sunday and the girls would bring the lunch. . . . It did not take much to have a good time those days." However, she made a point to specify that their activities were always morally

118 · CHAPTER 4

sound, and involved "clean sport . . . no taverns."[20] Young Scandinavian Americans like Hegborn illustrated agency in their struggle for recognition as legitimate, hardworking immigrants by their peers. This conflict represented the vital effort that Chicago's Scandinavians put into their bid for American favor. Yet, the fear of corruption and sexual misconduct bred by the white slavery panic of the 1890s into the twentieth century threatened to unravel the perfect image Scandinavians were in the process of creating for themselves.

Nordic Whiteness and the White Slavery Panic

The white slavery panic began in Chicago during the 1890s in conjunction with the mass immigration of young women eager to find work in the city. Two exposés of vice written by antiprostitution reformers formed the basis of the ongoing argument that independent women were too naive to survive on their own: *Chicago's Dark Places* (1891) published by the Women's Christian Temperance Union, and British journalist William T. Stead's book, *If Christ Came to Chicago!* (1894). In these narratives, women who worked long hours for low wages and greenhorns to the city were equally in danger of either falling into white slavery or being unwittingly lured into it by handsome "cadets."[21] In 1910, at the height of concern surrounding white slavery, Ernest Bell's *Fighting the Traffic in Young Girls* voiced the concerns of missionaries, law enforcement officials, and victims on the dangers immigrants faced in Chicago's red-light district. According to one of the anthology's accounts, Chicago faced a particular problem of French, Jewish, Italian, and Japanese "importers of women" who blatantly operated under the guise of foreign mystique in the Levee district at 22nd Street on Chicago's south side. Their most valuable commodity was dealing in American "girls" for American and Chinese men; women from Italy, Sweden, and Germany were in equal demand. Whether it was true or not, the author knew of no resorts controlled by English, Scottish, German, or Scandinavian men.[22]

The buying price for a young girl on the white slave market was connected to their perceived whiteness. A woman from southern or eastern Europe could "sell" for $200 to $600 while a "girl" who was "especially attractive," otherwise from northern or western Europe, could garner a price of $800 to $1,000.[23] The underlying theme of Bell's anthology emphasized the diversity in ethnic and racial background, class and intelligence, and propriety of women lured into white slavery but warned the American public of the practice rather than protecting those in danger. Warnings heeded to young immigrant women did not reach them by way of white slavery narratives because the majority of newly arrived immigrants could not read them. In standard fashion, the conversation surrounding fears over female independence operated around young immigrant women but did not involve them.

Scandinavians, on the other hand, did involve those who were most threatened by white slavers but from a much different perspective. Scandinavian emigration handbooks also warned young women of the dangers of these "*kadetter*" but employed a distinctive tone, providing comprehensive advice on basic language skills, working conditions, housing, trade unions, and other points of concern for the newly arrived immigrant.[24] The reasoning behind the cautionary tales provided in emigration handbooks was part of anti-emigration propaganda that emphasized that the United States was a dangerous place for Scandinavian women and therefore they should not leave. The white slave trade was dependent on a collaboration of diverse ethnic groups, and thus official investigations of women forced into prostitution was understood as an ethnic problem rather than a political or social issue.[25] Migrant women were the commodity being acquired and sold, and immigrant men were the slavers; therefore, according to investigators, it was not America that was dangerous, it was world migration, particularly issues related to travel.

Fears surrounding young women being lured into a life of crime and white slavery were also felt in the Pacific Northwest, especially over those who traveled alone by train. At the end of the nineteenth century, a large influx of Scandinavians destined for the newly industrialized areas of Tacoma and Seattle drew the attention of the American press. In May 1891, the *Seattle Press-Times* called attention to this migration by reprinting an article from the *New York Sun*, which lavishly praised the qualities of Scandinavians who seemed "generally [to] have been seen by the established American community as desirable." Unlike immigrants from Poland, Hungary, and Russia, these "spirited" and "healthy" Scandinavians were destined to set an example of ideal racial qualities.[26] These assumptions regarding Scandinavian "health" resulted in positive assumptions on behalf of immigrants; however, those who wished to cash in on the racial collateral of young Scandinavian women, namely sex traffickers, also paid attention.

Helga Pederson Watney recollected her experiences as a young Scandinavian girl traveling alone by train along the Northern Pacific line destined for Tacoma, Washington. She specifically recalled a moment in Minneapolis, when a man dressed in a train conductor's uniform offered to take her suitcase and indicated that she needed to follow him. She described her luck in having involved parents who had read of such practices on the trains. The man was no train conductor, but instead a "white slaver" who intended to steal away young immigrant girls like herself and force them into prostitution. While Watney's parents educated her on the dangers of white slavery, some parents did not express such liberal attitudes in teaching their daughters how to respond to issues of sexual endangerment. Watney told of a neighbor from Sweden she described as "pretty, lovely, and from a good home, had class," whose parents never heard from her again after she arrived in America. Presumably, the young woman was stolen away by a kidnapper who used the same tactics to lure Watney away from the train; however, she had been saved and her previous neighbor had not.[27] The problems that young Scandinavian women faced in urban areas were twofold: many were innocently unaware of the threats they faced in traveling without friends or family, while clearly there were kidnappers who targeted women of a particular racial background.

Skandinaven published one of the first reports of a purported white slavery case involving Scandinavian women in November 1889, signaling the beginning of a massive campaign to prevent others from falling victim to such heinous crimes. The victim in question was not of Scandinavian descent, but her story was told as a cautionary tale to the workingwomen in similar situations. The article was unique in that it described an instance of human trafficking where a woman rather than a man forced a young migrant into prostitution. Intended to illicit shock from *Skandinaven*'s large readership, the article described "a white slave being held at the Harrison Street [Police] Station," a claim the author found unbelievable in the "modern city" of Chicago. It all began when a woman named Fawn Kittie (presumably a pseudonym) "lured" the young woman, Marie Dubhene, whom the author described as "small and good-looking" and "hardly fourteen years old" from Montreal, where she had been working. Dubhene told the police that she had no money to buy a train ticket, but that Kittie lured her to Chicago on the promise of a good job. When she arrived in the city, Dubhene soon realized that Kittie received money from another woman for her work in procuring Dubhene. Though the brothel owner warned that her escape would result in an arrest, Dubhene fled the brothel and police later arrested her for robbery. The author warned that this was a common practice to ground women in a perpetual system of sexual servitude. The brothel owners gave their "girls" clothing in return for their signature on a form that states it is their "mortgage" until they have earned enough money through prostitution to purchase their clothes.[28]

Joanne Meyerowitz explains that the experiences of young women living "adrift" like Dubhene combined elements of independence from family, naïveté, low wages, and sexual service work, which sparked the imaginations of Victorian, and later, Progressive writers. During this era, the woman adrift became a symbol of the threats that industrialization and urbanization posed to womanhood and the family.[29] While some viewed her as a threat, others depicted the independent wage earner as a poor, innocent victim whose virtue was the community's responsibility to protect. During the late nineteenth and early twentieth centuries, Scandinavian newspapers including *Skandinaven*, *Scandia*, and *Svenska Nyheter* filled pages with numerous tales of white slavery in an effort to warn young women about real dangers rather than victimize or blame them for their personal choices. While concerned about women living adrift, Scandinavian writers grew particularly concerned over some of the issues that domestic service raised. In 1915, Swedish scholar E. H. Thörnberg found in his study of Swedes in Chicago that domestic service was not nearly as "safe" as some had hoped. Instead, Thörnberg reported a significant problem involving the sexual exploitation of some domestic servants from statements he obtained from American employers, doctors, pastors, and social workers that resulted in a high illegitimacy rate.[30] Even outside of the job, women who sought work as domestics were in a tenuous position that put them in potential danger.

During mass immigration, competition for skilled and unskilled work became intense and many women eventually exhausted themselves looking for work. Traffickers trained to identify vulnerability sought out these women who were often out of money and in despair with nowhere to go. All too often, these women found themselves making a deal with the first person to approach them with a position despite their lack of credentials or references, much like four girls "found" at Sadie Richards's brothel. Richards, a notorious Chicago madam, was powerful in the white slave trade and used the tactic of hiring young women to work as maids in her private home on Washington Boulevard as a cover for her illicit business. In 1889, *Skandinaven* exposed Richards's tactics, which were especially useful in procuring Scandinavian girls, who often sought out domestic work. In the newspaper's exposé, instead of omitting the victim's names in order to protect their reputations, the author splashed their names across the headlines for all to see. Richards hired Clara Larson, Alma Peterson, Frida Hussen, and Minna Borg—all young Scandinavian women—to work as maids. The girls worked as proper maids for a period of time, until Richards introduced them to some "nice" men who Richards instructed them to "entertain." It was only a matter of time before the girls were "thoroughly broken in," according to the paper.[31] *Skandinaven*'s author intended to raise awareness by not publicly shaming and victimizing these girls. If young workingwomen like those found in Richards's brothel had been made aware of such scenarios, the unfortunate situation might have been prevented.

Tales of Scandinavian Vice, Delinquency, and Illegitimacy

Over the course of 1889, subsequent *Skandinaven* articles tracked stories of sexual vice, sometimes claiming that the young Scandinavian women were involved in kidnappings, and included graphic details for the time. One news item focused on a Norwegian, Fannie Eckstrom, who was kidnapped by a man and forced to live in a room at his hotel on West Madison Street, where "he and his friends would visit her and force her to have intercourse against her will." Other articles told of the devastation of young girls who were either "diseased or disabled" by several illegal abortions and by venereal diseases.[32] And while some American and immigrant newspapers denied the presence of any of their own being involved in sexual vice, Scandinavian newspapers by and large took full responsibility in acknowledging that an unfortunate portion of the community's young women were involved and, even sometimes, at fault. In most of the brothels or "schools of vice," as many newspapers called them, women were there because they were held against their will. However, as the article "Juvenile Delinquency" admitted, a few worked in brothels "because they liked [this kind of] life."[33] While this was a bold position to take, it was sometimes true, regardless of what brought the women or made them stay.

Another issue that came to the forefront of newspaper attention in Chicago was the problem of illegitimacy among immigrant women. In August 1880, the *Chicago Tribune* reported the cautionary tale of Mrs. Peterson, an unmarried Norwegian woman "without money or friends" who suddenly took ill in the middle of North Des Plaines street. Upon receiving temporary shelter in a nearby tenement house, the woman shortly thereafter delivered a baby. The newspaper reported that the attending physician refused to allow her to be moved due to her precarious condition; however, the people living in the tenement house "insisted upon the unfortunate woman's removal" and she was moved to the County Hospital.[34] While Norwegians nevertheless acknowledged this as a very public embarrassment for their community, the attention of their leaders focused much more closely on creating a solution to the issue of negative stereotypes in relation to young women. Furthermore, the embarrassment was one of differing social mores—for centuries, within Scandinavian cultures, there was a certain permissiveness given to illegitimacy, especially in old peasant and rural societies. Parishioners often viewed the arrival of a child as an occasion for official marriage in the church; otherwise, a marriage may not have taken place.

Other historians speculate that some parish records in Sweden reflected fines charged by the church for illegitimacy but no fees devastating enough to stop illegitimate births from continuing to occur in subsequent generations.[35] In Sweden, pregnancy was traditionally the first step toward marriage in rural regions, often publicly considered as a formal engagement between two people who planned to marry upon the birth of their child. The *Swedish Catalogue of the World's Columbian Exposition* acknowledged this practice; the number of births out of wedlock in Sweden was admittedly high at 10 percent of all births while matrimonial frequency was relatively low. In 1880, 49.3 percent of all western European men ages 25 to 30 were married compared to 40 percent of Swedish men, while only 47.7 percent of Swedish women in the same age range were married, compared to 62.5 percent of all western European women.[36] At the time, Swedish scholars exhibited a range of viewpoints on this cultural practice. E. H. Thörnberg remarked that Swedish women were no more immoral than other immigrant women, but they became pregnant out of wedlock more frequently because they considered conception as binding as marriage. Later community discussions would show that Chicago's Scandinavian citizens largely supported this ideology, especially in relation to Castberg's Laws in Illinois, which granted children born out of wedlock comparable rights to legitimate children.

Some Swedish women, however, were not as flexible in their moral viewpoints, such as Cecilia Milow who claimed that some women in her community had a "flagrant disregard for morals and were not ashamed of bearing illegitimate children" within American society.[37] Aside from Milow's viewpoint, the question remains as to why illegitimacy has not been further considered as a historical problem that affected the Scandinavian community. One of the most telling reasons is that the problem of illegitimacy often is associated with those living in poverty or occupying the "lower" races.[38] Dorothy Puttee and Mary Ruth Colby's study, *The Illegitimate Child in Illinois*, illustrated similar surprise as to the preponderance of illegitimacy among Chicago's Scandinavians in comparison to other groups of women. The authors note one reason for such an oversight was due to the typical association of poverty and illegitimacy. In doing so, their 1928 study supported the false stereotype—that all of Chicago's Scandinavians stood on a stable financial framework—and therefore would not produce illegitimate children. In the 1920s, as typical in times of prosperity, the birth rate was relatively high with 118 births per 1,000 women of childbearing age in the United States.[39] In 1928 in Chicago, there were 1,346 illegitimate births recorded, which totaled 22.8 illegitimate births per 1,000 babies born. Of those 1,346 illegitimate births, 73 percent of the birth certificates recorded "white" for the baby's race or color. Therefore, as Puttee and Colby underlined, the problem of illegitimacy was one shared by the "white race" and not by people of color as one may have assumed.[40]

124 · CHAPTER 4

Furthermore, the authors' findings overturned preconceived notions of racial hierarchy that charged people of Nordic and Anglo-Saxon descent with behaving in appropriate ways that fit American social norms. Out of 144 foreign-born mothers recorded as giving birth to illegitimate children, the majority were representative of the "old" immigrant classes: 26 were from Germany, 22 from Ireland, 20 from Poland, 17 from Scandinavia, 16 from Austria, and 10 from Canada. Of "new" immigrants or migrants who gave birth to illegitimate children, there were "only 4 Italians, no Greeks, 5 Mexicans, and 3 Czecho-Slovakians [sic]."[41] Even today, their conclusions could elicit astonishment when considering historic representations of northern and western European women in the context of attitudes toward whiteness. Due mostly to ethnocentrism, histories of white slavery, prostitution, and sexuality in urban spaces focus more closely on those from the latter groups. However, as *The Illegitimate Child in Illinois* illustrates, those from the "old" immigrant groups contributed to the problem of illegitimacy in far greater numbers.

Even more surprising, however, is the lack of analysis on a much larger and strategic plan that several domestic servants of Scandinavian descent knowingly engaged in. According to Matovic and the findings of *The Illegitimate Child in Illinois*, single marital status was a prerequisite for employment as a domestic, whereas marriage would normally mark the end of work for women. Yet, many Scandinavian women used the cultural tradition of illegitimacy as a means to earn more income prior to the birth of their children. According to Matovic, some women had stable relationships and even secret engagements, primarily with Scandinavian men, and postponed marriage to keep their employment. Puttee and Colby used their statistics (782 out of 2,381, or 32.84 percent) of the registered unmarried mothers who were also domestics to state their case that such positions put women in danger of such unfortunate situations, while also keeping them grounded in a never-ending cycle of manual labor.

Matovic's work has been the only recent research to suggest that Scandinavian women used pregnancy as an advantage in their positions.[42] In doing so, these women were able to earn greater income from their employers, many of whom pitied their workers for their seemingly dire situations as illegitimate mothers. As Puttee and Colby noted of this apparent arrangement, "there has long existed the belief that to enter the ranks of those engaged in domestic service is to invite illicit lovemaking, extramarital intercourse and subsequent unmarried motherhood," which the high percentage of unmarried mothers who were also domestics suggested. Their statistics pointed to the "unorganized" nature of domestic service as employment, which they argued offered "insufficient education to get further training." Yet, the positions offered Scandinavian domestics many opportunities for education and upward social mobility.[43] The media did not give adequate attention to discourse on the nature of illegitimacy and unsavory behaviors in connection to Scandinavian domestics, yet this was about to change. A number of crimes, both clandestine and dramatic in nature, took center stage in the early 1900s, when vice in Chicago reached international prominence.

One of the first tales of clandestine crime involving Scandinavians to appear in the American press recounted the charge of Mrs. Sarah Tarskey, who had reason to believe her husband had been living "in adultery" with a Norwegian woman on Randolph street. The story, which read in the *Chicago Tribune* as a popular multipart drama over the course of several weeks, followed the testimonies of the Tarskeys, as well as the accused adulteress, Mrs. Bergh, whom the press painted as a conniving siren out to steal Mr. Tarskey away from his wife and effectively end their marriage.[44] By the turn of the century, a series of murderous crimes gripped the Scandinavian community, effectively turning attention away from comparatively inconsequential stories of adultery to much more heinous crimes that had the potential to shatter the positive image they cultivated. The first focused on Fred Hanson, who was found guilty of manslaughter in the shooting death of an Irishman, Edward O'Connor. While the Swedish-language newspapers admitted to the fact that Hanson was one of their own, the series of articles emphasized that Hanson was actually born in Iowa to Swedish immigrants in 1875. In an effort to create additional distance, the newspaper explained that Hanson was not a part of their community but rather had lived in Minneapolis for nineteen years prior to his move to Chicago just three months before committing the crime. The article went on to define the crime as one of passion motivated by jealousy—"both men were in love with the same girl," explained the news, and the murder was committed in her room.[45] The most sensational crime was yet to come, one that would bring national attention to the dangerous position of single Scandinavian women within the city.

The murder of Carrie Larson struck fear in the Norwegian community as a heinous crime brought against a young, single woman whose only crime was trusting herself alone in the presence of her boss. Louis Thombs, an American cook who worked aboard the steamer "Peerless," had hired the young Scandinavian woman to assist him on the boat docked on the Chicago River during the icy winter months. On a cold night in January 1902, Thombs attempted to force his way into Larson's room; she refused his advances. After ordering her to prepare a meal for him, he was angered by her denial of consent. He strangled Larson and "mutilated her body horribly."[46] Upon realizing that another boat

126 · CHAPTER 4

worker, Robert Keissig, had witnessed the murder, Thombs compelled Keissig to help him throw her body overboard into the icy river. All of Chicago's daily newspapers and newspapers as far as Richmond, Virginia, published salacious details of the horrible crime.

The American press at the turn of the twentieth century illustrated a tendency to focus on all of the gory details of murderous fouls while listing the outcome of the criminal process in terms that were more generic. In the case of Louis Thombs, Carrie Larson became the unfortunate victim of a man who could not contain his masculine desires while the defense sought to portray Keissig as an imbecile by employing racial taxonomy. According to one Chicago police officer's notations, Keissig was "tall and loose jointed" while his head was "small in proportion to his body" and therefore not credible as the only witness to the crime.[47] As newspapers like the *Chicago Tribune* generally reported the details of the case, *Skandinaven* expressed its outrage over a flawed American justice system that allowed for the murderer to acquire two stays from Illinois' governor despite his "absolutely conclusive" guilt.[48] The response of the Scandinavian press was to condemn Thombs for his heinous crime and blame his numerous successful appeals to his death penalty on the sympathies of "foolish women" and a flawed justice system. *Skandinaven* reported in August 1902, just days before Thombs was to be hanged, that the "deplorable state of affairs" that allowed for Thombs to receive respite twice before was due to the "sickly sentimentality of hysterical women who lionize criminals . . . to the delay and uncertainty of justice in our courts of law."[49] As Carrie Larson's murder illustrates, Americans who attempted to harm members of the Scandinavian community would receive no immunity for their crimes, regardless of the scenario.

Other murderous crimes involving members of the community as assassins would draw interesting parallels—in two specific cases, regardless of the details, the press stood by the accused, rather than the victims of the crimes. For instance, upon initial reports of the death of one Swedish man's wife, Mrs. John A. Nordgren, writers for *Svenska Nyheter* and *Skandinaven* came to the unflinching support of Nordgren, depicting him as a victim of the same corrupt system that had worked in the community's favor in the conviction of Carrie Larson's killer. In November 1904, *Svenska Nyheter* reported that the Swedish National League came to the aid of Nordgren, "convinced of his innocence" and was able to "engage competent counsel and bring the case before the Illinois Supreme Court" where he was granted a new trial and later acquitted of all charges.[50]

Another high-profile case involving a Scandinavian illustrated the community's support of the convicted, regardless of sex or extenuating circumstances. Helga C. Anderson, whom the *Chicago Tribune* described as a "pretty Norwegian woman, 24 years of age," was accused in May of 1907 of attempting to kill Julius C. Darby, an elevated railway motorman. The circumstances of the crime read like the pages of a romance novel: Darby and Anderson were engaged in an extramarital affair and, after Darby convinced Anderson to obtain a divorce so she could marry him, he jilted her, according to the paper. In an effort to garner sympathy on Anderson's behalf, the *Tribune* told of the events that led to Darby's injury. Upon hearing through gossip that Darby was spending time with several other women, Anderson unwrapped a revolver from a newspaper in her lap and shot Darby three times. She even attempted to shoot herself after realizing what she had done, but the bullet imbedded in her heavy coat and she was not injured. In eloquent prose, the newspaper reported that a sobbing Miss Anderson cried out, "I love him yet, I can't help it," as she left the hospital and that she "gave herself up without any trouble" as police took her to the station while they investigated the matter further. In a follow-up article, "Ex-husband approves of shooting," the reporter agreed, seemingly with her soon-to-be-ex-husband, that Anderson had done the right thing in shooting the reckless philanderer. At her cell, he shook hands with her and after listening intently to her story, promised to give her "all the aid he could," because as he remarked, "you did right in shooting him."[51] Not at any time did accounts of the crime paint Anderson as a criminal or even an adulteress, but instead she was portrayed as a woman promised the commitment of marriage by a man who rescinded his promise—a crime depicted by the newspaper as much worse that the shooting. Instead, the press recognized Anderson as a heroine for her bold gesture, regardless of the fact that she was arrested and admittedly guilty of the crime.

Just days later, another crime of passion took center stage as police arrested the Reverend Alfred Dahlstrom, minister of three Evangelical churches in both Chicago and Rockford, for the attempted kidnapping of Marta Petersen, a seventeen-year-old Swedish girl from Chicago. The response from the community was not as supportive as it had been of Anderson's crime. Not only was Reverend Dahlstrom a respected minister within the community, but he had also been living a secret life with Petersen, much to the dismay of his wife. Upon the report of Petersen's mother that the minister had kidnapped her daughter, he denied knowing the whereabouts of Miss Petersen, but added that he intended to marry the young girl upon her eighteenth birthday, when she would reach legal marrying age.[52] One would gather, given the amount of high-profile crimes involving Scandinavians in the early years of the twentieth century that Chicago's citizens would have judged Scandinavians in a negative light. However, due mostly to racial stereotypes of Nordic superiority, Chicago's citizens continued to see Scandinavians as exceptional. In 1907, Chicago's

128 · CHAPTER 4

Scandinavians began the process of combating the social evils that threatened their youth through their contributions to the settlement house movement. Through these establishments, the Scandinavian community remained conscious of its public image, which was apparent in the outpouring of press releases to Chicago newspapers that brought attention to the establishment of ethnic settlement homes. Scandinavians aimed to build settlement homes that appeared to Americans to acculturate its patrons to American norms but, inside, maintained the traditions and even languages of home.

The Scandinavian American Settlement House Movement

With the numbers of young, single Scandinavians on the rise in Chicago, Progressive-minded reformers grew wary of the potential ramifications of young immigrants living "adrift." However, the differences in approach by groups who sought to help the newly arrived pointed to distinctive gendered divisions in thought and practice. Such city reformers increasingly emphasized the need for homes intended for young women; at the turn of the century, reformers viewed young "women adrift" in Chicago as helpless victims under constant threat of the dangers of the city.[53] One of the best ways to keep young migrants on the correct moral path was to offer them safe housing options where they would be guaranteed a bed and a meal but, most importantly, the guidance of other women who operated the settlement houses. In support of their own, a number of settlement houses built for newly emigrated Scandinavians opened their doors in Lake View, Lincoln Park, and on the south side under the guidance of several Lutheran organizations. As early as the 1890s, such organizations began to develop plans to build boarding houses for Scandinavian working-women, but the implementation of such plans would require both funds and significant voluntary help.

In the opening years of the 1900s, an impressive number of Lutheran settlement homes opened their doors out of need, with many operating under the leadership of the Augustana synod such as the Augustana Central Home, Augustana Lutheran Mission Home, and Augustana Women's Home. Other homes like the Immanuel Women's Home, Swedish Covenant Home of Mercy, Susanna Wesley Home, Home of the Vikings, and the Young Ladies' Ebenezer Home of the Free Church functioned through the support of community church offerings or groups committed to maintaining the moral sanctity of the various enclaves. Newly arrived immigrants learned of these homes through word of mouth or through the various advertisements in Chicago's Scandinavian newspapers, many of which carefully pointed out the intentions of their organizations. The

Augustana Central Home was to be a "a safe place, a Christian home for young people where they can stay at very reasonable expenses and be among friends that are willing and ready at all times to give information, advice and help in every way possible."[54]

Following the lead of several other Progressive reform organizations in the city, homes like Augustana emphasized the potential dangers faced by newly arrived immigrants to the city, especially those who came to the city unaccompanied without knowledge of English. As the advertisement warned, "every year, thousands of young girls come to Chicago, go down to destruction just because of lack of these things . . . it prevents much evil, and here it is true that "an ounce of prevention is better than a pound of cure."[55] Similarly, the Susanna Wesley Home described itself as an institution that served a great need within the city for young women "sorely in need who find themselves homeless in a great city where so many grave dangers and temptations lurk."[56] For these new immigrants, settlement homes offered a temporary and safe retreat from the harsh conditions and potential dangers of boarding houses or shoddy hotels, but, in exchange for safety, workers expected immigrants to obey their rules during their stay.

One of the largest and most successful Scandinavian-operated settlement organizations for female migrants in Chicago was the Chicago Immanuel Woman's Home, which by 1911 had become the largest Lutheran hospice for girls in the United States. The idea of a Lutheran settlement home for young women living adrift first came to the attention of the pastor of the Immanuel Lutheran Church by youth who inquired where they could find a safe home in the city. The pastor later recalled that, "if [the visitors] were well and had sufficient money, their question was easily answered. They could be taken to the YWCA. But if they were ill or out of funds, the question was not so easily answered."[57] In considering viable options for a safe, yet inexpensive place of respite for young Scandinavian women, he called upon a group of prominent women of the church's congregation to undertake the needed project. The Immanuel Woman's Home Association was organized in January 1907 to find a suitable location for a home where workingwomen of the community could go when out of employment or in need of rest.

The purpose of the association mirrored the fears of American Progressive reformers as they looked to provide a "Christian hospice with a homelike atmosphere for young women in Chicago, who are away from the protecting influence of their parental home and former friends." The association pointed out that they "visualized the many dangers and temptations to which the friendless young woman in a metropolis like Chicago" were exposed on a daily basis.[58]

130 · CHAPTER 4

According to the association, a safe settlement home was in such demand that the thirty-three charter members immediately footed the sum of $7,500 for the three-story home at 1505 La Salle Avenue and were able to open its doors to their patrons by August of the same year.[59] The association also carefully planned the location of the home as both convenient for its working patrons to travel to from the business section of the city and peaceful as a home set next to the sprawling gardens of Lincoln Park.

As was the practice of many settlement homes in Chicago during the Progressive era, the association expected its patrons to follow a number of strict rules and adhere to specific social mores before they would receive admission to the home. While Lutherans of no particular denomination organized the association, its management remained Scandinavian and Lutheran. Similarly, the association emphasized its invitation to women of all nationalities and backgrounds to stay at the home. However, the majority of its patrons were of Scandinavian descent due to the insular nature of the home. It did not advertise its services aside from a few paid advertisements in the yearly Swedish Almanac published by the Augustana Book Concern. The home expected patrons to pay the fee of $3.50 to $4.00 a week for room and board, and the bylaws of the association stressed that the home was a "Christian hospice" and not a rescue home. The majority of those who shared in the hospitality of the home were able to pay the full price according to set lodging rates, as opposed to a rescue home, where patrons would pay what they could.[60] While the association would later emphasize that no woman was ever turned away from the Immanuel Woman's Home out of need, it enlisted the help of outside agencies, such as the Woman's Protectorate, Traveling Bureaus, and, in the worst-case scenarios, Police Matrons to "take charge" of those who arrived at the home destitute, friendless, and homeless.[61] Regardless of the tendencies of the home to allow only a certain selection of workingwomen through its doors, it was an incredibly successful endeavor; over the course of thirty years, the home hosted 18,435 patrons and would later encompass the surrounding properties to expand the space of the home.[62] One Norwegian woman who came to the home when it first opened in 1907 remembered it as almost a mirage for her and her friends, but she found that the home was a small blessing in her otherwise unfortunate series of circumstances: "At the Immanuel Home we were taken care of in every way at a low cost. We loved the Home."[63]

Similarly, homes opened at the turn of the century intended for Scandinavian workingmen under the auspices of settled members of the community to ease the process of settlement and provide a safe housing choice. In 1904, a group of Swedish newspaper men conceived of a Scandinavian "People's House" modeled after those in many Swedish cities that served as a meeting place and settlement home run by Scandinavian volunteers. From the beginnings of the process of planning, the group intended for the house to serve the needs of all Scandinavian newcomers to the city—Norwegians, Danes, and even Finns—in creating a brotherhood of Scandinavians, regardless of animosities from home toward other groups.[64] In planning their home, the group lamented over the struggles of the new immigrant to Chicago, yet pointed out regional divisions within the city among Scandinavians. One writer for *Svenska Nyheter* reported on the disorienting process of migration: "When the young Swede, the young Finn, the young Dane, and the young Norwegian set their feet on American soil they usually lose track of the friends and acquaintances which they have acquired during the voyage across the ocean. They scatter to the north, south, east, and west, and our immigrant finds himself among complete strangers." Rather than isolating himself, it was better for the Scandinavian immigrant to find a fraternal organization "where he may find sympathy and strike up new friendships . . . so it would be a great boon to Scandinavian brotherhood and cooperation if this plan could become a reality."[65] From its origin, community planners involved with construction of the Scandinavian People's Home stated their intentions to build a community center that adopted the same spirit of altruism as Jane Addam's Hull House, and yet it was established by Scandinavians for Scandinavians. The planners wanted to feel as though they were solely focused on serving the needs of newly arrived Scandinavian immigrants and not selfish desires to appear as martyrs to the cause of the poor.

In a full-page call to organize in *Svenska Nyheter* in June 1904, the planning committee established its intention to battle against the consequences of capitalist greed. In its statement, the committee argued, "the weak have to protect themselves against the abuses of the strong, and the lower, underprivileged classes are gradually becoming conscious of the fact that they are potentially many times as strong as the so-called upper classes." The committee called upon "brother Scandinavians, imbued with that same spirit" to come together to build a Scandinavian People's House in Chicago "to serve as our social and political center."[66] Over the next few years, as plans for the home came to fruition, the central idea of a general meeting place would transform into something much more vital to Scandinavian workingmen—a fraternal center that bred labor organization and socialist rhetoric. The Scandinavian People's Home, like other organizations aimed toward common workers, embraced education, socialist thought, and fraternity as the driving forces behind "getting ahead" in Chicago society. Historian Pehr Nordahl stressed in his study of social networks among Swedish American radicals that organizations like the Scandinavian People's

Home served as vehicles for socialist mobilization and working-class unity, thereby serving a much different purpose than clubs that catered to Scandinavian women.[67] Supported by many of Chicago's labor unions who came to the aid of Scandinavian workers during previous strikes and lockouts, such community organizations operated under the same goal of helping others rather than necessarily showing concern over the moral respectability of those they helped.

While organizations such as the Scandinavian People's Home and Café Idrott in Lakeview maintained a strict policy that no alcoholic beverages be sold or consumed on premises, the reasons for such standards lay with Scandinavian policies and not necessarily out of religious tenets. In the article, "To the Scandinavians of Chicago," the planning committee pointed out the vital necessity of a settlement organization that could help those without ties to any church by emphasizing that, out of 150,000 Swedes who lived in Chicago in 1904, 40,000 did not belong to any church that would be able to offer support.[68] Nordahl examined this relationship as representative of a larger trend in Lake View that emphasized the growing importance of social and political organizations. Between 1890 and 1919, various organizations established approximately twenty fraternal lodges in the area but only two churches, compared to the four erected during the 1880s alone. Nordahl saw this "mosaic of organizations" as instrumental in community building, but also in the formation of a strong campaign of labor organization grounded in the overlapping influence of trade unions, culture, and politics.[69] Therefore, the church, which was the driving force behind community organization for first-generation Scandinavians, was now secondary to fraternal organizations for men looking to change their social positions and experiences at work.[70]

Comparatively, this relationship greatly differed from that of women's organizations that continued to place religious tenets at the forefront of immigrant aid and assistance. While an emphasis on piety and moral public behavior continued to shape the experiences of women who sought the aid of Scandinavian women's homes, construction of the Scandinavian People's Home similarly blended elements of education and Scandinavian traditions.[71] To that end, the Scandinavian People's Home and the Immanuel Woman's Home of Chicago took a similar approach to settlement—to offer aid to the newly arrived workers by surrounding them with the comforts of home. Regardless of sex, the settlement house movement driven by Progressive-minded individuals sought to keep their youth from falling into lives of deviant behaviors and bad choices. While settlement home programs stood as a testament to the strength of immigrant communities, vice continued to be an all too familiar problem on the minds of Chicagoans by the 1910s. When the Vice Commission of Chicago was charged with the task of reporting on the problems of crime, white slavery, and poverty within the city, their revelations published in 1911—and subsequent "closing" of the vice district shortly after—drew continued attention to the connections of vice and immigrant youth. As Chicago's Scandinavians renewed their commitments to combating vice within their neighborhoods, a new movement was underway that was focused on intellectual growth and socialist ideals. These ideologies involved a new generation of Scandinavian youth in a movement their Chicago neighbors did not always understand.

Before publication of the Vice Commission of Chicago's study, *The Social Evil in Chicago*, many Scandinavians directly involved in the settlement homes continued their work in an effort to combat vice, which could potentially cast a poor light on the community. These Progressive-minded individuals worked with other groups of middle-class women within the city to fix the problems of urban sprawl, including sweat labor and illegal saloons, and used the power of major social programs such as the Swedish and Norwegian National Leagues to continue to prevent white slavers from encroaching on their neighborhoods. Through the pages of *Skandinaven, Svenska Tribunen, Svenska Nyheter,* and *Scandia*, articles submitted by social reformers emphasized the continued need of the community's involvement in combating such issues throughout Chicago. From a call that "the sweat shop must go" to an exposé that specifically blamed immigrants from southern and eastern Europe for "working their children like slaves," Scandinavians used their platform to become vocal and active participants in shaping the social future of their city.[72] Using the power of the press, Scandinavians turned the public's attention to the dangers of "concert halls" and various saloons, which operated under the radar of an ignorant and corrupt police force. Community social reformers did not give leeway to members of their own community who committed similar crimes. In 1900, an article in *Scandia* identified T. M. Swanson's Swedish "Concert Hall" at 226 Milwaukee Avenue as an illegal cabaret, where police found Scandinavian girls ("none of them over twelve years") being forced to drink and dance with men, most of whom were "pimps . . . and crooks of every description."[73] By the time the city shut down the vice district in 1912, Chicago's Scandinavians had become seasoned social reformers armed with a useful understanding of the problems of the city that held victims and criminals accountable for their actions.

Looking back at revelations on crime in Chicago, Walter Reckless revealed, in his study of seventy-seven white slave cases in Chicago between 1910 and 1913, an accepted pattern of procuring or pandering as part of a larger system of patriarchal rule within modern urban society. As he remarked, "it seemed to be the customary thing in the underworld" for a man to have one or several women on his arm as his public exploits.[74] Furthermore, Reckless corrected several misconceptions about white slavery according to the selected cases; one of the most important to this study was that, while only six of the sixty-three girls were reported as immigrants, three of those six were from Scandinavia. Conversely, none of the men reported as procurers or pimps in the cases were of Scandinavian descent, or even of northern or western Europe, but instead were largely represented by Italians, Poles, and Greeks.[75] Reckless explicitly stressed that police considered women involved in the white slave cases under investigation as "wayward" rather than "virtuous" victims. In the sixty-three cases (with the girls telling their own stories with lawyers and officers helping them), only four instances were reported where the procurer was actually responsible for violating the girl's chastity. The findings of both Reckless and the Vice Commission of Chicago marked an ideological shift in Chicago's society, where crimes committed against seemingly "virtuous" women in Chicago were given a second glance.

Conversations involving race, whiteness, and representation continued to shape the experiences of Scandinavians into the Great War. This first world conflict forced the community to come to terms with new questions about their loyalties to America and their commitment to "becoming" American. The newly constructed Scandinavian residence homes served as powerful examples of the persistence of ethnic identity into the twentieth century among a group otherwise noted for their seamless inclusion in American society. Out of these organizations grew a significant movement of Scandinavians who desired intellectual, social, and political enlightenment within their own community, grounded in the socialist traditions of home. One of these social clubs, the Swedish Educational League, was formed in an effort to espouse the ideologies of their ancestors who believed work and society needed to remain "free and unhampered from all forces that might cause it to stagnate."[76] The forward-thinking group often made public declarations throughout community advertisements that Scandinavians needed to demand both freedom of thought and absence of fear in thinking and expression in order to achieve personal and professional success. As a large segment of the community, especially second-generation youth, came to embrace the tenets of the Swedish Educational League for its grandiose gestures toward modern ways of thinking, more conservative-minded individuals did not view the actions of the group with such excitement.

Swedish writer Edith Janson would later comment in her recollections of Chicago during the 1920s that such groups were often comprised of "self-imposed exiles" who had somehow "found" their way to the United States. When such "agitators and young radicals," whom Janson recalled as members of the intelligentsia, found themselves to be "misfits" and far too forward in their thinking, they either returned to Scandinavia or retreated from public life.[77] At the same time, intellectuals within groups like the Swedish Educational League scoffed at such classifications that deemed their activities radical and explained that the group was radical "only in a constructive sense." In contrast to other "radical" socialist organizations, it advocated no political or religious creed but never hesitated to bring into discussion "progressive and even extreme viewpoints in order to acquaint its audience with the problems of the day and their possible solutions."[78] The interactions between these two groups—conservative and more liberal-minded—culminated in a much larger ideological discussion at the beginning of World War I. The loyalties of Scandinavians would be challenged in light of insinuations that some involved themselves in radical organizations prior to the war. For a brief period, the positive image Scandinavians cultivated for themselves within their adopted home of Chicago seemed on the brink of collapse amid tension and panic over loyalties to the American flag.

CHAPTER 5

World War I, Nativist Rhetoric, and the "White Man Par Excellence"

Between 1914 and 1917, the American and foreign-language press engaged in a discourse on racial fitness that adopted a sense of urgency. Chicago, like all of urban America during World War I, became a site of growing ethnic tensions that surrounded suspicious foreigners, especially Germans or allies of Germany. Now more than ever, racial and ethnic distinctions became part of a common narrative used by Americans and Europeans who employed nativism to question the loyalties of others. Many ethnic Chicagoans struggled to defend cultural traditions while nativists deemed their efforts inappropriate and selfish in a time of international conflict. Scandinavian Americans found themselves embroiled in a dangerous situation as America moved closer to entering the war. Due to Scandinavia's proximity to Germany, as well as previous declarations of support for the country, its people were placed in a difficult position. In 1917, the Scandinavian language press began to employ racial discourse that positioned Scandinavians away from the enemy. Publication of the most damning piece of scientific racism of the twentieth century, Madison Grant's *The Passing of the Great Race*, came at the same time Scandinavians constructed this argument and unwittingly shaped their arguments in the press. Though editors of the remaining Scandinavian language newspapers did not publicly admit to reading Grant's study, his decree that the Nordic race represented "the white man par excellence" undoubtedly seeped into their discourse about a shared "Nordic" bloodline.[1]

During the first two years of the war, most of Chicago's Scandinavians expressed ambivalence and were inclined to place blame equally on both sides of the conflict. According to one 1918 *Skandinaven* editorial, some remained on "friendly terms" with Germans due to Lutheran connections. Still, Scandinavian American newspaper editors possessed "great knowledge" in advance of its constituency and took positions that ranged from cautionary to intensely anti-German.[2] As early as July 1914, *Decorah Posten* and the *Minneapolis Tidende* joined the newspaper in placing blame on Kaiser Wilhelm for the war. Danish newspapers *Nordlyset, Revyen, Ugebladet*, and the *Danish Pioneer* printed violent attacks on the Kaiser, while *Svenska Amerikanaren* also defended its position against Germany.[3] Hidden in the articles was a plea for both relevance and loyalty in the shadow of suppression of the foreign-language press, racial conflict, and intense patriotism. Editors of *Skandinaven, Revyen*, and most of the Swedish-language newspapers implored their readers not to shy away from racialized discourse but to embrace it.

Four months after America's declaration of war, a *Skandinaven* editorial called those of "Nordic blood" to action, rallying their patriotism "as good American citizens" and acknowledging their obedience to law and loyalty to America. Those Scandinavians who stood in opposition to the American cause were outcast and considered traitors.[4] This insular argument was similar to others expressed in the foreign-language press at the time, yet *Skandinaven*'s use of "Nordic" in reference to race was new. Consciously or not, Scandinavians began to refer to themselves as part of the Nordic race for the first time in an effort to link racial fitness to American loyalty. Furthermore, the Scandinavian-language press took a remarkably nativist stance that mirrored the American campaign for 100 percent Americanism. What was most significant about the entire campaign was that it was all a ploy for Americans to exempt Scandinavians from suspicions of disloyalty to the allied effort.

American Nationalism, Pluralism, and Nativism before the War

From 1914, Americans began to question the patriotism of all immigrants or "hyphenates" who retained loyalties to their ethnic heritage, and Scandinavians were of no exception. After the United States declared war on Germany in April 1917, questions of loyalty escalated into mass hysteria evidenced through anti-immigrant propaganda, vigilante violence, and funding cuts to foreign-language programs in American public schools. Backlash led to fear, and, in response, foreign-born and hyphenated Americans submerged all remnants of ethnic cultural identity during and even after wartime. According to Russell Kazal, for German Americans of Philadelphia, the erasure of German ethnic identity in response to backlash reshaped their sense of self to adhere to a more conformist American nationalism and assimilation. Even today, there is a noted submergence of German American ethnicity.[5] Whereas German Americans and other European ethnic groups found refuge in the "monolithic whiteness" Matthew Jacobson identified as flattening racial distinctions, Scandinavian Americans redefined themselves as "Nordic" during and after the war.[6] Nordic was a "safe" identity, one that reflected upon Madison Grant's and Lothrop Stoddard's embrace of Scandinavian "racial" purity and consciously employed by Scandinavian Americans as a strategy for ethnic survival.

The Scandinavian American response to nativism and anti-ethnic hysteria during World War I is well documented for much of the urban Midwest except Chicago.[7] The few existing studies end in 1920, methodologically arguing that Scandinavians assimilated and, therefore, were no longer ethnic.[8] Instead, as this chapter and the next illustrate, pluralism did not end with the 1920s, but instead grew more complex as the onset of the Great Depression forced Scandinavian Americans to once again reconsider whiteness in the face of economic turmoil. The racial construction of Nordic identity by Scandinavian Americans during World War I was one built upon the acceptance of American culture and ideals through patriotism, loyalty, and participation in the war effort. Scandinavian Americans made use of derivations of the term *Nordic* as a way of ensuring their safety, of distancing themselves from their European neighbors to the south. In fact, Scandinavian Americans in Chicago embraced "Nordic" before Americans. The term did not come into vogue until the 1920s when it was used almost interchangeably with *Aryan*.[9] After the war, those of Nordic descent, especially from the middle and upper classes, used the term as a plural identity that equated to racial and physical fitness, as well as shared ethnic values. Nordic identity meant that Scandinavians could act "American" by speaking English in public, achieving success in education and business pursuits, and moving to suburban Chicago, all while privately embracing Scandinavian traditions.[10] Whereas other ethnic Americans experienced significant pressure to fully assimilate, as one 1921 editorial in *Svenska Tribunen-Nyheter* observed, Scandinavian Americans were able to "preserve the best of native qualities" after the war, even if it was in private.[11]

By the beginning of World War I in 1914, according to the U.S. Census, Chicago's foreign-born and native-born Scandinavian population was the largest to date and continued to grow. Foreign-born Scandinavians living in Chicago consisted of 116,740 Swedes, 47,235 Norwegians, and 20,772 Danes, while native-born Scandinavian Americans grew rapidly to 62,239 Swedish Americans, 24,748 Norwegian Americans, and 11,277 Danish Americans.[12] America's Scandinavian population also reached its peak prior to America's involvement in the war. According to the census of 1910, the country's Swedish-born population alone included 665,000 individuals, which together with nearly 700,000 of their American-born children comprised a total Swedish American population of nearly 1,363,554, or 1.48 percent of the population of the United States.[13] Just when the size of the Scandinavian American population grew to have a significant cultural impact on the Midwest, immigration fell off drastically. Immigration from Sweden, which in 1913 totaled 16,329 persons, declined to 9,589 in 1914 and was down to 4,538 by 1915 after the sinking of the Lusitania brought transatlantic migration to a standstill. By 1918, after America entered the war, Sweden's immigrants numbered a mere 1,416—the lowest figure since the Civil War era.[14] Between 1914 and 1917, Scandinavians and their families faced intensified pressures to assimilate during wartime from Americans who grew increasingly nervous about long-standing European alliances.

Prior to the war, the Scandinavian communities of Chicago welcomed young newcomers into vibrant, outwardly ethnic neighborhoods. In the middle-class community of Lake View, much like in the German community of Wicker Park or Ukrainian Village, new immigrants could easily locate newspapers written in their language, services that appealed to their needs, and businesses that carried familiar products from home. In 1910, Lake View businesses appeared untouched by time, comprised of the same bakeries, butcher shops, fish markets, and general stores once transplanted from the downtown neighborhood of the nineteenth century.[15] As Lake View retained much of its old-world charm, class divides among working-class immigrants and established intellectuals in the business community reflected a difference in preference to retain ethnic identity. New immigrants sought the familiarities of home, such as a shared language and consumer products, whereas middle-class Scandinavian American businessmen maintained a more symbolic identity that reflected Scandinavian ethnicity of their parents' generation. The upper classes grounded Scandinavian American identity in material cultures like food, ethnic celebrations, and fraternal organizations that embraced a love of singing and athleticism rather than "true" Scandinavian ethnicity. To Scandinavian Americans, new Scandinavian immigrants often appeared to be out of step regarding both class and ethnic divisions. However, these new immigrants purposely distanced themselves from an ethnic identity that was more nostalgic than authentic.

In the early 1910s, the Scandinavian American press aimed at a more liberal, intellectual audience began to reflect this nostalgic ethnicity. The Norwegian-language newspaper, *Scandia*, sought to "speak the truth" to "the Norwegian businessman, the doctor, the lawyer," and "last but not least," the worker and the farmer.[16] One *Scandia* editorial declared the importance of insular ethnic institutions within the community, such as two of the community's Norwegian restaurants. The editor remarked that such ethnic institutions were essential in that "men and women from all parts of the Scandinavian countries, yesterday's arrivals or the old pioneers" could meet and partake in old-world delicacies, albeit symbolically for many. The editor's nostalgic tone emphasized that "only he who has loved the mother country can truly learn to love the new home of his choice," and urged those who were new to America to assimilate while retaining their love of Scandinavia.[17] Whether authentic or symbolic, Scandinavian Americans began to cast off their Nordic ethnic identity during World War I and in its place grew ideological, racial connections of "Nordic blood."

In the early 1910s, the American press contributed to nativist discourse depicting the people and races of Europe as either fit or unfit for citizenship in the United States. Filiopietistic Scandinavian American authors such as Kendric Babcock added similar viewpoints that nurtured the tumultuous ethnoracial climate of the wartime era, positioning "fit" Scandinavians in America as distinctly separate from "unfit" immigrants. Using nativist rhetoric, Babcock argued that the "progress of civilization in America" relied on "those who reinforced the strength and virtue of the nation" and who supplemented the country's "defects" with desirable elements.[18] Furthermore, Babcock identified three groups within specific contexts who lowered America's standards and "prevented its advancement," which included the Chinese of California, the Hungarians "in the mines," and "the Hebrews in the sweatshops."[19] Mass immigration compiled with economic issues, urban sprawl, and political corruption soured the attitudes of even the most filiopietistic writers of the late nineteenth and early twentieth centuries who previously preferred to romanticize the virtues of Scandinavian origin.

Babcock and other writers like him blamed the "lower" races of southern and eastern Europe and of Asia for the buildup of an urban proletariat rather than the industrial robber barons who exploited their labor. Before the war, many middle-class Scandinavians positioned themselves as "American" in contrast to Hungarians, Jews, and other "new" immigrants. In extreme measures, this stance employed racialized language to recast Scandinavians as one race who shared "Nordic blood." In the years prior to publication of Madison Grant's racist master narrative, *The Passing of the Great Race*, numerous Scandinavian American authors spoke in similar terms as a response to anti-German hysteria that escalated into full-blown postwar xenophobia. America's participation in the European conflict unleashed a bevy of antiforeign sentiments aimed at those

The Scandinavian American Press and Nordic Identity during the War

who remained loyal to their country of origin. In an effort not to end up like their ostracized German neighbors, Scandinavian Americans harnessed the power of the press to promote an all-important wartime message: Scandinavians were good American citizens and those who acted out of character would be excommunicated.

The Scandinavian American Press and Nordic Identity during the War

Prior to the war, Germans were one of the most respected ethnic groups in America and were part of the distinctive "old" immigrant group to which nativists assigned them by 1900. Germans were biologically "old stock" in the words of Frederick Jackson Turner and occupied the same "scientific" racial typology as Scandinavians according to nativist lore. German was the most commonly taught foreign language in American public schools and, like Scandinavians, Germans built a diverse network of voluntary associations and other organizations driven by ethnic pride. The dynamics of World War I coupled with pressure for absolute Americanism created a significant impact on public education, outward ethnic identity, and symbolic representations of pride in German nationality. Likewise, Scandinavians and Scandinavian Americans who rallied in support of the German cause faced severe consequences for their loyalties.

In the years preceding America's entrance into the war, each Scandinavian American newspaper differed in its discussion of ethnic and national alliances given the time and European proximity to Germany. Early into the war in Europe, the Swedish-language press boldly adopted a pro-Germany stance in spite of a wide diversity in political and ideological rhetoric. The Swedish Lutheran-Republican weekly, *Hemlandet*, vocalized initial support for Germans despite America's stance of political neutrality. In August 1914, the *Hemlandet* writer expressed that Germans did not fall into the ranks of the uncivilized immigrant masses that Babcock described and hoped that a higher power would assist Germany and its Kaiser, "for in this war they battle for everything that a civilized people holds sacred." The author went on to express that, in the event that Sweden was forced to rescind its wartime neutrality, he hoped that his country of origin would join the Central Powers of Austria-Hungary, Germany, Bulgaria, and the Ottoman Empire.[20] Others, like reporters for the Minneapolis-based *Svenska Amerikanska Posten*, mirrored the general sentiments of *Hemlandet* but none so much as the writers for the secular and highly influential paper, *Svenska Amerikanaren*. On New Year's Eve of 1914, the newspaper's editor went as far as to declare Swedish Americans to be "the most pro-German of all nationalities in

142 · CHAPTER 5

the United States" as tensions between Germany and the United States escalated on the high seas.[21] The early pro-German stance of the Swedish-language press eventually took its toll. In Chicago as well as Minneapolis, dailies and weeklies that favored Germany witnessed financial decline as propaganda against the foreign-language press scared off advertisers.[22] Between 1914 and 1917, those newspaper editors in support of Germany generally spoke in terms of long-standing political alliances and European proximity rather than connections of race in underlining the basis of their stance. By February 1915, early pro-German sentiment of Scandinavian newspapers began to sour due to backlash against Germans in America.

That winter, after several articles in Chicago's newspapers insinuated shady trade agreements involving Holland and Scandinavia by which American goods were smuggled into Germany, the editors of *Skandinaven* announced their disdain over the allegations. By 1915, official and public hostility toward foreign-language newspapers resulted in the formation of a congressional committee charged with investigating the press and its editors. Under pressure from the U.S. government threatening to conduct covert monitoring of the foreign-language press, Scandinavian American editors began regularly publishing editorials in English and in the language of the newspaper as a means of defending the immigrant press.[23] *Skandinaven*'s editors used an article to protest the allegations in Norwegian and specify that statements made in Chicago's newspapers outlets were false, at least in regard to Scandinavia's role in the matter.[24] That April, in a public relations move intended to appease nativists, *Skandinaven* took a pacifist stance, publishing a full-page article translated into English and signed by 373 foreign-language editors in Chicago. The article expressed the consensus of the undersigned editors to end the war, asking the American nation to stop the production of war materials intended to "murder our brothers, to make our mothers and sisters widows and their children fatherless."[25] This reminder that the community still had loved ones living in Europe was bold in wartime, when questions of loyalty to the American cause abounded. The strategy of writing an article as an appeal to the American press was one of many efforts Scandinavians made to put themselves in the good graces of public opinion. However, this article was not initially enough to sway the American public to consider Scandinavians as being loyal to the Allied cause. In the aftermath of the sinking of the Lusitania in 1915 by a German submarine torpedo, any lingering sentiment held by Scandinavians toward the German campaign cooled, thereby solidifying Scandinavian loyalty to the side of the Allied forces. Even so, isolated incidents such as the arrest of Theodore H. Lunde for wartime espionage caused Americans concern regarding Scandinavian loyalty to America.

In November 1917, Chicago police arrested Lunde, a Norwegian manufacturer of piano metal parts in Chicago, for a breach in regulations involving espionage. The *Chicago Daily Tribune* reported that the "Pro-German" was released on a bond of $25,000 put up by Dr. Karl F. M. Sandberg and Leonard Hoerdt, owner of a saloon and restaurant on Belmont Avenue in Lake View, after federal operatives searched his residence. While the names of Lunde's bond posters and Hoerdt's residence implied that the three men were Scandinavian, nowhere in the article was Lunde's Scandinavian background mentioned forthright. According to the article, authorities arrested Lunde for his ideological stance as an avowed socialist and not because he was Scandinavian.[26] In *Skandinaven*'s reporting of the arrest, the paper admitted to Lunde's guilt in making unfounded statements of support for Germany in the midst of wartime after the police confiscated a letter in which he declared his admiration for Germany's Kaiser. In the letter, Lunde blamed England for encouraging the beginning of the war, admitting that he considered the Kaiser to be the "greatest social politician" of the day, "a Socialist on a large scale."[27] Despite his implicating letter, the newspaper expressed confidence that the authorities would clear Lunde of any crime. In a time when American nativists equated socialism with anarchy and social upheaval, the American press interpreted Lunde's private musings on the successes of the Kaiser as a social politician to be subversive, thereby creating further suspicion about Scandinavian Americans as true citizens loyal to the American cause. Furthermore, in Chicago's earlier labor movements, numerous Scandinavian names littered the papers of those involved in socialist activities and rallies. From the Scandinavian perspective, many within the community faced a highly uncomfortable situation, which caused many to overreact or to become vehemently silent regarding any position on the war.

As discussions regarding loyalty to the American cause reached its wartime apex, some news outlets expressed indignation over the supposition that Scandinavians were not entirely loyal citizens of the United States. Theodore Roosevelt's concept of "true Americanism" was at the forefront of growing nativist rhetoric during the war. The ideology, framed by the influx of "new" immigrants during the 1890s, offered a pronounced distinction of immigrant groups considered "desirable" and those who were not, which formed the basis of nativist thought and xenophobic reactions during a time of war with the Central European powers. One *Svenska Kuriren* editorial railed against the concept, conveniently readdressed during an election year, as a blatant attack on "hyphenated citizens" who were otherwise fully loyal to their adopted country. Agitated with the constant reaffirmations of loyalty to the American flag, *Svenska Kuriren* urged its readers to overlook "all this foolishness" and reminded

144 · CHAPTER 5

them, "We cannot be deprived of our rights as citizens, unless it is through our own shortcomings." Rather than to focus on proving their worth as hyphenated Americans, Scandinavians needed to distance themselves from those with "Bohemian and Polish names" for the sake of their own self-preservation.[28] In doing so, the editor asked readers invited to attend a meeting by the Committee for the Promotion of Loyalty to the United States to politely decline, reminding readers that they had no solidarity or common ties with eastern Europeans.[29] In this indignant expression, the editor, knowingly or not, took a position that many citizens within the Scandinavian community agreed with: that the need for excessive reaffirmations of loyalty were unnecessary and beneath the level of their racial position within America.

At the center of the debate of nativism and "true Americanism" stood a racial discourse based on the assumption of the superiority of the northern European races. Previous racial "science" posed in 1899 by economist William Z. Ripley and anthropologist Joseph Deniker classified people who originated from Scandinavia as part of a northern "Teutonic" or "Nordic" race of "tall, blond longheads."[30] Nativist writers like Madison Grant transformed the typology that elevated the races of northern Europe using the emerging "science" of the eugenic movement to connect race to the inner dynamics of history. In his infamous 1916 text, *The Passing of the Great Race*, Grant employed classifications of race based exclusively on human physical characteristics to posit "Nordics" were "the Great Race." "Nordic," in Grant's application, signified the epitome of whiteness but was also interchangeable with "old stock" to point to America's original pioneers.[31] Race was now linked to "intelligence, enterprise, and daring," according to Grant and could be used to determine racial "fitness" in America. Grant opined that the American nation forfeited its "birthright of Nordic racial purity by opening its doors to unrestricted immigration to gain cheap labor" but recognized Scandinavians as "splendid human material."[32] Sweden was home to the "purest Nordic type," Grant stated; he added that these individuals were characterized by prized physical features that included "blondness, wavy hair, blue eyes, fair skin, [and] a high, narrow and straight nose," which nativists associated with great social stature.[33]

Much like earlier Social Darwinist discussions, Grant equated physicality with an aptness or ability to succeed within society by nature of historically proven capabilities. One of the most unfortunate results of Grant's racist connotations about those who were fit for American society was the resurgence of the Ku Klux Klan in 1915, which agitated not only for white but for Nordic supremacy. Scandinavian Americans did not gloat about their racial superiority after Grant's publication made headlines in American newspapers, however.

Editors of the Scandinavian American press were indeed aware of Grant's racial discourse that served to benefit them during a chaotic era, noted by shift in the racialized language used in the press. Prior to the war, articles used discourse regarding ties of ethnicity more than of racial connections of "Nordic blood" or "Nordic stock." The shift in racialized language that occurred post-Grant indicates that Scandinavian Americans positioned themselves as "Nordics" in order to distance themselves from southern and eastern Europeans and create a position of protective exceptionalism.

One of the most contested issues surrounding Scandinavian loyalty to the American war effort hinged upon American citizenship. By 1910, the majority of Scandinavians in Chicago had begun the process of gaining American citizenship, as illustrated in table 5.1. In October 1918, the Augustana Synod's magazine for young adults, *Ungdomsvännen*, expressed outward indignation toward Swedish Americans who were eligible for citizenship but had not yet claimed it. "They are not Americans," the newspaper declared, while also arguing that "they are scarcely Swedes either, for then they ought to stay where they belong."[34] The article then took a radical position that the U.S. government should force Swedes who had not become American citizens to choose between forced citizenship or deportation to "where they are entitled to live."[35] For some immigrants, it was a much more difficult process to relinquish citizenship to their native country than it was for others, especially those who had not fully settled upon permanent residence in the United States.

Other outlets spoke of American citizenship as a symbolic badge of honor. Scandinavians deserved high regard as some of the most loyal immigrant groups to their adopted home. One article in *Skandinaven* boasted in 1917 that Americans ranked Scandinavians among the best citizens; they were "loyal, hardworking people, obedient to law," and took great pride in their "willing patriotism" to the country and its flag.[36] The newspaper used the article as a means of defending its citizens after nativist rhetoric had begun to cast its gaze on the Lutheran Church as an "object of suspicion" due to the predominance of Lutherans in

Table 5.1: Citizenship of foreign-born white males 21 years of age and over, by country of birth, for Chicago, 1910 (*Females not naturalized until 1920*)

	Total	Naturalized	Have 1st Papers	Alien	Citizens (no record)
Norway	11,193	6,924	1,319	2,059	891
Sweden	29,436	19,441	3,294	4,408	2,293
Denmark	6,126	3,870	797	1,002	457

Source: Burgess, *Census Data for the City of Chicago, 1920*, 26.

146 · CHAPTER 5

Germany.[37] While the article acknowledged that outsiders could potentially view the institution and its foreign nature as suspicious and anti-American, it also sought to negate such claims with a plea of support to the American cause.

With pressure mounting on issues of citizenship, American patriotism, and pledging loyalty to the allies, Scandinavian Americans redirected the public's attention to its assistance in the Allied war effort. The campaign, which reached its apex in 1918, focused on raising funds through liberty loan drives. During World War I, vigilante groups focused on anti-German and antisocialist rhetoric took it upon themselves to incite violence against groups who did not express outward loyalty to the American cause. Ethnic organizations that failed to raise sufficient Liberty Bond funds to show sufficient respect for the war effort became victims of small-scale riots and became the target of increased surveillance.[38] Aware of such threats, Chicago's Scandinavian Americans were vehement in their drive to support the war effort. One such drive reported in *Skandinaven* in May 1918 illustrated the extent to which Norwegian women were able to raise funds through liberty loans. The Daughters of Norway, along with other Norwegian women in the community, gathered together at the Chicago Norwegian Club on April 9th for a fundraising drive and were subsequently able to raise $43,300 within the span of only a couple of weeks.[39] As the overall push for liberty loans slowed by the fall, Norwegians continued to show their support by continuing with the drive. In October 1918, the Norwegian Club reported in *Skandinaven* that the members of the club purchased over $20,000 in less than a week, pushing the overall amount of loans purchased by Norwegians in the third liberty loan drive to over $5 million.[40]

In the spirit of competition between ethnic groups, that fall *Svenska Kuriren* published a list of the amounts subscribed by the different nationalities for the Third Liberty Loan. Germans were by far the most apt contributors to the cause with $87 million in loans purchased, while Swedes contributed $6 million, Norwegians contributed $5 million, and Danes bought almost $3 million.[41] Chicago's newspapers published the amounts of funds earned by ethnic groups comparatively, noting the extensive amount of money Scandinavians were able to raise. Through these pledge drives, Scandinavian groups understood the symbolic benefit of their association with such massive liberty funds. When one editor discovered that 55 percent of liberty loan subscribers chose to omit their nationalities from their subscriptions, the Swedish Committee for the Fourth Liberty Loan Campaign published a plea to the community, which asked each citizen to record their nationality when subscribing to loans.[42] In doing so, Swedes and other Scandinavians illustrated the importance of recognition in the charitable campaign, because a positive public image during wartime was just as vital as the drive itself. Throughout each of the campaigns for the Liberty Loans, groups were careful to express to the community the symbolic importance of contribution through subscription to loans as both patriotic and a vital outward expression of one's citizenship as a Scandinavian American.

As the war ended, an intriguing celebration took place, which illustrated the outward expression of Scandinavian whiteness as a carefully blended sense of ethnic identity. In a parade that combined the celebration of Foreign-Language Day in Chicago and the drive for the Liberty Loan, Scandinavians came together on April 24, 1919, to display the combination of old and new. The pages of *Skandinaven* proudly recalled, "A chorus of two thousand voices, consisting of foreign-language singing societies, participated in the foreign-language parade yesterday. There were no pedestrians in the parade; everybody rode on floats."[43] The fear and paranoia of such associations with European foreignness disappeared for an interim period. Through war bond drives and public appeal for recognition, Scandinavians were able to relinquish ethnic pride without forfeiting their rights to citizenship. The featured float of the parade, a sixty-feet-long Viking Ship with a costumed Leif Erikson at the helm, stood as the constant symbol of Norwegian heritage driving down the streets of the adopted homeland. Yet, as wartime ended and international migration reconvened, a new battle against the foreign began in the 1920s, forcing many Scandinavians to reconsider their loyalties to the notion of ethnic and cultural persistence.

Scandinavian Americans in Chicago after the War

Following World War I, Chicago's citizens delighted in the return of America's soldiers and of peace, yet nativist rhetoric and scientific racism persisted and boiled over into an urban crisis. Between 1914 and 1919, Chicago's African American population had grown by 70,000, mainly due to the draw of northern industry by migrants from the South. The massive influx of black migrants increased racial tensions, especially among working-class men who felt the pressures of job competition following the war's conclusion. Despite the proximity of working-class Scandinavian Americans who lived on Chicago's south side, there was very little public discussion of racial tensions. Largely in spite of class, most Scandinavian Americans saw themselves outside the context of Chicago's racial conflicts because they occupied a position of white exceptionalism and therefore did not concern themselves with matters of racial competition. The largest points of conflict between white and black individuals in Chicago emerged among white ethnic groups who directly experienced nativist vitriol such as Italians, Poles, Hungarians, and Russians.

148 · CHAPTER 5

Chicago's most well-known Swedish American, Carl Sandburg, covered the 1919 race riots in Chicago for the *Chicago Daily News* and later published his articles in the full-length report, *The Chicago Race Riots, 1919*. Sandburg had a Swedish immigrant upbringing in the more rural area of Galesburg, Illinois, which did not provide much contact with African Americans. Later, Sandburg became an avowed socialist and associated with leaders of the Industrial Workers of the World, which was the most radical union of the prewar era. In spite of his radical politics and progressive worldview, Sandburg was not sympathetic with the black cause. His reports of the riots, which erupted when a young black man crossed an invisible racial barrier on a crowded beach on July 27, downplayed the seriousness and extent of the violence on Chicago's south side. As black newspapers reported racial chaos, Sandburg noted the riot lasted only three days and claimed twenty black deaths. In actuality, the riot went on for fourteen days and culminated in thirty black deaths, seven of police, and no rioters killed.[44] In his mainstream articles, Sandburg positioned himself as white, though not "Nordic" as some Scandinavian American writers had begun to identify themselves. When he spoke publicly of African Americans, he used hierarchical terms that came from a position of understood privilege and therefore did not feel it necessary to specify categories of whiteness.

Privately, however, Sandburg expressed racist viewpoints on racial categories that mirrored the nativist rhetoric and racial categorizations of Madison Grant. In a series of letters to his brother-in-law, Edward Steichen, Sandburg spoke of spending ten days in the black belt and writing articles "on why Abyssinians, Bushmen and Zulus are here."[45] Aldon Nielsen argued that Sandburg was "operating within the poetic tradition of white speech" and that his writings transmit racism even as he appeared to speak out against it.[46] Much like other lesser-known Scandinavian Americans, Sandburg had begun to see himself both publicly and privately in a position of ultimate racial hegemony as a person of white Nordic descent. His whiteness, like that of the rest of Scandinavian Americans, would go uncontested from this point forward in American history according to the discourse of race. Even in contrast to other European ethnic groups, Scandinavians now occupied an untouchable position of white privilege.

As the debate in response to the position of immigrants within American society grew to a frenzy by the mid-1920s, Scandinavians responded in a surprising manner. Instead of retreating to a thoroughly American way of life, Scandinavians witnessed a cultural revival, albeit one that worked to combine the two national identities into one palpable sense of self. Scandinavians constructed this combined national identity with the understood approval of

Americans, whose discussion grew as to the importance of Nordic whiteness as raised by racial theorists and nativists. Repeatedly, Scandinavians used the language of nativism to their advantage in ways they had not done before, often speaking of their own racial features as a reminder of their cultural preference in American society.

In reflecting upon the past, Nordics made a distinct effort to frame their ties to America within the context of Scandinavian whiteness in an effort to retain ethnic heritage. A continuous argument that Scandinavians pressed was the notion that Leif Erikson was the first to discover America 300 years before Columbus, thereby solidifying the position of Scandinavians in the social fabric of America. In 1917, Norwegians adapted the argument to one that emphasized the racial grounding of Americans as Anglo-Saxon. As the editor of *Skandinaven* wrote in October 1917, "we cannot allow it to be forgotten that our continent was discovered by the Norwegians, and that our country is Anglo-Saxon, *not* Latin," linking racial preference to the past as well as the present.[47] Scandinavians also expressed a desire to maintain ethnic traditions in Chicago, especially in relation to the cultural importance of foreign language within the community. That same year, the Chicago Norwegian Club, by a majority vote, moved to use Norwegian instead of English within the confines of the club after a period of English-usage as a way to make a point.[48] For foreign-born club members, it was a way to revisit the past and relinquish ethnicity, yet for native-born members, the move alienated those who did not have as firm a grasp on the language as their parents' generation.

At war's end, the push for the revival of foreign language remained strong among Scandinavians despite growing nativist sentiment. In a call to the Norwegian community, the editor of *Skandinaven* spoke out in August 1920 against the intolerant "two-hundred-percenters," who, during the war, moved to convert Norwegians to full Americans. In the piece, the editor contended, "The time has come to restore real Americanism at home . . . some of [the two-hundred-percenters] took the position and said they wanted a law to forbid the use of any other language than English in the church, the school, and the newspaper. That is ridiculous and absurd. Can't a man fight equally well regardless of what language he uses?" The editor also argued that the ancestors of the Norwegian community deserved the right to speak their native language and practice the corresponding cultural habits. He adamantly declared, "does Americanism demand that we turn our hearts into stone and say to father and mother and to our grandparents: 'We are smarter than you now; we want a law to forbid you to use the language you like to use!' That is not Americanism. It is

150 · CHAPTER 5

intolerance."[49] Regarding the argument to revive use of foreign language, some Scandinavians considered it backward to turn one's back on their past. This was very different from the desires of American nativists whose expectations included abandoning one's ethnic past. Why would Scandinavian Americans have prioritized ethnic revival over their own personal safety? Given the tense climate of postwar America, the importance of Nordic whiteness was so great that their racial characteristics outweighed any declarations of ethnic pride. In the midst of such confusion, the number of immigrants in Chicago rose in the postwar years to an all-time high.

According to the 1920 census, there were approximately 130,000 Swedes, 72,000 Norwegians, and 29,000 Danes in Chicago. These staggering numbers, which did not include the second generation, came close to outnumbering some of the other major cities of the Midwest by comparison.[50] The new influx of immigrants sparked the discussion of American citizenship once again, especially in 1920 when women received the right to naturalize. A majority of Chicago's Scandinavians were naturalized citizens, while nativists publicly ostracized those who did not take the necessary steps (see table 5.2).

As an influx of immigrants swelled newcomers to Chicago, nativist discussions regarding citizenship and the desired and undesired immigrant classes grew to a frenzy. Growing sentiments exacerbated by World War I led Congress to set the first of many restrictive immigration quotas for each nationality on May 19, 1921, through the Emergency Quota Act. The act limited the annual number of immigrants who could be admitted from any country to 3 percent of the number of persons from that country living in the United States in 1910 according to the U.S. Census, favoring immigrants from northern and western Europe. Scholars have long criticized the American Quota Laws that established the concept of national origin as a discriminatory process. Both John Higham and Mae Ngai have pointed out that the central theme of the quota process was a race-based nativism, which favored Nordics of northern and western Europe over the "undesirable races." The result would culminate in a hierarchy of Europeans ranked by racial desirability—a concept long discussed but not formalized in legislation.[51]

Table 5.2: Number and percent naturalized among foreign-born white males and females 21 years of age and over, for Chicago, 1920 (*Denmark not listed*)

	Male Total	Naturalized	Female Total	Naturalized
Sweden	28,040	20,366 (72.6%)	28,833	19,774 (68.6%)
Norway	9,473	6,886 (72.7%)	10,102	6,893 (68.2%)

Source: Burgess, *Census Data of the City of Chicago*, 1920, 27.

Therefore, the initial quotas actually worked to benefit Scandinavian immigration, which reached the peak of its final wave in 1923. For Sweden alone, the first law of 1921 gave the country a quota of 20,042—a number far larger than waves in previous years. The final surge of Scandinavian immigrants represented accumulated demand; those who had planned to emigrate prior to the war could now do so at war's end. However, in 1922, only 43.8 percent of the quota requested admission. The following year witnessed a surge in immigration with 24,948 admitted into the United States; however, the subsequent quota law of 1924 reduced the quota to 2 percent instead of 3 percent, limiting Sweden's portion to only 9,561.[52] After 1924, the number of migrants returning to the Scandinavian countries was greater than those coming to America. Following the final adjustment of immigration quotas by the National Origins Act of 1927, which drastically reduced the quotas for Germany, the Irish Free State, and the Scandinavian countries, the number of immigrants from the Nordic countries continued to shrink drastically.

The Scandinavian newspapers of Chicago initially illustrated a positive response to the regulation of immigration by Congress because of the benefits such quotas offered Scandinavians as a desired ethnic group. One such reaction came after the publication of a now infamous editorial in the *Saturday Evening Post* that encouraged the U.S. government to increase the quota of the "more desirable" Nordic immigrants and decrease the quota of the "less adaptable." The author, Kenneth Roberts, declared that such a law would "signify a deserved tribute to those past generations of immigrants to which this country is so greatly indebted. It would express our appreciation of the excellent qualities of the Scandinavian peoples, who have contributed so much to the development of the Northwest."[53] Much of the favorable response to Scandinavian immigration came from the perspective of industrialists who viewed them as a group of diligent and specialized workers. A particularly favorable section of the annual report of the Bureau of Immigration in Washington, "Trades and Occupations of Immigrants of Various Countries," came to the attention of the editors of *Svenska Tribunen-Nyheter*. As the editors shared with their readers, national figures showed that the Scandinavian population contained a higher percentage of individuals with special occupational training than any other ethnic group in America.[54]

In comparison to other European ethnics, more Scandinavians held white-collar and other non-service positions, signifying the intelligence and dedication of the group to the American workforce and economy. Many of Chicago's Scandinavians did not view immigration quotas that favored further immigration from Scandinavia as a positive measure. Instead, the older generation viewed the new wave of immigrants in the 1920s as a menace to the established status quo—young people who would have to endure the arduous tasks of learning English and becoming Americanized. One editorial retorted that such newcomers often attracted unfortunate public attention and stood to give the community a bad name. Of these Scandinavian newcomers, the majority represented a certain "hoodlum" element, made up of young, working-class men who made passes at women on the street and indulged in ungentlemanly conduct. The author retorted that while these men may have gotten away with "that sort of thing in Sweden," they needed to learn appropriate manners and customs of Scandinavian American life in Chicago.[55] According to such viewpoints, an older generation of Scandinavians desired an insular community who acted "American" to nativists.

The National Origins Act of 1927, which effectively reduced the quota granted to the Nordic countries, caused many of Chicago's Scandinavians to express their outrage and even blatant racism toward other European groups. Some chose to place the blame on the disparate groups previously outraged by their own low quotas. One such reaction came from a member of the community who indignantly inquired within the pages of *The Lutheran Companion*: "Can anyone calculate wherein the United States will be benefited by the immigration of more Italians, Poles and Irish, Belgians and Dutch, and by reducing the quota of Germans and Scandinavians?"[56] While such editorials downplayed the element of competition among ethnic groups for jobs, it was clear that the once accommodating Nordic community felt threatened by the presence of other European races and chose to highlight the benefits of Nordic whiteness.

A later, more hostile editorial in *Svenska Tribunen-Nyheter* pushed the argument that the revised quotas were not only inconvenient but also impractical in building a country of "desirables." Mirroring the language of nativism, one editor sternly argued: "For a long time the immigrants from northern Europe have been hailed as forming the backbone of our nation. Are these highly valued Danes, Norwegians, and Swedes now going to be thrown aside to make room for Lithuanians and long-bearded, half-wild newcomers from Soviet Russia?"[57] Other outlets expressed greater concern for the potential loss of cultural practices and heritage, and therefore the community needed to equate ethnicity with positive institutions as well as with race. One newspaper warned that, if the 1924 quota were not relinquished, "all our socially constructive Swedish American institutions, including the press, societies, fraternal orders, churches, old people's homes and orphanages—in a word, all that the Swedish Americans from the earliest times down to the present have with such great sacrifices built up, will slowly but surely wither and die."[58] As the potential threat of the loss of cultural identity gained recognition, the community responded in a surprising manner—in the shadow of nativist rhetoric regarding immigrant "backwardness," Chicago's Scandinavians witnessed a cultural revival that built upon the ideal of a truly dualistic sense of citizenship in America.

In the years that followed the persecution of ethnic diversity in America, Scandinavian Americans once again celebrated the culture of home within the neighborhoods of Lakeview and Andersonville in Chicago. Membership in Scandinavian churches and societies steadily grew throughout the 1920s due to an influx of newcomers, native-born children, and those influenced to return to the church.[59] The Norwegian community used the 1925 centennial of its establishment in America to reflect upon its own hyphenated American identity. The Centennial was what historian April Schultz describes as a "specific site of contestation" that could not be understood outside the context of American nativism and the immediate tensions surrounding communities of foreigners.[60] Celebrations such as the 1925 Norwegian Centennial became commonplace in this period, while the actual practices of the homeland fell off, especially the use of Scandinavian languages in the public sphere.

The previous public emphasis on the use of native languages and literary culture dwindled in the postwar years; however, many continued to speak Nordic languages in the home and privately taught it to their American-born children. In spite of this private emphasis on ethnic heritage, Scandinavian American children had a far different image of America than that of their parents' generation during the 1920s. Entertainer Lydia Hedberg, who toured America from 1920 to 1923 as a Swedish folk singer and storyteller, recalled the vision of second-generation Swedish Americans as a confused space in between cultures. Most of them, she wrote, behaved in a manner unbecoming to public spaces; the young women quickly adopted every Americanism, bobbing their hair and sporting horn-rimmed glasses while speaking a "mish-mash slang" that combined English and the language of their parents. Hegberg was most disturbed in her travels by the "panicky anxiety" she encountered among the children of "well-to-do" Scandinavian immigrants who sought to conceal their Swedish origins and avoid any identification with newcomers from the homeland.[61] Despite her encounters with such insecure youth, Hegberg noted her failed perception that the process of becoming "well-to-do" would require full Americanization in moving into the upper classes of Chicago society. Instead, she found successful Scandinavians who mapped out a new direction in America—one that did not require the loss of Nordic whiteness or Scandinavian ethnicity.

By the 1920s, the last of the new arrivals from Scandinavia made their way into a complex ethnic community that was quite different from the segmented

154 · CHAPTER 5

communities of the 1880s. The centralized enclaves that Scandinavians shared had now grown to accommodate diverse groups of citizens and the community that was once desperate to hold onto ties to the homeland had found other ways to express cultural heritage. Newly developing suburban regions of Chicago allowed Scandinavians to exert social power over their environment and re-create their community affiliations outside the city. In doing so, these former immigrants were able to strengthen ethnic consciousness in areas removed from central Chicago and assert Scandinavian presence within the city as well as outside of it.[62] The importance of this inner-migration to suburban regions of Chicago proved vital in continuing the traditions of the homeland in a uniquely American way, emphasizing the benefits of the potential in America to become "well-to-do." Many Scandinavian Americans joined others in the early flight to the suburbs; the urban ethnic neighborhoods, once sites of substantial ethnic businesses and institutions, gave rise to ethnic elite who dominated the pub-lic life of the neighborhood and claimed to represent the group in its dealings outside of it, according to April Schultz and John Jenswold. Suburbanization, they found, proved to be a paradox for such ethnic elites; on one hand, flight from the centralized urban community had the potential to weaken their hold on the community, but on the other, they could express a truly Scandinavian American pluralistic identity in suburban regions through participation in the new lifestyle of American consumer culture.[63] As Liz Cohen questioned the standard view of the 1920s as a decade where mass consumer culture worked to assimilate ethnic Americans, she also discovered that Chicago's ethnic citizens interpreted consumer behavior differently than their American neighbors.[64] Therefore, as suburban flight for Americans would largely symbolize class mo-bility, Scandinavians grounded their move to the suburbs in rural traditions of the homeland where home ownership had very different meanings.

For many of these former immigrants, upward mobility held the possibili-ties to enjoy the finer things that the booming consumerism of the 1920s now had to offer. During this era of opulence, members of Chicago's Scandinavian elite took the steps to separate themselves from the city and their neighbors in forming their own insular community, even in the wake of nativist calls to be-come American. For members of this group, the opportunity to take advantage of the celebratory culture of the 1920s was far too tempting. They would soon set out to create a private space where high-class leisure and social interaction would offer the chance for new beginnings, however reminiscent of the culture of home.

CHAPTER 6

The New Nordic Man of the 1920s

On May 10, 1925, in the spirit of America's postwar affluence, a group of prominent Scandinavians prepared to break ground on a wooded site in the northwest Chicago suburb of Itasca, Illinois. A little over a year later, on Memorial Day 1926, the founders would celebrate the opening of the Nordic Country Club—a bucolic establishment set upon 120 sprawling acres of golf courses and parkland. Chicago's new Scandinavian elite, who included a group of successful doctors, lawyers, and businessmen, conceived of the Nordic Country Club as a weekend retreat from the rigors of city life. Their ideal "home away from home" became a vital cultural institution that developed out of two larger social movements in American cities during the 1920s: the great suburban migration and the growth and popularity of country clubs for America's upper classes. The construction of the Nordic Country Club was unlike any other affluent suburban escape of the day. The Club, built almost exclusively by Scandinavian Americans, symbolized the acceptance of an immigrant group into Chicago's elite; however, it was established deliberately apart from the social set of the North Shore. While the gentlemen of the Nordic Country Club purposely chose the club's name to reflect a racial, rather than ethnic, presence within the elite, they also founded the mostly fraternal organization as a means of adopting a new cultural identity during the 1920s, which I refer to as the "new" Nordic man.

The new Nordic man placed an emphasis on outward appearance, reflected through success in the American business world but also through the ability

Figure 13: An artist's rendition of the planned front lawn of the Nordic Country Club. The Club's founders wanted a large porch where club members could enjoy the pastoral surroundings of the country. Courtesy of F. M. Johnson Archives and Special Collections, North Park University, Chicago.

to maintain insular ethnic ties that connected to old-world culture. After work and on weekends, Chicago's Scandinavian elite enjoyed participation in popular social clubs as a marker of success within the community. However, a select group of men sought an outlet for a Scandinavian way of life that embraced the old and the new. This dream culminated in a suburban organization that blended markers of success in both cultures, which the name itself exudes: the Nordic Country Club. American and foreign-language newspapers both reported on the establishment of the club, whose name emphasized the adoption of the image of Nordic whiteness by Scandinavian Americans at the height of nativist fervor. After the initial fear of subversion subsided during World War I, Scandinavians went about cultivating an image that would illustrate their loyalties to their American citizenship while also embracing ethnic ties. Adopting one of the American values most celebrated during the 1920s, that of prosperity, affluent Scandinavian men participated in numerous leisure clubs as a means of networking, sharing in the cultural traditions and languages of home, and celebrating their rise into a new social class.

Anita Olson Gustafson, whose work focuses on the religious and ethnic affiliations of Chicago's Swedish citizens, agrees that while Swedes had the means and ambition to move their families into the suburbs, the process of suburbanization did not equal assimilation or loss of a Swedish ethnic identity. Instead, Gustafson likewise found that "their adaptation to life in Chicago was a synthetic development which combined the old with the new, creating a different kind of culture which was neither completely Swedish nor American." However, as this chapter further illustrates, the Swedish community and their Scandinavian neighbors were able to express their ethnic identities in unique ways that did not erode under the force of modernization, using social clubs and affiliations to benefit Scandinavians as a whole.[1] Furthermore, historians who explore the 1920s often look for certain markers in defining class mobility during this historical moment; often, the achievement of education, professional qualifications, and an embrace of bourgeois values are practices used as markers in defining class status and the desire to move up the social ladder. One common marker used to distinguish the entrance of immigrant groups into the middle to upper classes is their sense of cultural identification, or the degree to which they are willing to accept American standards over those of home.[2] However, as this chapter argues, this final indicator of class distinction was negotiable for Scandinavians in Chicago, and in most cases, did not apply. The establishment of the club, the activities and traditions practiced, and the people who gained membership to the club were, in every sense of the word, Scandinavian. The notion of separation from the rigors of city life had become popular since the earliest years of the population boom in Chicago, especially for groups like Scandinavians who had both the means and the desire to become suburban.

Planning the Scandinavian Utopia

As early as the 1880s, those Scandinavians who could afford to do so retreated to the new suburban areas outside the city limits including Lakeview and what later became Andersonville. When Scandinavians moved outside the city, they "brought" their community affiliations with them, including churches, secular clubs, labor unions, temperance societies, and professional associations. Rather than losing their ethnic affiliations and assimilating into American society, the process of suburbanization gave them a window of opportunity in the city's development to create the ethnic communities they so desired.[3] In 1893, a real estate company called the Swedish University Association (SUA) purchased land in the newly established neighborhood of North Park with the intention to transform the land acquisition into "an entire Swedish Covenant colony" within Chicago. Gustafson attributed this plan to the process of using an American institution, the urban-style subdivision, to "shape the needs of an ethnic sectarian community."[4] While the suburb and the educational institution of North Park eventually flourished into one of the most successful endeavors of the insular

Figure 14: A photograph taken for the founding members of the Nordic Country Club to show the natural beauty of the surrounding area. Before builders broke ground on the project, the area was quite rural with sprawling countryside perfect for the prospective Scandinavian American playground for the elite. Courtesy of F. M. Johnson Archives and Special Collections, North Park University, Chicago.

Swedish group, the notion of creating a completely homogeneous community within a growing urban area created immense internal conflicts complicated by economic and demographic forces. The early social experiment of the North Park group nevertheless created a model for Scandinavians who also desired a temporary escape from Chicago's city limits, either through home ownership or through membership in an association like the Nordic Country Club. For potential members, the club offered an insular community, as well as the privacy to practice ethnic traditions outside of the watchful eye of American nativists who would not approve of such affiliations.

From the initial stages of planning, the Nordic Country Club's founders publicly acknowledged a genuine need for such a foundation. For many prominent Scandinavian Chicagoans, the once exciting culture of the city neighborhoods and streets transformed over time into a nuisance, especially for those who expressed nostalgia for simple, rural Scandinavian life. In the planning stages of the project, Nordic's investors looked to other prominent Chicago social clubs (such as the Evanston Golf Club) for cues in execution and maintenance. While many of the club's founders could have belonged to any given one of the private membership clubs in the Chicago metropolitan area, the founders intended the club as the Nordic alternative. One of the most enticing elements of a country club was its distance from the city. Such distance, along with more rural, natural surroundings reflected more of the emphasis on Scandinavian natural living the investors were looking for.

In one of the early promotional maps of the Nordic Country Club and the surrounding housing developments, the club's investors encouraged potential members to move from Chicago to the suburb of Itasca, or to purchase a second home. Unlike Chicago, the quiet suburb was not plagued with the dirt and smoke of suburbs surrounding Chicago, and was only a short commute to the city, but most importantly, it was "an American community of substantial, prosperous people, who live modestly but well."[5] Their publicity raised an excellent point of marketing toward elite Scandinavian men looking to have their cake and eat it too. They could symbolically engage in a wholly American way of life and participate in ethnic activities at the club on the weekends. Another announcement promised a "very attractive location, close to the city," easily accessible by train and plans that would make the club "one of the most attractive and complete clubs in the country." Investors in the club also expressed a modern emphasis on transportation by automobile, noting that the club was "far enough away to lose the noise and dirt and din of the city, yet near enough to be within an hour's easy drive," assuming that most of its members owned cars.[6] Most importantly, the investors expressed the discourse of prominent Scandinavians of the city who "appreciated for some time the need of a club of this kind."[7] To such affluent Scandinavians, the need for a beautiful retreat from the city was just as important as the proposed features of the club, which embraced both American and Scandinavian culture.

In the earliest years of planning, the founders proposed the Nordic Country Club as an organization conceived by Scandinavian men for Scandinavian men. Advertisements for the club touted it as "a place where the busy man of today [and his family] can get the recreation, the play, the fun, the pure air and sunshine, and the social atmosphere of a summer or winter resort within easy reach of home." The club built by a group of men "with vision and foresight" offered opportunities for fraternal camaraderie and networking, set in "an ideal outdoor playground" for the successful Nordic man.[8] In doing so, the club would become an escape for Scandinavian men of a particular social and economic standing who sought an outlet for the sporting pastime of their adopted class and Scandinavian ethnic culture. At the club, members and their

160 • CHAPTER 6

families could partake in golf, tennis, "saddle and kindred" sports embraced by the upper classes as appropriate leisure activities. By the 1920s, according to the club's publicity, "places of wholesome and public playgrounds had been taxed beyond their limits" within Chicago, and therefore the club's investors proposed a new opportunity for sophisticated leisure that combined class and a renewed sense of cultural heritage.[9]

In 1925, the club's campaign and publicity director, Carl Collier, put out an eager rallying call to the charter members in a push to sign up the 375 members of the club needed for its opening. In his speech, Collier reiterated the genuine need for a club in revitalizing body and mind for Scandinavian Americans plagued by the rigors of city life. Collier emphasized that the club offered an opportunity to appropriate more of the advantages of America, while providing the Scandinavian benefits of physical fitness. Collier reflected on the nativist language of Nordic whiteness, pointing out that the "ideals of perfection," included a sound mind in a sound body. Scandinavian American men could attain this masculine ideal through physical exertion in the spacious outdoors of the Nordic Country Club. With exposure to sunlight, exercise, and fresh air not available in the skyscraper-blocked downtown of Chicago, Scandinavian men could restore the "natural balance of life, [which] nourishes the moral fiber of mankind."[10]

Collier and the founding members viewed citizenship as something earned, not merely given away, and leisure as a practice that could actually strengthen the quality of citizenship for Scandinavian Americans. Furthermore, the founding members embraced both leisure and sport as a piece of cultural heritage passed on to Americans, as they had with Ling Gymnastics and sauna bathing. As Collier wrote, "we can go a long way in that direction by getting [Americans] out of doors and really interested in nature. We can make still further progress by engaging them in sports."[11] In establishing a club focused on the importance of the natural world and Scandinavian culture, Nordic men could embrace their heritage and express to their American neighbors the benefits of maintaining ethnicity in America.

Nativism, Nordicism, and Excess in America during the 1920s

Publication of studies such as William Ripley's *The Races of Europe*, Madison Grant's *The Passing of the Great Race*, and Lothrop Stoddard's *The Rising Tide of Color against White World-Supremacy* combined racial science with nationalism to form the basis of a flawed racial hierarchy. The linguistic and ideological differences between Ripley and Deniker's anthropological studies undoubtedly influenced Madison Grant's establishment of the most damaging nativist rhetoric of the twentieth century. His argument that the earliest Americans were purely Nordic resonated with those who considered themselves part of the old stock, thereby linking Anglo-Saxon heritage with the Nordic race. In the 1920s, nativist doctrines reiterated these characterizations through the eugenics movement, the Immigration Act of 1924, and the Nazi movement, which regarded the Nordic race as superior to all other races. Eugenicists in America, who believed in the study and practice of selective breeding applied to humans with the aim of improving the species, helped to inspire the Immigration Act. Created out of the eugenic belief in the racial superiority of "old stock" white Americans as members of the Nordic race, the Immigration Act strengthened the position of existing laws prohibiting miscegenation. Many anthropologists and racial scientists applauded Nordics for their "responsible" reproductive habits; around the turn of the century, nearly 90 percent of Scandinavians married within their racial and ethnic group.[12] The imagined racial hierarchy, which became even further delineated with the passage of the Johnson-Reed Act of 1924 linking country of origin to proclivity for U.S. citizenship, was vastly damaging for those who fell into the "lower" races of such definitions. Yet, there are two elements often omitted from consideration within the history of nativist thought, which pose different frameworks for our understandings of American positions on race and ethnicity during the early twentieth century.

In the midst of conflict over immigration restrictions placed on "new" immigrants, it was especially in vogue to be "Nordic" in America. In his play on Oscar Wilde's ironic rhetoric, Aldous Huxley wrote on "The Importance of Being Nordic" in America in 1925. Huxley found it quite comical that Americans everywhere now claimed to have Nordic heritage based upon little evidence other than the benefits of what newspaper articles and public discourse promised people who could claim such racial ties. Huxley lamented the anthropological philosophers and nativists and their books "full of perfectly groundless generalizations" that influenced many to regard the Nordic race as superior to all other races.[13] By the 1920s, "the Nordic races," Huxley wrote, "have now, in their own imagination, taken the place of the Greeks and Romans. All virtue and intelligence belong to them."[14] Similarly, F. Scott Fitzgerald saw through such veiled attempts of modern Americans in understanding race, or at minimum in expressing anxiety over racial difference. Tom Buchanan, the pompous villain of *The Great Gatsby*, insisted to the book's protagonist, Nick Carraway, that "we're Nordics, I am, and you are . . . we've produced all the things that go to make civilization," and because of that, the "dominant" race needed to "watch

162 · CHAPTER 6

out or these other races will have control of things."[15] Fitzgerald deliberately borrowed Buchanan's nativist rant, based upon the work of "this man Goddard," from contemporary discourse of the late 1910s and 1920s. Lothrop Stoddard's *The Rising Tide of Color against White World-Supremacy* built upon Grant's scientific racism and warned of the collapse of the "white world" that could be brought about through further "colored migration."[16] Because more Americans read fictional works like Fitzgerald's and Huxley's narratives, they were more likely to be influenced by such ideologies, regardless of satirical intention.

Such understandings of race were closely tied to wealth and social class. A lifelong social climber of his day, Fitzgerald himself exposed a confused stance on racial whiteness in his personal letters to longtime confidant Edmund Wilson, expressing his dissatisfaction with his first visit to Europe in 1921 before publication of *The Great Gatsby* and after publication of his first novel. He lamented, "God damn the continent of Europe. It is of merely antiquarian interest . . . raise the bars of immigration and permit only Scandinavians, Teutons, Anglo-Saxons and Celts to enter."[17] Fitzgerald's elitist position illustrated the utter confusion many "old-stock," white, Anglo-Saxon, Protestant Americans expressed toward racial difference during the 1920s. According to such Americans, they were Nordics because they were of the "old-stock," and if Scandinavians represented the purest of the Nordic race, they were not a threat, nor a draw on capitalist society like other ethnic groups and had the potential to reap the benefits of American consumerism.

The Nordic Country Club's founders advertised the club in Chicago's newspapers as "the first 100 percent Swedish country club in the country," with every intention of limiting the club's membership to privileged Scandinavians.[18] Carl Collier specifically expressed that neither he nor the charter members would accept just any "Tom, Dick, or Harry" as a member of their club. It would be easy, in his opinion, to find people willing to enroll in the club because "hardly an intelligent man in the entire loop district" would turn down such an opportunity. However, he reiterated, "We don't want that. We want to build this organization for your friends and our friends."[19] According to both Collier and the bylaws of the club, "friends" were of a particular standing in the Scandinavian community. The bylaws of the club indicated that any individual over the age of 21 was eligible for membership; however, the fine print of the bylaws noted that the potential members were required to endure a lengthy process, which included a vote by the board of directors, with three negative votes resulting in the denial of membership. The reasons for such staunch eligibility requirements for charter membership were clear: charter members of the club would actually hold a stake of the club's land. For $1,000 paid in eight installments at the beginning of the building process, members could become permanent shareholders—a wise investment for the time but also a hefty price to pay for membership to a social club.[20] For that price, a shrewd businessman could instead flaunt his wealth by purchasing a luxury model sedan. Regular social memberships (without a stake of the club) to the club were additionally costly. The price of membership in the initial years of the club increased with every 100 people who joined, beginning at $350 and going up to $550 for the last to commit to annual membership. The investors in the club knew that creating an affluent country club grounded in the cultural heritage of the homeland would require a significant amount of collateral in order to guarantee long-term success.

Initial membership in the Nordic Country Club was also limited to men, with visiting rights extended to ladies of the immediate family. In doing so, the club maintained an image of a family atmosphere on the surface yet operated as more of a fraternal organization. In campaigning for social members, the investors (all of whom were men) produced membership recommendation cards, which expressed their desire for a "congenial, social atmosphere where the business and professional man and his family may have all the advantages of an ideal Country Club away from the din of the usual crowds."[21] The bylaws of the club made it clear that women and children of members were more than welcome to enjoy the privileges of the club without membership, but they would be subject to additional rules and regulations that actual members were not. Such exclusions included golf tournaments and various weekend activities where the male members of the club did not appreciate the presence of women and children. The bylaws were also very specific about the extent to which the club's ancestors desired to maintain a morally upstanding façade. In 1930, the club's board added an amendment to the bylaws, which specified, "Ladies of the immediate family shall be construed to mean the wife and daughters of a member residing with him."[22] This amendment illustrates that Scandinavian men still exuded an image of old-world piety, and even in the modern era, members of the Nordic Country Club continued to hold onto their moral beliefs despite the introduction of modern social mores.

In addition to the fraternal undertones of the goals of the club, it was clear that the charter members looked to fill its ranks with athletically and culturally minded citizens of the Scandinavian community in Chicago. In a letter of correspondence, written in July 1925 between director Carl Hjalmar Lundquist and the rest of the charter members, Lundquist urged the men to instill pride in their recruitments. To Lundquist, it was a privilege to belong to the Nordic Country Club, and therefore members needed to encourage their friends within the business community to join "as to keep up the quality of our members on the same high plane as it is now."[23] In doing so, there was a specific demographic that the charter members were especially eager to recruit within Chicago. While socioeconomic status was crucial, recruiters targeted groups such as the United Swedish Singers of Chicago and the Swedish-American Athletic Association, comprised of Scandinavian men of important social standing in the community. After the club opened in 1926, an article in the club's newsletter, *The Nordic Fairway*, discussed the pride of the club in having members that represented virtually every business and industry due to the keen maneuvering of early recruiters. The most important outcome of their recruitment tactics, according to the newsletter, was the caliber of modern gentlemen they located to fill their ranks. Admittedly, the club aspired to recruit self-assured members of the Scandinavian elite—bankers, manufacturers, small business owners, lawyers, brokers, managers. Whatever the business or profession of its members, Lundquist emphasized that "the secret of success for Nordic lies in the fact that they are real men; real friends, good companions and gentlemen. And that, after all, will make any enterprise successful."[24] Ultimately, success in American business made you a real Nordic man.

The Nordic Country Club was not without its competition from other Scandinavian social and leisure clubs that required private membership. In June 1927, *Scandia* announced the opening of a summer resort intended to cater to the needs of Chicago's Norwegian elite. Despite the resort's inclusive name, Scandia Community Beach, described as a "summer resort for members of Chicago's Norwegian colony," was a private beach club in the north woods of Wisconsin. The lush resort perched on Lake Michigan was made possible by L. H. Lund, editor of *Scandia*, as a vacation destination for Chicago's Norwegian families who had the means to travel the almost 300 miles north of the city. One firsthand testimony published in *Scandia,* clearly intended to market the resort, told of the modern conveniences in the rural location and evoked remembrances of the old country. The resort's staff treated the "big party" of would-be members to a royal reception including a big fish breakfast and, afterward, a tour by automobile. The contributor claimed that they "heartily recommended" that anyone who had the means to spend their summers at Scandia Beach should purchase a lot or two, which included a year's subscription fee.[25] The establishment of private clubs like Scandia Community Beach and the Nordic Country Club illustrates that while elite Norwegian and Swedish men could have chosen to be members of American country clubs, Scandinavian culture was more important as a means of identity.

However, planning such private clubs did not come without class-related disputes. Despite the façade of rational planning and execution of the Nordic

Country Club's goals in the early stages of recruitment, the charter members did not escape the occasional squabbles, often sparked by egotism and jealousy over rank in the hierarchy of the club. One such disagreement arose in June 1925 between Carl Hjalmar Lundquist and Chas Fellowes when Lundquist, who was both a director and major investor in the club, discovered that Fellowes printed Lundquist's name on every piece of letterhead and publicity for the club. Lundquist wished to be more of a silent partner in the dealings of the club and intended to downplay his role in an effort to maintain an image of financial modesty. Noting his own ethnic stubbornness, Lundquist scribbled a terse letter to his once close friend. In the letter, Lundquist referenced a confidential conversation between the two during which Fellowes suggested that Lundquist not take such an active part in the organization.

Previously, Lundquist worried over his rise to leadership in the somewhat risky financial investment. Lundquist explained to Fellowes that he would be obliged to "lay low so as to give those a chance who wanted to be in the limelight." He was appalled when the board of directors approved a listing of the entire board on all correspondence of the Nordic Country Club—a move Lundquist accused of "smell[ing] something akin to egotism." Lundquist ended his letter with a word of advice to Fellowes and, more broadly, to the other directors: "Let's do business like businessmen—not kids."[26] This early animosity expressed between Lundquist and Fellowes exploded into a much larger issue in later years, when the club and its members faced the massive problem of maintaining an affluent social club in the midst of the country's greatest economic depression. In the years leading up to the stock market crash, however, the Nordic Country Club prospered under the guidance of its charter members, eager to transform the club into an oasis dedicated to Scandinavian heritage away from the confines of city life.

In a push to mark the inaugural season of the Nordic Country Club, the charter members distributed a commemorative booklet to each new member of the club separated into features for men and women. In the booklet, the members could view the architectural sketches of the new clubhouse—a palatial Nordic chalet reminiscent of structures in the homeland with classic Tudor lines of Scandinavian architecture. The booklet touted the many possibilities for leisure and relaxation that the club had to offer to its members. For those who wished to stay indoors, the club provided a spacious lounge complete with billiard and card rooms for rainy days or evening play. Catering to members' wives, the booklet described that the dinner dances and social affairs of interest would take place in the club's opulent ballroom. Down the hall from the ballroom, the club's female patrons could find a library and reading and writing rooms adver-

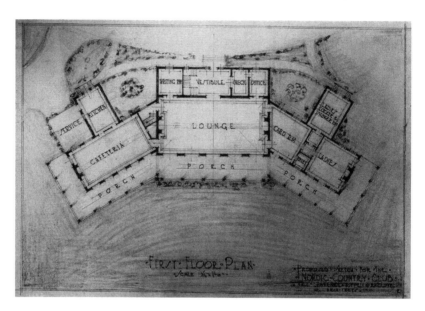

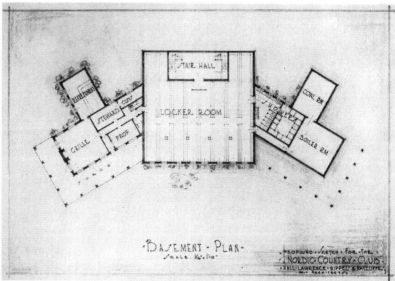

Figures 15 and 16: Architectural blueprints for the first floor of the Nordic Country Club. A small "ladies' area" was located on the first floor, while the entire basement was set aside for the male club members. Courtesy of F. M. Johnson Archives and Special Collections, North Park University, Chicago.

The New Nordic Man of the 1920s • 167

tised as a cozy respite complete with wide, open fireplaces. The central part of the club for all its patrons was the main dining room, where husbands and their families could come together to reconnect after a long day of outdoor activities. As the booklet advertised, the dining room was one that catered "to the inner man" with the finest foods, comfort, and cuisine—it was a place "to chat and smoke and while away a pleasant hour."[27] Sketches accompanied the booklet's description of the club's amenities, alternating between scenes of men in full dinner dress smoking pipes in the lounge, and elegant couples dancing in the grand ballroom. The propagandist booklet reassured the club's newly anointed members that their investment was a sound one that the club would celebrate in its opening.

Beginning in 1925 and continuing through the 1930s, the club published a monthly newsletter for its members, which combined ethnic humor and current events and featured prominent club members. Over time, the newsletter would shift from a simple retelling of events to become a vital reflection of the changes the affluent Scandinavian members faced in the economic downfall of the country. In the first edition of the newsletter, the newly recruited members of the club were introduced to the "who's who" of the organization—biographical sketches of each prominent man on Nordic's board. One biography after another told a similar story of emigration with their families and concluded with a statement that each considered Chicago to be his permanent home. Similarly, they all told stories of Scandinavian men who became highly industrious and successful through their acculturation into American life, which thereby rewarded them with fine homes and healthy, happy families, while also pointing out the duality of their ethnic identities as Scandinavian Americans.

The *Swedish Blue Book*, a widely read community directory, which highlighted well-established Swedish American leaders and businesses, mirrored the descriptions of this network of businessmen who created a vital "old boys club" inside and outside of the community. The biographical sketches of Scandinavian American high society followed a marked pattern in the path its members took in achieving social success. The descriptions of mostly men in metropolitan Chicago painted a picture of business success in American society and interpersonal achievements in Scandinavian fraternal groups. Almost all of the men belonged to prominent Swedish fraternal clubs in Chicago, including the Vikings, the Svithiods, the Svithiod Singing Club, the Odd Fellows, and the Fish Fans Club. A selection of businessmen from the *Swedish Blue Book*, such as C. Hilding Anderson, were not even born in Scandinavia but nevertheless desired membership in a club that symbolically embraced ethnicity. Many narratives told a similar tale of personal triumph in America, beginning with higher education at Ivy

168 · CHAPTER 6

League institutions or those revered by the Scandinavian community (i.e., North Park and Augustana Colleges) and active participation in American politics. In the professional world, several individuals placed an emphasis on building a business from the ground up or on work in a number of positions that signaled achievement in the American workforce, including law, business, or economics. Participation in any of the major fraternal groups, especially the Scandinavian male choirs, became a symbol of Lutheran camaraderie, and shared Nordic whiteness.[28] Through endeavors like the Nordic Country Club, fraternal orders, and male choirs, elite Scandinavian American men created distance between their ethnic group and the rest of Chicago's society as a means of celebrating Scandinavian culture as they remembered it. These groups were able to embrace their ethnic heritage in a tumultuous era for underprivileged European ethnic groups. Similarly, the "who's who" section of *The Nordic Fairway* published by the Nordic Country Club illustrated the capability of Scandinavian Americans to walk a very fine line in American society between appearing racially American while embracing Scandinavian ethnicity.

The Nordic Fairway contributed to an insular discussion among its members that embraced Scandinavian ethnic discourse through cultural jokes and took a lighthearted approach to the difficulties of navigating within a society that held preconceived stereotypes of Scandinavians. One such joke played on the common assumption that Nordics were typically taller in stature than the average person:

CONDUCTOR: "How old is your little boy?"
FOND MOTHER: "Four"
CONDUCTOR: "How old are you, my little man?"
BOY: "Four"
CONDUCTOR: "Well, I'll ride him free this time, but when he grows up he'll be either a liar or a giant."[29]

Other jokes featured in the newsletter poked fun at a more unfortunate stereotype—that of the rural, and therefore not fully acculturated, Scandinavian:

Ole Oleson came into a drug store in a Minnesota village and inquired if they had any "squirrel" whiskey. "No," said the clerk, "but I can slip you a little Old Crow." "Aye don't want to fly," said Ole. "Aye yust want to yump around a little."[30]

In the late 1920s, the club's newsletter took on a more masculine, rough tone aimed at the club's male members in spite of the fact that their wives also read *The Nordic Fairway*. In the September 1926 edition, colorful jokes that addressed sexuality and alcohol consumption during prohibition were scattered throughout the newsletter. Many of the jokes appeared to drift away from cultural stereotypes to focus more on American discourse and mores in society, including a view of youth culture:

> The first thing a freshman learns in college is how to judge good whisky. This is how it's done: One drops a hammer in the whisky, if it floats it's fair whisky; if it sinks, the whisky is poor; but if the hammer dissolves—that's whisky.[31]

This particular brand of humor was reminiscent of a shift in discourse over the course of the 1910s and 1920s when Scandinavians became more accepting of the consumption of alcohol. Scandinavians, once known for their strict temperance, now embraced American social customs, especially in references to sneaking alcohol during prohibition. Several jokes also featured a more open interpretation of sexuality than that expressed in previous years by Scandinavians, including satire that addressed premarital sex and flirtatious public interactions. One anecdote featured a father asking his daughter's suitor for an explanation as to why his daughter was sitting on the young man's lap. To the father's question, the man replied, "I got here early, sir, before the others."[32] Another satirical piece appeared at first glance to be a serious letter to the editor of the newsletter from a young member looking for an answer to his personal dilemma:

> **DEAR EDITOR:** I cannot get over being sleepy about two o'clock in the morning. What do you suggest?
> **ANSWER:** Marry the girl and then you can stay at home nights.[33]

The pages of *The Nordic Fairway* offer an invaluable glimpse into the social discourse of an ethnic group in the process of blending two dominant national identities. Humor in the newsletter focused on common jokes from Scandinavia seamlessly blended with new jokes about Scandinavians in uniquely "American" situations. Joy Lintelman explained that ethnic humor was a tool used to bring the community together into a common discourse about those outside of the margins; yet, for this group of privileged Scandinavians, the humor focused on their own social class. In doing so, the two identities would combine into one ethnic persona.[34] However, this did not necessarily mean that everyone was in on the joke.

Despite the pretense that the Nordic Country Club was a place for both men and their families, the pages of *The Nordic Fairway* maintained the appearance of a fraternal organization with chauvinistic discourse centered upon its female attendants. In one article, a club member joked about the possibility of an annual ladies' "stag" where the members' wives could play the men for a day: "Turn the club over to the ladies for the day. Give them the whole layout and tell them to go to it. We wonder how many of them would be speaking to each other by evening."[35] In another article from the same issue, the editor talked about the chance for "the boys" to reacquaint themselves with their homes as winter was on the horizon, canceling the opportunity for golf. The editor lamented that winter would mean that the members would be required to "become the head of a household once more, and to get on speaking terms with the wife. So, taking it all in all, perhaps it is just as well to have a bit of winter for a change."[36] While the majority of the newsletters focused almost exclusively on golfing merits and personal briefs on its members (including weddings and birth announcements), the newsletters also publicized cultural events that celebrated Scandinavian traditions. The club held an annual crawfish dinner as a way to bring together members and their families for a traditional Scandinavian Midsommar celebration outside of the city. *The Nordic Fairway* boasted about the extensive amount of money the club set aside to import crawfish from Sweden and Norway for the occasion but truly embraced the opportunity to gather with fellow Scandinavian Americans. The spirit of celebration during the 1920s could not, however, be maintained forever. As the effects of the stock market crash and the Great Depression took hold in metropolitan Chicago, Scandinavian Americans found themselves in complicated financial situations, even in great need.

The Curtain Falls: The Great Depression and the Scandinavian Community in Chicago

Upon entering into major financial investments, many of Chicago's most successful businessmen encountered some degree of hesitation about the age of excess that defined 1920s financial decisions. Even before entering into one of his most successful social and professional endeavors, Carl Lundquist hesitated before making such a significant investment. In a document prepared by his lawyer and good friend, Chas Fellowes, it was clear that the Nordic Country Club had the potential to be viable, but this was only contingent on the cooperation of Lundquist and his colleagues. Fellowes reminded Lundquist and the other investors that "there are several members of the Organization committee of the Nordic Country Club who are widely known and stand very prominently among the Swedish population of Chicago."[37] In other words, if the potential investors did not choose to invest their funds in the club's properties, as well as the club itself, it would set a negative precedent. Along with their investment, the charter members agreed to receive a physical claim to the club in the form of 50-by-150-foot property lots in addition to their share in equity. For shrewd

The New Nordic Man of the 1920s • 171

lawyers like Lundquist, the bank could rescind rights to the property, and their homes, if the deal fell through. Lundquist was a dynamic thinker when it came to anything that involved the potential for failure in business. Following Fellowes's document in his files, Lundquist attached a handwritten note, which read as somewhat of a nervous stream of consciousness as to the consequences of this business endeavor:

> I am organizing this thing. Getting my friend into it. Assuming the responsibility of having them put $7,000 into it with a chance of loss $700 I stand to lose. May have to do $700 of work to save it. Put up $25.00 each [month] and will have to put up more for committee work. I am attending banquets and meetings 3 nights a week to put it on. I am obligating myself to Hilding [Anderson] and others on behalf of this and making enemies out of some people I would rather be friends with.[38]

Despite his skepticism, Lundquist eventually entered into the business deal and unwillingly became a major leader in the enterprise. In hindsight, however, Lundquist would regret his early decision later when the dismal years of the Great Depression quietly diminished his portfolio and wreaked havoc on his professional relationships with his business associates.

Lundquist's rise to professional and political success read very much like a page of the "who's who" section of *The Nordic Fairway*: a distinguished Swedish American journalist, author, engineer, and later lawyer, Lundquist was highly educated and well respected. Lundquist's professional career was indicative of the extent to which Scandinavians had the ability to navigate between Scandinavian and American cultures. After working as the city editor of *Svenska Tribunen*, *Fosterlandet*, and *Svenska Posten* of Rockford in the early 1900s, Lundquist made the bold decision to put himself through Chicago Law School. For years, Lundquist attended school during the day and worked as a tool-and-die maker at night. After his admission to the Illinois Bar in 1922, Lundquist worked as an assistant corporation counsel for the City of Chicago.

In his leisure time, Lundquist prioritized his identity as a Swedish American by becoming an active member of the Svithiod Singing Club, serving as chairman of Verdandi Lodge #3 and Värmlands Nation, and organizing the Chicago branch of the Swedish Cultural Society in 1923. Through his participation in these groups and his work in the legal field, Lundquist became adept at professional networking, which later informed his participation in the investment deal surrounding the Nordic Country Club. Like many of his colleagues and Scandinavian American neighbors, by the late 1920s Lundquist had the means and desire to live outside of the city in the comfortable suburb of Rockford

172 · CHAPTER 6

with his family. Yet, his move to Rockford would become both a physical and metaphorical separation from his colleagues at the Nordic Country Club. Over the late 1920s, his social participation lessened and he visited the club only on rare occasions. In 1930, as many of the club's members began to experience the early effects of the Great Depression, Lundquist was no exception. For him, the devastating effects came in the form of public humiliation by his colleagues.

The significant economic hardship and social upheaval of the depression transformed the Nordic Country Club in negative ways. The once carefree, elite membership, who dedicated their time to combining Scandinavian customs with the traditions of American consumerism, now focused solely on economic survival. During the early 1930s, the club's regulations forced many of its members to withdraw their social membership in the club or face the embarrassing consequence of delinquency from failure to pay club dues. Like other members, Lundquist encountered similar financial woes that his distance from the club and its board of directors did not abet. On May 28, 1930, the board of directors charged Lundquist with the first of several notices of debt to the club over the course of the 1930s. In the terse letter, Lundquist was informed of the board's resolution that unless his indebtedness to April 1, which amounted to a staggering $462.95, was paid within ten days, he would be suspended from "all the rights and privileges of the Club."[39] The papers of the Nordic Country Club are indicative of both the financial climate and contrast of the 1920s and the 1930s. While the majority of the papers claim that the club was a prosperous and successful financial endeavor, the inclusion of Lundquist's personal financial woes stands out. While Lundquist's struggles with the club to release him from debt would surprisingly not haunt him later in his political career, his personal papers illustrate an era when financial crisis could outweigh interpersonal and business relationships.[40]

Instead of appearing in person at a board meeting to refute the issue, Lundquist sent a letter of resignation as a member of the board of directors and requested that his membership transfer to a "non-resident member" of the club. Upon his request, the board agreed to reinstate him a few months later as a "non-resident member" of the club, yet, by January 1931, Lundquist was once again delinquent with payments that now amounted to $546.70, resulting in his denial of membership. After years of this back-and-forth financial struggle between Lundquist and the board of directors, Lundquist later filed legal papers in August 1941 for the club to release him from his monetary commitment, promising his son, Donald, a membership transferal and thereby releasing himself from further payments.[41] While the club never made its private financial dealings public to its members, the telltale signs of social embarrassment were present in simple omission. The pages of *The Nordic Fairway*, once sprinkled with regular accolades of the successes of Lundquist—such as his invitation to meet the Crown Prince of Sweden in June 1926—were now devoid of any mention of Lundquist or his family, even as most of the club's members suffered the effects of the depression in one way or another. As Ulf Beijbom argued, many Scandinavian Americans who had the means to do so returned to northern Europe early on in 1930, while by 1932 all emergency relief funds were diminished and the cost of unemployment enormous.[42] Even those who returned to Scandinavia eventually felt the massive effects of the worldwide financial collapse. There was no escape from the devastation of the Great Depression, not even for the most resourceful and competent Nordics.

Marketing of the Nordic Country Club delivered to Chicago's newspapers attempted to avoid discussion of the financial problems the club and its members faced. William Randolph Hearst's first Chicago newspaper, the *Herald Examiner*, published an article about the Nordic Country Club in 1933 that highlighted the benefits of the club in ways that Americans could appreciate. The club, which the article described as being built in Chicago's "boom days" by Scandinavian contractors, had become far more inclusive in recent years as a "melting pot" that welcomed other ethnic groups with open arms. In a clear publicity move aimed at increasing membership, the article claimed that at the Nordic Country Club, "Irishmen rubbed elbows with Swedes, Germans fraternized with the Irish, and everybody was happy" until the depression hit. The article concluded with a promise that "new and substantial refinancing" among the members of the Nordic Club was "in full bloom."[43] Yet, according to *The Nordic Fairway*, the club was *not* taking a Progressive step toward ethnic inclusivity. Instead, the club's leadership constructed this insider/outsider discourse as a means of positioning their racially exclusive club above the fray of the collapse of American capitalism. By appearing to nativist Chicagoans that their club was inclusive of problematic European groups such as Germans, the Nordic's investors took a somewhat arrogant position. The Nordic Country Club would not collapse, unlike similar private American clubs, because Scandinavian Americans were shrewder in business and more adept in handling their finances than Americans.

As a last ditch effort, the club's newsletter declared that membership of the largely Scandinavian club was holding strong and that there would be no need to market the club to other European ethnic groups. While the Nordic Country Club never explicitly pronounced its exclusivity as a club founded for Scandinavians by Scandinavians, its name alone was enough to deter other groups from joining out of fear of conflict or exclusivity. Furthermore, the most successful

174 · CHAPTER 6

marketing tactic the club used in gaining new members was through word of mouth: therefore, the club remained wholly Nordic. The club's directory was almost entirely comprised of Scandinavian names.[44] Even in the grips of the Great Depression, the Nordic Country Club remained selective in its membership by ethnicity and social standing in the community, even though there was no explicit mention of this practice. The economic problems that the Nordic Country Club faced were representative of a much larger issue that was unfolding back in Chicago.

The Great Depression for Scandinavian Chicago's "Other Half"

In the years following World War I, immigration resumed across America and brought a new wave of Europeans eager to join their friends and family and take part in the American dream. Much like the first Scandinavian settlers, these "greenhorns" would have to prove their worth in a society plagued by nativist rhetoric. One of these new immigrants was Bror Johansson, a Swede who immigrated to Chicago in 1926 and would later tell the story of the shift he witnessed from prosperity to the "starving years" of the depression. In a series of interviews conducted with Johansson in the 1980s, co-authors Lilly and Lennart Setterdahl described their subject as "a big and tall man with clear-cut features, a blond Viking with blue eyes and a warm and friendly smile that definitely contradicts the roughneck vision one can get from hearing his story."[45] Playing upon stereotypes still prevalent in America's social consciousness, Johansson took pride in the fact that he was not a "typical Swedish-American." He did not attend church, was a lifelong Democrat, and chose to remain in Chicago after "almost all other Swedes" had moved to the suburbs.[46] Johansson arrived a "greenhorn" in the 1920s, offering a stark contrast to the new Nordic men of Chicago's Scandinavian elite. His reminiscences as a late immigrant to Chicago, however, provide a similar framework of masculine ethnic pride within the world of work and leisure.

Upon arrival by train from New York in August 1926, a former neighbor met Johansson and took him immediately to Lake View in preparation for a card party later that evening. As he prepared to go to the party, Johansson mistakenly put on a hat he brought from Sweden; his brother warned: "You can't wear it. It doesn't look American."[47] His reflections on the Scandinavian neighborhood in the 1920s offer a glimpse of an ethnic community that was beginning to embrace modern American cultural standards. While Johansson described the neighborhood as a place where "Swedes could find anything they needed," it was an area that appeared more American than Scandinavian in several ways. He went to the Dalkullan store, which had the best snuff imported from Sweden; continuing on throughout the community, he noted walking past the Vic Theater and Mary Garden Dancing Place, "a nice place with good music." He noted Café Idrott, the "famous cooperative" his friends told him about in letters prior to his arrival where, as a new immigrant, he could pick up his mail and provide an address. The café was still dominantly ethnic in character; Johansson described its library, where "there was always a crowd of people reading newspapers" in Swedish and English, while the café continued its rules of temperance—"no dancing or whiskey in that place," Johansson lamented. Altogether, he counted seventeen Swedish restaurants within walking distance of his new home, all of which retained their ethnic names, including Gästis's Smörgåsbord, Gufstafson's, and Mrs. Swanson's, illustrating the ethnic persistence of Scandinavian culture in Chicago.[48]

Upon settlement, Johansson found work after only one weekend and moved to 3221 Sheffield Avenue in the heart of Lake View, where he shared a first-floor "bachelor" apartment with four other men from Sweden. During the late 1920s, Johansson recalled his experiences in the apartment on Sheffield as that of perpetual mischief, while his work experiences were not nearly as enjoyable or rambunctious. Beginning in a construction job, which Johansson labeled "slave work," he was able to hold his job until he received his first paycheck, when he was also fired. In the late 1920s, well-paying, union-supported positions in manual labor were difficult to attain in Lake View. Johansson was finally able to come into a good position by lying about his ethnicity to a potential German employer and posing as a German in a unique turn of events.[49]

As financial woes of the Great Depression set in, Johansson refused to leave his new home as others had done, despite the fact that he was working only temporarily for a printing company for three to four months a year. Johansson, like many other Scandinavian men, remained vehemently stubborn in accepting handouts, and in his words, "never stooped to the level of standing in a soup line."[50] A characteristic feature of the depression era was the way in which men suffered in contrast to women, according to Beijbom, who became more responsible for family expenses.[51] Johansson was forced to swallow his pride and took a job working at a laundry, where he made only 12-1/2 cents an hour washing clothes and working as the foreman, which he felt was beneath him even as a still-recent immigrant. At his job, Johansson endured constant theft from laundresses employed at the laundry. In one instance, the laundresses had rolled blankets and sheets around their bodies and underneath their skirts, and upon the end of their shifts, casually "walked away with the loot." Rather than accusing the women whom Johansson admitted "probably had to steal" in

176 · CHAPTER 6

such dire times, he instead defended himself to his boss by explaining that he thought the women were pregnant. He exclaimed to his boss, "You can't expect me to look under their skirts, can you?"[52] After his inevitable dismissal from the laundry, Johansson resorted to theft when he and another Swede, Swan Donell, became partners in the business of buying and selling gold and silver.

Between 1933 and 1934, the two admittedly "swindled their way through the Depression," going door to door in suburban regions of the city and taking advantage of people who "made the most money," but were also most afraid of losing their homes if they did not meet their mortgage payments. Johansson and his partner "appraised" jewelry for their customers who were desperate to make ends meet: "If it was worth $35, we paid $5 and sold it to a jeweler for $35."[53] Johansson expressed no remorse for his underhanded business tactics but also realized the potential for arrest and admitted to never patronizing the streets of Chicago. When times grew incredibly dire, Johansson and the four men who lived in the "bachelor apartment" retreated to a more primitive way of life when they purchased five piglets from a farmer in Wisconsin. Over the next year, they kept the five pigs in the basement of the house, fed them scraps from the food they brought home, and one by one, they slaughtered the pigs to provide food. Johansson later defended the actions of his roommates and himself in such times of need by explaining that "times were hard, but all of us survived . . . except the pigs."[54] The story of survival Johansson told of his experiences as a Swede in Chicago during the Great Depression stand as a testament to the marked contrast between established and greenhorn Scandinavians as two different classes of ethnic Americans. While all groups suffered to a certain extent, the diversity of their experiences and the ways they chose to cope with economic loss illustrate vital issues pertaining to identity, image, and social class in the midst of the Great Depression.

H. Arnold Barton put it best when he referred to the era that encompassed the Great Depression as "the afterglow" for Scandinavian Americans.[55] During its early years, many of Chicago's Scandinavians reflected on the great migrations of the past and began to reconsider their ethnic past. For some, improving economic conditions in the Scandinavian countries prompted them to return home. For those who refused to give up on their adopted homes, the strong support system established in the earliest years of the financially dire epoch helped many to cope with economic and social issues that would soon follow. Within the city, the sole remnants of the once thriving Scandinavian communities appeared to be on a downturn as time went on.

In 1930, the remnants of Scandinavian culture in Lake View included the Swedish Club on North LaSalle Street, a few rooming houses on North Clark

Street, and several small businesses, while the majority of Scandinavian businesses moved to Andersonville during the 1920s where rent was cheaper. Those who had not migrated to the suburbs moved their homes and businesses north to Andersonville and Lakeview, south to Englewood, and west to Irving Park and Albany Park.[56] Bror Johansson, who survived the depression by becoming a pawnbroker, noted that not every Scandinavian was so lucky. Some had to sell their handcrafted homes, and he recalled instances where up to five men shared a single room in local boarding houses to get by. Other more unfortunate souls "walked until their hats floated" in Belmont Harbor rather than become a failure in their community.[57] While community missions like Fyrbåke distributed basics such as food and clothing, many Scandinavians stuck to their cultural tendencies toward stubborn pride, often refusing to ask for charity of any kind. To historians who study Scandinavians in Chicago during the Great Depression, this stubbornness creates difficulty in comparing the experiences of former immigrant groups in the midst of economic and social struggle. On the surface, it appears that few needed aid, but in looking deeper, it becomes more apparent that many simply did not ask for it until their ultimate survival hinged upon it.

The practice of re-migration, for those who had the means, was a common tactic of avoidance. Advertisements in the pages of the *Swedish Blue Book* from 1926 and 1927 stood as a testament to a simpler and more prosperous time. The practice of summer excursions and periodic visits back home had grown incredibly popular among Scandinavians as early as 1914, when grandiose passenger liners like the *Skandinavien-Amerika Linien* attracted customers to take "an ideal vacation trip this summer . . . enjoy the healthy, invigorating climate of the North Lands!"[58] Simple summer excursions were now out of reach for the majority of Scandinavians, and a number put together all of their funds in an effort to escape the economic depression with every intention of returning when the financial climate improved. Yet, for a small group of dedicated loyalists in the homeland and in America, as Barton explained, the emigration became a "kind of modern morality play," a "collective tragedy of the hapless masses who escaped capitalist oppression in their native land only to be swallowed up by the insatiable American Moloch."[59] For most, the grand movement of people became transmuted into a story of dreams fulfilled in a vast Midwestern city.

Conclusion

The Contemporary Importance of Nordic Whiteness

In June 2015, what originated as a local news item out of Spokane, Washington, gained national coverage in the wake of a new wave of race-related conflicts in American society. Rachel Dolezal, a 37-year-old woman who had worked as a civil rights activist and served as president of the Spokane Chapter of the NAACP, resigned her position following allegations that she had lied about her racial identity as being African American. For an entire week media poured over the side-by-side photographs of present-day Dolezal and the contrasting images of her as a young girl. Baffled and angered, journalists focused their attention on what appeared to be a blatant form of inverse racial passing. The photographs of Dolezal illustrated a process by which a white American woman of Czech, German, and Swedish descent appropriated African American racial identity over the course of her young adulthood. Her skin became darker through use of makeup, her hair was worn in braids or a weave, and when questioned by NBC Nightly News' Savannah Guthrie about her racial identity, Dolezal replied, "I definitely am not white."[1] Dolezal considered her racial identity to be genuine even though it was not based on biology or ancestry. Because race is a social construction rather than a biological absolute, Dolezal felt that she was simply adopting a racial category with which she most closely self-identified. Media outlets and the American public expressed outrage for several reasons, all of which intertwined in the complexity of understandings of race and ethnicity in America today.

180 · *Conclusion*

Though Dolezal was not solely of Scandinavian descent, her Nordic whiteness was what drew the most public attention, albeit in covert ways. Many expressed anger and outrage, not because Dolezal had successfully passed for years as a black woman, but because she denied the most privileged position in the imagined hierarchy of race. As a young girl, Dolezal's physicality fit the stereotype of the "typical" Scandinavian American with freckles and curly blonde hair, which angered her critics even further. To her opponents, Dolezal treated race simply as a costume that one could put on or take off at the end of the day because of her heightened white privilege, especially from the perspective of African American observers. Darryl E. Owens, a reporter for the *Orlando Sentinel*, spoke of Dolezal as a "melanin-masquerader" and "Nordic-Teutonic princess" who had suffered "racial Stockholm syndrome."[2] Professor emerita of Columbia Nell Irvin Painter wrote that the problem, moreover, was with the inadequacy of white identity. "Everyone loves to talk about blackness, a fascinating thing," Painter explained, "but bring up whiteness and fewer people want to talk about it. Whiteness is on a toggle switch between 'bland nothingness' and 'racist hatred.'"[3] Two days after Dolezal's parents exposed her racial secret to the national media, a young man who professed an avowed white supremacist agenda gunned down nine people in a historically African American church in Charleston, South Carolina. When one contrasts the Dolezal case with the Charleston church massacre, we are reminded of how remarkably trivial her case was and how both stories illustrate the sheer divisiveness and hatred espoused in America's racial consciousness in the early twenty-first century. While there is an urge to deny that the hierarchy of race that William Ripley, Joseph Deniker, and Madison Grant constructed long ago still exists, when we see the complexity of racial and ethnic self-identification from a contemporary perspective, it is clear that this hierarchy is alive and well.

Today, Nordic whiteness remains as the ultimate position of unquestioned racial hegemony and privilege, even though use of the term "Nordic" as a racial qualifier has fallen out of fashion for obvious reasons. The idea of unquestioned whiteness from a historiographic perspective is quite significant; however, far less scholarship explores immigrant groups like Scandinavians whose whiteness was beyond doubt.[4] As this study poses, between the late nineteenth century and the 1920s, Americans considered Scandinavians as part of the white majority; they may not have been "American," but their whiteness was undeniable. During World War I, American self-identification as *Anglo-Saxon* dwindled due to its Germanic associations. In its place, nativist rhetoric applied the language of Madison Grant's subtext on the Nordic race. *Nordic* was a term Scandinavian groups employed to denote ethnic pride during the interwar period that witnessed the rise of Nordicism, or the belief that the Nordic race constituted a master race. This shift in terminology gave way to the interchangeability of the terms *Nordic* and *Aryan*, influencing government policy. During the 1920s, passage of the Johnson-Reid Act proved to be especially damaging to southern and eastern European ethnic groups while Scandinavians remained in favor with American policymakers.

Nordicism led to an international eugenics movement and influenced German eugenicists Erwin Baur, Eugen Fischer, and Fritz Lenz to author *Human Heredity* in 1921, which argued for the innate racial superiority of the Nordic race and later influenced Adolf Hitler's writing of *Mein Kampf*.[5] By the 1930s, during the Great Depression and before Hitler's reign of terror, criticism of Nordicism grew in the United States and in Britain. After World War II, the term *Nordic* fell out of use as a means of defining a master race of Caucasians, even as tensions erupted surrounding race relations in the South during the 1950s and into the 1960s. In contemporary society, white supremacists are the only group that still embrace use of the racial term *Nordic* to justify their bigotry. People of Scandinavian descent do not employ the term as a badge of racial honor but do use it to qualify ties of ethnicity. Ronald Bayor suggested that, with many white, European "ethnics," a nationality-based ethnic identity existed longer than thought, and ethnicity became one of many identities.[6] Therefore, Scandinavian ethnicity has become the identity by which Americans signify their white privilege in a more politically correct context than use of the word *Nordic*.

Nordic whiteness connects to Scandinavian ethnicity as a marked point of entitlement. As this book argues, to be of Scandinavian descent in America is to claim a heritage that is untainted by an unfortunate history, unlike other northern European ethnic groups such as German Americans or Irish Americans.[7] When Americans self-identify as Scandinavian, it is another way of noting structural advantage and race privilege and typically a source of self-pride. According to the authors of *Seeing White*, white people who, as a group, hold more social and economic power than people of color, often perceive whiteness as normative—ordinary, typical, what is expected.[8] It is American culture, and not race, that has elevated Scandinavian Americans to a position of ultimate white privilege in the twenty-first century. So, this concept begs the question: Does Scandinavian heritage lead to social, economic, and even political success in America? According to selected data from the U.S. Census and the American Community Study of 2015, the answer is a resounding "yes." Historically speaking, the pervasive nature of Nordic whiteness as an indicator of success in America is astonishing when one takes into consideration the statistical data shown in table C.1.

Figure 17: A watercolor painting of the iconic water tower in Andersonville, Chicago, which is a constant reminder of the neighborhood's Swedish ethnic presence. Courtesy of Kevin Haller, "A Hint of Sweden," 2011.

There are clear societal benefits for native-born Scandinavians and Americans of Scandinavian descent living in the United States today. According to statistical data on household median income, Scandinavian Americans are ranked eleventh in the list of most financially successful ethnic groups in America.[9] The more generalized response of having "Scandinavian" ancestry, rather than the more specific responses of "Swedish," "Norwegian," or "Danish" indicate respondents who may have been unsure of their specific country of origin, though somewhat certain of Scandinavian heritage. Even so, when compared to the generalized "white" population of America, people of Scandinavian heritage constitute a mostly native-born group of individuals who predominantly speak English, are well educated, and earn far more annually than other white Americans earn.

Many of the reasons for these correlations are culturally driven. First, there remains a close association of Nordic whiteness and Scandinavian ethnicity. Racially, Nordic whiteness is indicative of ultimate white privilege that is unquestioned, even if a white person claiming to have a Scandinavian background

Table C.1: Ethnic groups in the United States by household income: selected survey of Scandinavian, Swedish, Norwegian, and Danish ethnic groups, 2015

	White Alone	Scandinavian	Swedish	Norwegian	Danish
Total Number of Races Reported					
Total population	234,940,100	630,845	3,829,029	4,432,738	1,315,302
Place of Birth					
Native-born	214,607,102	626,087	3,778,400	4,397,649	1,282,408
Foreign-born	20,332,998	4,758	50,629	35,089	32,894
Foreign-born; naturalized	9,232,159	2,318	23,602	16,296	13,426
Foreign-born; not a U.S. citizen	11,100,839	2,440	27,027	18,793	19,468
Language Spoken at Home and Ability to Speak English					
Population 5 years and over	221,793,779	588,870	3,644,546	4,189,213	1,250,093
English only	84.3%	97.2%	96.9%	97.6%	95.8%
Language other than English	15.7%	2.8%	3.1%	2.4%	4.2%
Speak English less than "very well"	6.0%	0.3%	0.3%	0.3%	0.4%
Income in the Past 12 Months					
Households	91,023,564	254,526	1,744,722	1,966,266	603,962
Median household income	$59,698	$71,190	$67,908	$67,403	$68,558
Educational Attainment					
Population 25 years and over	163,862,749	438,089	2,817,006	3,159,393	968,994
High school graduate or higher	89.1%	97.2%	96.6%	96.5%	96.9%
Some college or associate's degree	29.3%	35.3%	33.1%	34.6%	33.9%
Bachelor's degree	19.9%	28.4%	26.9%	25.6%	26.4%
Bachelor's degree or higher	31.9%	45.6%	43.1%	39.8%	43.3%
Graduate/professional degree	12.0%	17.2%	16.3%	14.3%	17.0%

Source: Findings selected from the "Selected Population Profile in the United States, 2015," American Community Survey 1-year estimates, United States Census Bureau, 2015.

does not stereotypically appear to be Scandinavian. Conversely, public figures like celebrity chef Marcus Samuelsson, a Swede of Somali descent, often confuse some naive Americans who assume that Scandinavians can only be white. Second, Scandinavian culture in and of itself evokes the epitome of whiteness for most Americans. The clean lines of Ikea's furniture, the purity of Nordic food and clean eating embodied in world-renowned restaurants, and references to the physicality of Scandinavians in American culture typically focus on racial beauty and strength. Ultimately, American culture reinforces the notion that

184 · *Conclusion*

the whiter you are, the more successful you will be—in work, in school, and in life.

Another reason for the veritable success of Scandinavian Americans has to do with assumed intelligence and the persistence of racially charged ideologies. Every twenty years or so, a study is published that creates a problematic link between race and one's capacity for intelligence, such as the 1994 bestseller, *The Bell Curve*. In their eugenicist text, Harvard University psychologist Richard J. Herrnstein and well-known conservative political scientist Charles Murray argued that intelligence is innate, something we are (or are not) born with. According to Herrnstein and Murray, intelligence is heritable, fixed in our chromosomes, and can be measured through intelligence tests like the Binet-Simon Intelligence Scale.[10] This line of argument is highly problematic given the social and cultural constructions encompassed in these tests for intelligence, and yet these ideas persist because they justify and reinforce an extremely unequal and unfair material reality.[11] With such false assumptions, one might be led to inaccurate conclusions about the intellectual capabilities of people of Nordic descent. One example of the complexity of this argument regarding intelligence and Nordic whiteness is encompassed in the Scandinavian and Nordic Studies programs in the United States noted in table C.2).

When examining table C.2, two elements of significance stand out: the prestige of many of the institutions as well as the heavy regional concentration of institutions in the Midwest and along the Pacific Coast. Historically speaking, it makes perfect sense that all of the colleges and universities in the first

Table C.2: List of colleges and universities in the United States with Scandinavian, Nordic studies programs

Scandinavian American Schools	American Schools
Gustavus Adolphus College	University of Washington
Augustana College	University of California–Los Angeles
Pacific Lutheran University	University of California–Berkeley
Concordia College	University of Wisconsin–Madison
St. Olaf College	Minnesota State University–Mankato
Finlandia University	University of Illinois–Urbana-Champaign
Luther College	The Ohio State University
Augsburg College	University of Wisconsin–Milwaukee
North Park University	University of Oregon
	University of Minnesota
	Columbia University
	Harvard University
	University of Colorado–Boulder
	University of Alberta

column have such interdisciplinary programs. All of these schools started out as Scandinavian American institutions intended to further the education of Scandinavian American youth while maintaining their cultural and ethnic heritage, particularly language retention. Because Scandinavian Americans settled in these areas of the country in larger numbers than those who settled in the South or West, this process led to the persistence of Scandinavian language and culture in these regions of the country. Attendance at Scandinavian American schools such as St. Olaf, Augustana, and North Park continue to be part of a rite of passage for Scandinavian American youth to this day.

However, one might falsely associate intelligence with Nordic racial whiteness based on the educational reputation of American institutions like Columbia, Harvard, and Berkeley, which also have Scandinavian and Nordic Studies Programs. One could draw inaccurate or culturally specific conclusions about intelligence given this prestigious list without further understandings of the historical reasons behind the establishment of such programs. Scandinavian Americans may have a greater array of advantages available to them because of the persistence of biological essentialism, or the belief that "human nature," personality, or some specific quality (such as intelligence) is innate rather than a product of upbringing and circumstance.[12] However, as most scholars of race and ethnicity argue, race is not a biological category but a cultural one. Race is a social construction that derives from the cultural communities in which individuals socialized, and not primarily from genotype or biological ancestry.

Biological Essentialism, Ethnicity, and Nordic Whiteness

In 1998, the American Anthropological Association published the following statement as a measure of combating biological essentialism:

> In the United States both scholars and the general public have been conditioned to viewing human races as natural and separate divisions within the species based on visible physical difference. With the vast expansion of scientific knowledge in this century, however, it has become clear that human populations are not unambiguous, clearly demarcated, biologically distinct groups. Evidence from the analysis of genetics (e.g., DNA) indicates that most physical variation, about 94% lies within so-called racial groups. Conventional geographic "racial" groupings differ from one another only in about 6% of their genes. This means that there is greater variation within "racial" groups than between them.[13]

The position of the American Anthropological Association emphasized the contemporary scholarly understanding that human cultural behavior is "learned,

186 · *Conclusion*

conditioned into infants beginning at birth, and always subject to modification," and therefore, our personalities are shaped by our surroundings rather than genetics.[14] Yet, American consumer society continues to perpetuate the myth of biological essentialism by playing upon the lure of symbolic ethnicity. After the Civil Rights Movement, many Americans sought a tangible ethnic identity to attach themselves to out of support for the multitude of movements, but others chose out of conservative fatigue over liberal rhetoric regarding diversity. Whiteness had become bland and uninteresting in an era where activists embraced racial and ethnic differences. As the baby boomer generation has come of age and embarked on a new, strangely familiar environment of racial tension, many have turned to genealogy and ancestry as a way of coping with this new, yet strikingly similar, world.

In recent years, ancestry has become a big business in America. In 2015, a popular commercial for Ancestry.com told the story of "Kyle," described as a member of the website since 2011, who told the following story of tracing his family's lineage:

> Growing up, my family was German. We danced in a German dance group, I wore lederhosen. When I first got on Ancestry, I was really surprised that I wasn't finding all these Germans in my family tree. I decided to have my DNA tested through Ancestry DNA. The big surprise was, we're not German at all. Fifty-two percent of my DNA comes from Scotland and Ireland. So I traded in my lederhosen for a kilt.[15]

The focus of the commercials produced for Ancestry.com follows a very similar model to Kyle's story. Most of the commercial spots follow the short story of an American who always self-identified as a member of a European ethnic group, symbolically wearing the group's "traditional" garb, and informing others of their cultural identity as a way of differentiating himself or herself as uniquely white. Because white racial and ethnic identity is remarkably malleable (as opposed to shifting identity across racial lines in the case of Rachel Dolezal), it can be customized to fit the parameters of how white Americans choose to identify, regardless of whether or not those biological markers are legitimate. The idea Ancestry.com is selling through their DNA test is therefore problematic, even dangerous, and further perpetuates biological essentialism.

DNA testing cannot definitively prove whether a person is German, Irish, or a member of any other ethnic community. While our genes can determine our eye color, for example, ethnicity is our perception of a collection of specific physical traits. Ancestry's DNA test compares segments of a subject's DNA to the DNA of people of known origin and who are looking for similarities.[16] Therefore, when Kyle's DNA report told him that 52 percent of his DNA indicated that he was Scottish and Irish, not German, it simply meant that 52 percent of it was most like that of a person living in Scotland or Ireland. The intention of the test's results should be fun but not taken as essential truth of one's racial or ancestral origins. Still, since 2005, DNA testing has gone from being outside of the realm of Middle America's budget to a $99 simplified test kit. Ancestry.com, which is the world's largest for-profit internet genealogy company today, markets its DNA tests as scientific proof of a subject's "sense of identity," while global sales of the kits are slated to reach $60 billion in the next four years.[17] Television shows like PBS's *Finding Your Roots* and TLC's *Who Do You Think You Are* further emphasize the use of DNA analysis in conjunction with historical findings in reconstructing genealogy and ethnic identity. When examining this popular culture obsession with finding one's "roots," it becomes clear why the hierarchy of race and biological essentialism persist in white American society. White Americans want to identify as anything other than the simplistic category that whiteness offers. Being able to tell other Americans that you are of Scandinavian descent is a tangible ethnic identity that another white individual can appreciate because of the assumed racial privilege that pairs with it.

Whereas the American press vilified Rachel Dolezal for turning her back on her Nordic heritage and choosing to masquerade as a black woman, other more high-powered individuals have adopted a Nordic identity as a means of purposely costuming themselves in white privilege, namely President Donald Trump. Today, Americans tend to focus their attention on connections of economic wealth and a more generic whiteness encompassed in the privileged identity of the white Anglo-Saxon protestant. This ethnic and racial identity, often used in derogatory terms as *WASP*, is a derivative of the more socially appropriate term *Yankee*, which Americans of English descent used between the nineteenth and early twentieth centuries to denote privilege. Popularized as a disparaging term used to denote a closed group of highbrow, typically East Coast Americans, this elite brand of individuals came to dominate politics and the economy. The Trump family epitomizes the rise of the white Anglo-Saxon protestant in American society with one major exception—Trump is decidedly *not* Anglo-Saxon. By his own claim, he is Nordic.

In an article published in August 2016, *New York Times* writer Jason Horowitz outed Trump as a German American by parlaying the story of how Trump's family cast off their German heritage for an adopted Swedish one. The namesake to the Trump legacy, Friedrich Trump, emigrated from Germany in 1885. During the interwar period, Friedrich's son, Fred, chose to bury his German identity in the face of nativist discrimination expressed toward Germans. This practice was common—many German Americans altered their surnames during and after World War I. However, as Horowitz wrote, for years, the Trumps "went out of their way to avoid disquieting their Jewish friends and customers by burying their German identity," and that "they told anyone who asked that they were Swedish."[18] The family's self-identification as Scandinavian snowballed into a carefully constructed ethnic lie. In his infamous 1987 *New York Times* best seller, *The Art of the Deal*, Trump called his father's story a "classic Horatio Alger" tale of a rise from a humble, ethnic background and that his grandfather "came here from Sweden as a child," all the while knowing the story was untrue.[19] In a brave new world of "Trumpisms," Trump's story reads as a poignant tale of racial and ethnic appropriation for an individual whose campaign vehemently focused on racial difference and categorization of good versus evil. In January 2018, Trump drew attention to this continued racial preference in immigration policy when he opined that America "should have more people (emigrate) from Norway."[20] Trump's concealment of his "true" ethnic identity is an all-too-common occurrence for white Americans who have the luxury of portraying themselves as any white ethnic group they best identify with, or gather will bring them the most success.

Over the past decade, it has become increasingly clear that many Americans' understandings of their own racial and ethnic background can often diverge completely away from reality by way of confusion or misinformation, but also as a means of portraying oneself in more positive racial terms for social gain. Recently, D'Vera Cohn, a researcher at the Pew Research Center, found in a study coauthored by University of Minnesota sociologist Carolyn A. Liebler that millions of Americans change their race or ethnicity from one census to another. While their study focuses mostly on Americans of mixed race, it illustrates the utter confusion some Americans encounter when completing the census because of separate questions about race and ethnicity. It is not so much that respondents lie about their racial background, but, instead, many have an evolving self-identity over the course of ten years' time. Though the phenomenon varies by group, the researchers found clear correlations between self-portrayal of race and ethnicity and benefits associated with identification with some individualized groups. As confusion grows over understandings of race and ethnicity in America, this marked shift in self-identity will continue to occur unless we begin to have more unilateral discussions of whiteness and divisiveness of white privilege in our country.

This study's intention is to help bridge the gap in our understandings of white racial identity by analyzing the history of those who benefited most from a social constructed hierarchy of race in America. As evidenced in the election

Conclusion • 189

cycle of 2016, America is a country staunchly divided by economic background, ideological positioning, political beliefs, and racial difference, as well as in our understandings of those differences and how we got to where we are today. This book should *not* be taken as a dialogue on how to succeed as a Nordic in America. Instead, my hope is that the topic of this book will raise further awareness of how Americans have constructed white privilege out of problematic stereotypes that are all a facade in the end. The meaningless categorization of humans into distinct "races" created a powerful ideologue of thought that ultimately does not prove one group of individuals is more racially fit than another.

With that said, the second "character" in this study, Chicago, simply serves as a backdrop, albeit an essential one, in illustrating the process by which people of Scandinavian descent became the embodiment of whiteness in the United States between the late nineteenth and early twentieth centuries. At this time, Chicago was one of the most Scandinavian-centric cities in the country and like its urban counterparts, Minneapolis and Seattle, the city provided opportunities for vast advancement in a time of great social and industrial change. During the early twentieth century, Scandinavians in Chicago and throughout America used this beneficial rhetoric to their advantage to achieve professional and social success; yet, we cannot forget the role their hard work played in allowing them to get ahead in immigrant America. Still, Americans afforded Scandinavians opportunities denied to other Europeans. We cannot ignore the privileges their whiteness granted them. With that, more than anything, my hope is that this book will illustrate our similarities as Americans and contribute to a growing body of work that has begun to bring these divides back together in tangible, constructive ways across barriers of race, sex, class, and political thought.

Notes

Introduction

1. "Will the World's Most Beautiful Living Woman Be Found in Sweden or Norway[?]," *Chicago Daily Tribune*, January 19, 1908.

2. For further discussion of divisions in social class, public and private spheres, and the beauty culture of the late nineteenth and early twentieth centuries, see Lois Banner, *American Beauty* (New York: Knopf, 1983); Kathy Peiss, *Cheap Amusements: Working Women and Leisure in Turn-of-the-Century New York* (Philadelphia: Temple University Press, 1986); Sarah Banet-Weiser, "Miss America, National Identity, and the Identity Politics of Whiteness," in *"There She Is, Miss America": The Politics of Sex, Beauty, and Race in America's Most Famous Pageant*, eds. Elwood Watson and Darcy Martin (New York: Palgrave Macmillan, 2004), 67–92.

3. "Will the World's[?]"

4. William Z. Ripley, *The Races of Europe: A Sociological Study* (New York: D. Appleton and Company, 1899), v, 121.

5. Ibid., 130; Joseph Deniker, *The Races of Man: An Outline of Anthropology and Ethnography* (first published in French as *Les Races de l'Europe* [London: Walter Scott Ltd., 1900]).

6. Matthew Frye Jacobson, *Whiteness of a Different Color: European Immigrants and the Alchemy of Race* (Cambridge: Harvard University Press, 1999), 7.

7. Noel Ignatiev, *How the Irish Became White* (New York: Routledge, 1995); James R. Barrett and David Roediger, "Inbetween Peoples: Race, Nationality, and the 'New Immigrant' Working Class," *Journal of American Ethnic History* 16, no. 3 (Spring 1997): 3–44.

192 · *Notes to Introduction*

8. In her book, Frankenberg defines whiteness studies as the converse of black studies in its focus on the ways that white normativity and normalcy reproduce themselves. See Ruth Frankenberg, *White Studies, Race Matters: The Social Construction of Whiteness* (Minneapolis: University of Minnesota Press, 1993), 1; Catrin Lundström, *White Migrations: Gender, Whiteness and Privilege in Transnational Migration* (New York: Palgrave Macmillan, 2014), 163.

9. Jørn Brøndal, "The Fairest among the So-Called White Races": Portrayals of Scandinavian Americans in the Filiopietistic and Nativist Literature of the Late Nineteenth and Early Twentieth Centuries," *Journal of American Ethnic History* 33, no. 3 (Spring 2014): 5–36. Similarly, Arne Lunde acknowledges that the history of Scandinavian immigration carries "strong cultural assumptions and expectations" in American popular culture about their essential whiteness. See Arne Lunde, *Nordic Exposures: Scandinavian Identities in Classical Hollywood Cinema* (Seattle: University of Washington Press, 2010), 8–9.

10. Lunde, *Nordic Exposures*, 9.

11. Thomas Guglielmo, *White on Arrival: Italians, Race, Color, and Power in Chicago, 1890–1945* (New York: Oxford University Press, 2003); Peter G. Vellon, *A Great Conspiracy against Our Race: Italian Immigrant Newspapers and the Construction of Whiteness in the Early 20th Century* (New York: New York University Press, 2014).

12. Steven H. Corey and Lisa Krissoff Boehm, "Examining America's Urban Landscape: From Social Reform to Social History," in *The American Urban Reader: History and Theory* (New York: Routledge, 2011), 8.

13. *Swedish-American Life in Chicago: Cultural and Urban Aspects of an Immigrant People, 1850–1930*, eds. Philip J. Anderson and Dag Blanck (Urbana: University of Illinois Press, 1992), 1. While Nordic immigrants came to Chicago from all the Scandinavian nations, this study centers upon the social interactions and cultural ties of Swedish, Norwegian, and Danish immigrants, due to the preponderance of immigrants from those countries, and not Finland or Iceland. According to the Census records of 1900 and 1910, recorders placed Finnish-born immigrants within the population of Russia, while the ambiguous relationship of Iceland and minimal population of Icelanders recorded in Chicago provides little evidence of contribution to this study.

14. Odd S. Lovoll, *A Century of Urban Life: The Norwegians in Chicago before 1930* (Northfield: Norwegian-American Historical Association, 1988), 18; Philip S. Friedman, "The Danish Community of Chicago," *The Bridge: Journal of the Danish American Heritage Society* 8, no. 1 (1985): 33–52.

15. I use my narrative to emphasize the uniqueness of this conversation that took place in Chicago. Further research to determine the degree to which Scandinavian communities elsewhere followed the same patterns as those in Chicago is needed, particularly regarding the applicability of this process to other urban areas (i.e., Minneapolis and Milwaukee) and in rural America.

16. David Roediger, *Working towards Whiteness: How America's Immigrants Became White* (New York: Basic Books, 2005), 35–36; Brøndal, "The Fairest," 8–9.

17. Brøndal, "The Fairest," 10.

18. Some of the studies that followed the filiopietistic tradition in recounting what was then the most recent immigrant past include *History of the Scandinavians and Successful Scandinavians in the United States*, vols. 1 and 2, ed. O. N. Nelson (Minneapolis: O. N. Nelson and Co., 1893); Herbert N. Casson, "The Scandinavians in America," *Munsey's Magazine* (August 1906): 613–618; Kendric C. Babcock, *The Scandinavian Element in the United States* (Urbana: University of Illinois Press, 1914); Olaf M. Norlie, *History of the Norwegian People in America* (Minneapolis: Augsburg Publishing House, 1925); George M. Stephenson, *A History of American Immigration, 1820–1924* (Boston: Ginn and Company, 1926); Theodore Blegen, *Norwegian Immigration to America*, 2 vol. (Northfield, Minn.: The Norwegian American Historical Society, 1931); *The Swedish Element in America: A Comprehensive History of Swedish American Achievements from 1638 to Present*, 3 vols., eds. Erik G. Westman and Gustav Johnson (Chicago: Swedish American Biographical Society, 1931).

19. Dag Blanck, "A Mixture of People with Different Roots": Swedish Immigrants in the American Ethno-Racial Hierarchies, *Journal of American Ethnic History* 33, no. 3 (Spring 2014): 47.

20. *Scandinavians and Other Immigrants in Urban America: The Proceedings of a Research Conference October 26–27, 1984*, ed. Odd Lovoll (Northfield: Saint Olaf College Press, 1985), 196. A few exceptions to the rule include Jon Gjerde, *The Minds of the West: Ethnocultural Evolution in the Rural Middle West 1830–1917* (Chapel Hill: The University of North Carolina Press, 1997); Orm Øverland, "Becoming White in 1881: An Immigrant Acquires an American Identity," *Journal of American Ethnic History* 23, no. 4 (Summer 2004): 132–141.

21. See Ignatiev, *How the Irish Became White*; Guglielmo, *White on Arrival*, 15, 59–63 (Guglielmo similarly contests that Americans viewed Italians as white, albeit undesirable); Eric L. Goldstein, *The Price of Whiteness: Jews, Race, and American Identity* (Princeton: Princeton University Press, 2006). One study where the process of racial construction occurs backward is Russell Kazal, *Becoming Old Stock: The Paradox of German-American Identity* (Princeton: Princeton University Press, 2004).

22. David Roediger, *The Wages of Whiteness: Race and the Making of the American Working Class* (New York: Verso, 1991; 3–17); Roediger, *Working towards Whiteness*, 36; Brøndal, "The Fairest," 6; Guglielmo, *White on Arrival*, 7; Eduardo Bonilla-Silva, "Rethinking Racism: Toward a Structural Interpretation," *American Sociological Review* 62, no. 3 (June 1997): 465–480.

23. Eric Arnesen, "Whiteness and the Historians' Imagination," *International Labor and Working-Class History* 60, no. 3 (Fall 2001): 3–32.

24. David Roediger, "Race and the Working-Class Past in the United States: Multiple Identities and the Future of Labor History," *International Review of Social History* 38 (December 1993): 132.

25. Lundström, *White Migrations*, 19; Jeff Werner, *Medelvägens Estetik: Sverigebilder i USA* [The aesthetics of the middle way: Images of Sweden in the USA] (Hedemora: Gidlund, 2009).

194 · *Notes to Introduction*

26. In a 1751 essay, Franklin referred to Scandinavians (specifically Swedes) as having a "swarthy complexion" based on their unwillingness to Anglicize. For further discussion, refer to chapter 1. See also Benjamin Franklin, "Observations Concerning the Increase of Mankind and the Peopling of Countries, [1751]" in *The Autobiography and Other Writings by Benjamin Franklin*, ed. Peter Shaw (New York: Bantam, 1982), 290.

27. Jacobson, *Whiteness of a Different Color*, 68–69.

28. Blanck, "A Mixture of People," 44.

29. Instead of seeing race as an unchanging physical characteristic, Matthew Frye Jacobson posits that race is an invented category, "designations coined for the sake of grouping and separating peoples along lines of presumed difference." See Jacobson, *Whiteness of a Different Color*, 4; Milton M. Gordon, "Assimilation in America: Theory and Reality," *Daedalus*, 90, no. 2, Ethnic Groups in American Life (Spring 1961): 268; Roediger, *Working towards Whiteness*, 53.

30. Gail Bederman, *Manliness and Civilization: A Cultural History of Gender and Race in the United States, 1880–1917* (Chicago: The University of Chicago Press, 1995), 31.

31. Orm Øverland, *Immigrant Minds, American Identities: Making the United States Home, 1870–1930* (Urbana: University of Illinois Press, 2000), 8; Dag Blanck, *The Creation of an Ethnic Identity: Being Swedish American in the Augustana Synod, 1860–1917* (Carbondale: Southern Illinois University Press, 2006), 165–168.

32. Some of these representative works with a focus on single, wage-earning women include Harzig, *Peasant Maids*; Joy Lintelman, *I Go to America: Swedish American Women and the Life of Mina Anderson* (Minneapolis: Minnesota Historical Society Press, 2009). One of the most recent works focused on the experiences of specific ethnic groups is *Norwegians and Swedes in the United States: Friends and Neighbors*, eds. Philip J. Anderson and Dag Blanck (Minneapolis: Minnesota Historical Society Press, 2012), viii.

33. Joan Scott, "Gender: A Useful Category of Analysis," in *Gender and the Politics of History* (New York: Columbia University Press, 1988), 41; Joanne Meyerowitz, "AHR Forum: A History of 'Gender,' *American Historical Review* 113, no. 5 (December 2008): 1346, 1353). While there is an enormous body of literature on poststructuralist and feminist theory, a selection of works that helped shaped discussions of deconstructionism and power in this study includes Jacques Derrida, *Of Grammatology*, trans. Gayatri C. Spivak (Baltimore: Johns Hopkins University Press, 1998); Michel Foucault, *The History of Sexuality: An Introduction*, vol. 1, trans. Robert Hurley (New York: Vintage Books, 1990); Linda Nicholson, ed. *Feminism/Postmodernism* (New York: Routledge, 1989); and *Feminists Theorize the Political*, eds. Judith Butler and Joan W. Scott (London: Routledge, 1992).

34. Pertinent studies of masculinity, especially within the context of "civilization" influence this analysis, including Bederman, *Manliness and Civilization*, and Kristin Hoganson, *Fighting for American Manhood: How Gender Politics Provoked the Spanish-American and Philippine-American Wars* (New Haven: Yale University Press, 1998). Another guiding analysis is Kathleen Brown's, *Good Wives, Nasty Wenches, & Anxious Patriarchs: Gender, Race, and Power in Colonial Virginia* (Chapel Hill: University of North Carolina Press, 1996).

Notes to Introduction • 195

35. See Donna Gabaccia, *From the Other Side: Women, Gender, and Immigrant Life in the U.S., 1820–1990* (Bloomington: University of Indiana Press, 1994); M. Alison Kibler, *Censoring Racial Ridicule: Irish, Jewish, and African American Struggles over Race and Representation, 1890–1930* (Chapel Hill: University of North Carolina Press, 2015), 126–127 and 136, for more specific examples of gendered representations of the Irish and Jewish women in particular. Elisabeth Oxfeldt's work on Nordic Orientalism helps to complicate Nordic whiteness from an international perspective through analysis of travel narratives, *Nordic Orientalism: Paris and the Cosmopolitan Imagination, 1800–1900* (Copenhagen: Museum Tusculanum Press, 2005); Oxfeldt, *Journeys from Scandinavia: Travelogues of Africa, Asia, and South America, 1840–2000* (Minneapolis: University of Minnesota Press, 2010); Nikolas Glover and Carl Marklund, "Arabian Nights in the Midnight Sun? Exploring the Temporal Structure of Sexual Geographies," *Historisk Tidskrift* 129, no. 3 (2009): 487–510.

36. Lundström, *White Migrations*, 164.

37. Between 1899 and 1909, a total of 485,217 Scandinavians emigrated, from which 483,049 indicated that they could read and write; 2,168 (or .4 percent) indicated that they could not. See U.S. Immigration Commission, *Reports of the Immigration Commission: Emigration Conditions in Europe*, vol. 4 (Washington, D.C.: Government Printing Office, 1911), 30.

38. Leara Rhodes, *The Ethnic Press: Shaping the American Dream* (New York: Peter Lang Inc., 2010), 73.

39. Comparatively, the Sunday edition of the *New York Times* reached a circulation rate of 50,000. Statistics originate from N. W. Ayer and Son, *N. W. Ayer and Son's American Newspaper Annual and Directory* (Philadelphia: N. W. Ayer and Son, 1900), 1411–1413.

40. Marion Marzolf, "The Danish-Language Press in America," *Norwegian-American Studies* 28 (1979): 274.

41. Jørn Brøndal, *Ethnic Leadership and Midwestern Politics: Scandinavian Americans and the Progressive Movement in Wisconsin, 1890–1914* (Urbana: University of Illinois Press, 2004), 288.

42. Lloyd Wendt, *Chicago Tribune: The Rise of a Great American Newspaper* (Chicago: Rand McNally, 1979), 28; Frank William Scott and Edmund Janes James, *Newspapers and Periodicals of Illinois, 1814–1879* (Cambridge: Harvard University, 1910), 127.

43. The most useful contextual discussions of the influence of the Scandinavian press and the process of assimilation include Brøndal, *Ethnic Leadership and Midwestern Politics*, and Ulf Beijbom, "Olof Gottfrid Lange—Chicago's First Swede," in *Swedish-American Life in Chicago*, 26–27.

44. According to the 2010 U.S. Census, out of an estimated 223,553,265 individuals who responded that they were "white" (72.4 percent of the responding U.S. population), comparatively 11,920,524 census takers reported to be of Scandinavian or Nordic descent. See U.S. Census Bureau, "Race and Hispanic or Latino Origin, 2010," 2010 Census Summary File, accessed June 10, 2016, http://factfinder.census.gov/faces/table services/jsf/pages/productview.xhtml?src=CF; U.S. Census, 2006–2010 American Community Survey, Total Ancestry Reported, accessed June 10, 2016, http://factfinder

196 · *Notes to Introduction and Chapter 1*

.census.gov/faces/tableservices/jsf/pages/productview.xhtml?pid=ACS_10_5YR_
B04003&prodType=table.

45. Some examples of the process of "becoming" white include Ignatiev, *How the Irish Became White*; Roediger, *Working towards Whiteness*; Karen Brodkin, *How Jews Became White Folks and What That Says about Race in America* (New Brunswick: Rutgers University Press, 1994); Matthew Frye Jacobson, *Whiteness of a Different Color*; Guglielmo, *White on Arrival*; Russell Kazal, *Becoming Old Stock: Are Italians White? How Race Is Made in America*, eds. Jennifer Guglielmo and Salvatore Salerno (New York: Routledge, 2003). As further discussed in chapter one, the notion of Scandinavians becoming "civilized" rather than white is informed by Gail Bederman's thesis regarding imperialistic thinking of the late nineteenth century, which connected racial fitness to manliness. See Bederman, *Manliness and Civilization*.

46. Per Nordahl, "Swedish-American Labor in Chicago," in *Swedish-American Life in Chicago*, 212–213; Hartmut Keil, "The German Immigrant Working Class of Chicago, 1875–90: Workers, Labor and the Labor Movement," in *American Labor and Immigration History, 1877–1920s: Recent European Research*, ed. Dirk Hoerder (Urbana: University of Illinois Press, 1983), 163, graph 20.

Chapter 1. When Scandinavians Were Swarthy

1. Franklin, *Autobiography*, 226.

2. Matthew Frye Jacobson notes the contrast of exclusivity in regard to the 1790 naturalization law and its impact on migration for Asian peoples with the vast inclusivity of naturalized citizenship granted to "free white persons" with its unquestioned use of the term "white." For further discussion, see Jacobson, *Whiteness of a Different Color*, 39–40.

3. John Lewis Peyton, excerpt from *Over the Alleghenies and across the Prairies: Personal Recollections of the Far West One and Twenty Years Ago* (1848), in *As Others See Chicago: Impressions of Visitors, 1673–1933*, ed. Bessie Louise Pierce (Chicago: University of Chicago Press, 1933), 100–101.

4. Bederman, *Manliness and Civilization*, 24. See also George W. Stocking Jr., *Race, Culture, and Evolution* (New York: Free Press, 1968), 112–132, esp. 114, 121–122; George W. Stocking, *Victorian Anthropology* (New York: Free Press, 1987); Cynthia Eagle Russett, *Sexual Science: The Victorian Construction of Womanhood* (Cambridge: Harvard University Press, 1989), 144–148.

5. Jacobson referred to Richard Henry Dana Jr.'s sea travelogue, *Two Years before the Mast* (published in 1840 and reissued in 1859 with postscript) to illustrate that in twenty years, "Anglo-Saxon" had displaced "white" in political discussions of whiteness. See Richard Henry Dana Jr., *Two Years before the Mast* [1840, 1859] (New York: Signet, 1964), 139, 161, 316, 344, 345; Jacobson, *Whiteness of a Different Color*, 41.

6. Carl Hjalmar Lundquist, "Scandinavian Day at the Century of Progress" [1933], speech, MS30, Carl Hjalmar Lundquist Papers (hereafter cited as CHL), box 3, folder 26, Swedish-American Archives of Greater Chicago, North Park University, Chicago.

Notes to Chapter 1 • 197

7. Anthropologists did not introduce the term *Nordic* to racial discourse in America until 1898, with French anthropologist Joseph Deniker's racial classification of "Nordique" as brought to the attention of Americans by scholar William Ripley. Until this point, the racial classification of *Anglo-Saxon* occupied the highest status on the hierarchy. See Joseph Deniker, "Les races européennes," *Bull. Soc. d'Anth.* (Paris, 1897): 189–208; Deniker, "Les races de l'Europe," *L'Anthropologie* ix (Paris 1898): 113–133, with map; Ripley, Deniker's Classification of the Races of Europe," *Journal of Anthropological Institute of Great Britain and Ireland* 28, 1/2 (1899): 166–173.

8. Nelson, History *of the* Scandinavians, vol. 1: 1–2, 4, 11–12; Brøndal, "The Fairest," 13.

9. Some of the earlier works on Scandinavians in the United States are largely biographical and/or bibliographical, employing an older framework focused on revisiting the experiences of the Swedish, Norwegian, and Danish cultural elite of the East Coast and the Midwest, with the most well-known including *The Swedish Element in America*, eds. Westman and Johnson; Enok Mortensen, *Danish-American Life and Letters* (Des Moines: The Danish Evangelical Church of America, 1945); O. Fritiof Ander, *The Cultural Heritage of the Swedish Immigrant: Selected References* (Rock Island: Augustana College Library, 1956); Carlton C. Qualey, *Norwegian Settlement in the United States* (Northfield: Norwegian-American Historical Association, 1938).

10. *Swedes in Chicago* filled a historiographic gap by exploring the social institutions and interactions of Swedes with other Chicago immigrants between 1846 and 1880. During the four decades since Beijbom's book, the study of Chicago's earliest Scandinavians expanded; however, ambivalence remains in contextualizing the origins of Nordic immigrants in their adopted homes. See Ulf Beijbom, *Swedes in Chicago: A Demographic and Social Study of the 1846–1880 Immigration* (Stockholm, Sweden: Läromedelsförlagen, 1971).

11. Taylor published an impressive collection of travel narratives, poems, and other forms of literature in American and Britain focused on his international travels. He witnessed his greatest period of success during the 1850s, when he traveled to northern Europe to study Scandinavian life, culture, and ethnicity. The trip produced *Northern Travel*, as well as his narrative poem, "Lars." Bayard Taylor, *Northern Travel: Summer and Winter Pictures of Sweden, Lapland, and Norway* (London: Sampson Low, Son, and Co., 1858), 26, 32.

12. Lovoll, *A Century of Urban Life*, 4.

13. Margareta Matovic, "Maids in Motion: Swedish Women in Dalsland," in Harzig, *Peasant Maids, City Women*, 99.

14. See Beijbom, *Swedes in Chicago*; Lovoll, *A Century of Urban Life*; H. Arnold Barton, *A Folk Divided: Homeland Swedes and Swedish Americans, 1840–1940* (Carbondale: Southern Illinois University Press, 1994). For a systems approach model, see Christiane Harzig, "Introduction: Women Move from the European Countryside to Urban America," in *Peasant Maids, City Women*, 4; James H. Jackson Jr. and Leslie Page Moch, "Migration and the Social History of Modern Europe," *Historical Methods* 22 (1989): 27–36.

198 • Notes to Chapter 1

15. Dirk Hoerder, "Migration in the Atlantic Economies: Regional European Origins and Worldwide Expansion," in *European Migrants: Global and Local Perspectives*, eds. Dirk Hoerder and Leslie Page Moch (Boston: Northeastern University Press, 1996), 36.

16. The Royal Swedish Commission for the World's Columbian Exposition, *World's Columbian Exposition 1893, Swedish Catalogue, Exhibits and Statistics*, 8.

17. Ibid.

18. Ibid., 9.

19. The sixth stanza of the Norwegian National Anthem, "Ja, Vi Elsker Dette Landet," first adopted by Norway in 1864.

20. See Odd Lovoll, "A Scandinavian Melting Pot in Chicago," in *Swedish-American Life in Chicago*, 61; T. K. Derry, *A History of Modern Norway, 1814–1972* (Oxford: Oxford University Press, 1973), 1–16.

21. Nelson, *History of the Scandinavians*, 42.

22. Florence Edith Janson, *The Background of Swedish Immigration 1840–1930* (Chicago: The University of Chicago Press, 1931), 20.

23. Ibid., 14.

24. Ibid.

25. Nelson, *History of the Scandinavians*, 249. See also Kristian Hvidt, *Flight to America: The Social Background of 300,000 Danish Emigrants* (New York: Academic Press, Inc., 1977).

26. Lyman Beecher, *A Plea for the West* (Cincinnati: Truman and Smith, 1835), 11.

27. Beecher remarks in a footnote to his amended sermon that he received this perspective from a friend, "Judge Hall" from Illinois. See ibid., 19.

28. Nelson, *History of the Scandinavians*, 15.

29. According to the census of 1880, 6,029 Danes, 16,970 Norwegians, and 42,415 Swedes resided in the state of Illinois and 6,071 Danes, 62,521 Norwegians, and 39,176 Swedes lived in Minnesota in 1880 (with the combined population of Scandinavians numbering 65,414 in Illinois and 107,768 in Minnesota). See U.S. Census Bureau, *The Tenth Census of the United States: 1880* (Washington, D.C.: Government Printing Office, 1883).

30. Odd Lovoll, "Norwegians," *Encyclopedia of Chicago*, accessed July 14, 2015, http://www.encyclopedia.chicagohistory.org/pages/911.html.

31. Ulf Beijbom, "Olof Gottfrid Lange—Chicago's First Swede," in *Swedish-American Life in Chicago*, 20–21; Beijbom, *Swedes in Chicago*, 44; "Biography of Victor Freemont Lawson," Inventory of the Victor Lawson Papers, Newberry Library, accessed January 7, 2016, https://mms.newberry.org/xml/xml_files/Lawson.xml.

32. "Svenska-Amerika's Plymouth Rock," *Svenska Kuriren*, September 21, 1916; Roger Daniels, *Coming to America: A History of Immigration and Ethnicity in American Life*, 2nd edition (New York: Harper Perennial, 2002), 167–168.

33. Jon Butler, Grant Wacker, and Randall Balmer, *Religion in American Life: A Short History*, 2nd edition (Oxford: Oxford University Press, 2011), 285–286.

34. Beijbom, *Swedes in Chicago*, 119.

Notes to Chapter 1 · 199

35. U.S. Census Bureau, *The Seventh Census of the United States: 1850* (Washington, D.C.: Government Printing Office, 1853).

36. Beijbom, *Swedes in Chicago*, 10, 51–52.

37. Gustaf Unonius, *Minnen från en sjuttonårig vistelse i Nordvestra America*, v. II (Upsala: M. Schultz's Förlag, 1862), 568.

38. See Carl Smith, *Urban Disorder and the Shape of Belief: The Great Chicago Fire, the Haymarket Bomb, and the Model Town of Pullman* (Chicago: The University of Chicago Press, 1995), 65–67, and Lois Wille, *Forever Open, Clear, and Free: The Struggle for Chicago's Lakefront* (Chicago: The University of Chicago Press, 1972, 1991).

39. Harvey Warren Zorbaugh, *The Gold Coast and the Slum: A Sociological Study of Chicago's Near North Side* (Chicago: The University of Chicago Press, 1929), 4–6.

40. A. T. Andreas, *History of Chicago. From the Earliest Period to the Present Time*, 3 vols. (Chicago: A. T. Andreas Publisher, 1884–1886), 1, 595.

41. Elias Colbert and Everett Chamberlin, *Chicago and the Great Conflagration: With Numerous Illustrations by Chapin & Gulick, from Photographic Views Taken on the Spot* (Cincinnati: C. F. Vent, 1871), 60. For further study on the history of cholera, see Richard Evans, *Death in Hamburg: Society and Politics in the Cholera Years* (New York: Penguin Books, 2005).

42. Lovoll, *A Century of Urban Life*, 41.

43. *Nya Wexjö-Bladet*, December. 29, 1854.

44. Unonius, *Minnen från*, 372.

45. Bremer recounts her travels through the United States and Europe, which became a popular travel account in America during the 1850s. See Fredrika Bremer, *The Homes of the New World: Impressions of America*, vol. 2 (London: Arthur Hall, Virtue, and Co., 1853), 605–606.

46. Unonius, *Minnen från*, 372.

47. Wille, *Forever Open*, 40.

48. Anders Larsson, "Några minnen af en Svensk, som vistats 28 år i Amerika," *Nya Verlden*, December 22, 1873–June 8, 1874.

49. Ernst W. Olson, *History of the Swedes of Illinois*, vol. 1 (Chicago: The Engberg-Holmberg Publishing Company, 1908), 322.

50. Beijbom, *Swedes in Chicago*, 10.

51. Chicago Board of Health, *Report of the Board of Health 1867, 1868, and 1869 and a Sanitary History of Chicago 1833–1870* (Chicago: Lakeside Publishing and Printing Co., 1871).

52. Carl Hjalmar Lundquist, Speech to the Independent Order of Svithiod, December 3, 1955, MS30, CHL, box 4, folder 26, Swedish-American Archives of Greater Chicago.

53. Beijbom, *Swedes in Chicago*, 288; Beijbom, "Olof Gottfrid Lange," in *Swedish-American Life in Chicago*, 26.

54. "A General Scandinavian Mass Meeting," *Skandinaven*, October 6, 1869, 2; Lovoll, *A Century of Urban Life*, 91–92.

200 · *Notes to Chapter 1*

55. Beijbom, *Swedes in Chicago*, 9–11.

56. On ethnic tensions resulting from the Chicago fire, see Smith, *Urban Disorder*, 19–20, 25; Karen Sawislak, *Smoldering City: Chicagoans and the Great Fire, 1871–1874* (Chicago: University of Chicago Press, 1995), 44, 312 n. 129; Maureen Flanagan, *Seeing with Their Hearts: Chicago Women and the Vision of the Good City, 1871–1933* (Princeton: Princeton University Press, 2002), 13–30; Richard F. Bales, *The Great Chicago Fire and the Myth of Mrs. O'Leary's Cow* (Jefferson, N.C.: McFarland and Co. Publishers, 2005).

57. Olson, *History of the Swedes*, 301–312; newspaper article series on Swedish Week in Edgewater in the *Edgewater News*, Wednesday, September 4, 1935.

58. Edith Abbott, *The Tenements of Chicago, 1908–1935* (Chicago: University of Chicago Press, 1936), 23.

59. Sawislak, *Smoldering City*, 22–25; Flanagan, *Seeing with their Hearts*, 5.

60. Smith, *Urban Disorder*, 75.

61. Chicago Relief and Aid Society, *Report of the Chicago Relief and Aid Society of Disbursement of Contributions for the Sufferers by the Chicago Fire* (Chicago: Riverside Press, 1874), 122; *Tenth Census of the United States, 1880.*

62. See Sawislak, *Smoldering City*; Beijbom, *Swedes in Chicago*, 72–79; Lovoll, *A Century of Urban Life,* 105–138.

63. Richard Sennett, *Families against the City: Middle Class Homes of Industrial Chicago, 1872–1890* (Cambridge: Harvard University Press, 1970), 32–33.

64. Frederick Law Olmsted, "Chicago in Distress," *The Nation*, November 9, 1871.

65. Beijbom, *Swedes in Chicago*, 103.

66. "Vill bli av Italienarna: Svenskarna på Milton Avenue vill riva Grannarna av Italienarna," *Skandinaven*, May 8, 1900.

67. "Oönskade invandrare," *Svenska Nyheter*, October 6, 1903.

68. Beijbom, *Swedes in Chicago*, 11.

69. Ibid., 136.

70. Ibid., 11.

71. U.S. Immigration Commission, *Reports of the Immigration Commission: Statistical Review of Immigration 1820–1910*, vol. 3 (Washington, D.C.: Government Printing Office, 1911), 33–38.

72. Lundquist, speech to the Independent Order of Svithiod. For further context on the role of ethnic establishments in the process of settlement and acculturation, see Perry Duis, *The Saloon: Public Drinking in Chicago and Boston, 1880–1920* (Urbana: University of Illinois Press, 1983).

73. Chicago Plan Commission, The Report of the Chicago Land Use Survey, vol. 2, Land Use in Chicago (Chicago: Chicago Plan Commission, 1942–43), xvi.

74. Zorbaugh, *The Gold Coast and the Slum*, 25, 30.

75. Kerstin B. Lane and Carl Isaacson, *Andersonville: A Swedish-America Landmark Neighborhood* (Chicago: The Swedish American Museum and Center, 2003), 15.

76. Anita R. Olson, "The Community Created: Chicago Swedes 1880–1920," in *Swedish-American Life in Chicago*, 53.

Notes to Chapters 1 and 2 • 201

77. Ibid., 49–59.

78. See Harold Platt, *Shock Cities: The Environmental Transformation and Reform of Manchester and Chicago* (Chicago: University of Chicago Press, 2005); Wille, *Forever Open.*

79. Pauline Hegborn Nelson, memoirs, January 13, 1882, MS39, Hegborn-Nelson Family Collection (hereafter cited as HNF), box 2, folder 8, Swedish-American Archives of Greater Chicago, North Park University, Chicago.

80. Ibid.

81. Ibid. See also Margaret Garb, *City of American Dreams: A History of Home Ownership and Housing Reform in Chicago, 1871–1919* (Chicago: University of Chicago Press, 2005).

82. *Census Data for the City of Chicago, 1920*, eds. Ernest Burgess and Charles Shelton Newcomb (Chicago: The University of Chicago Press, 1931), 21.

83. Beijbom, *Swedes in Chicago*, 342.

Chapter 2. Vikings and Dumb Blondes

1. See Jacobson, *Whiteness of a Different Color*, 201–273.

2. See Lunde, *Nordic Exposures.*

3. Joanne Meyerowitz, *Women Adrift: Independent Wage Earners in Chicago, 1880–1930* (Chicago: The University of Chicago Press, 1988), xvii–xviii.

4. Margareta Matovic, "Embracing a Middle Class Life: Swedish-American Women in Lake View," in Harzig, *Peasant Maids, City Women*, 289. See also Ann-Kristen Wallengren, *Welcome Home Mr. Swanson: Swedish Emigrants and Swedishness on Film* (Lund, Sweden: Nordic Academic Press, 2014), 162–169; Gloria Swanson, *Swanson on Swanson: An Autobiography* (New York: Random House, 1980), 69–75.

5. As one of the leading eugenicists of his time, Madison Grant used the term *Nordic* as a synonym with the phrase "white man par excellence" to denote the purest of European white races. See Madison Grant, *The Passing of the Great Race; or the Racial Basis of European History* (New York: Charles Scribner's Sons, 1916), xx–xxi.

6. Swedish women were the most common group of Scandinavians to work in domestic service during the late nineteenth and early twentieth centuries; however, Americans used the term *Swedish* as representative of a sort of indefinite, catch-all Scandinavian identity.

7. "Englewood's Field Day," *New York Times*, September 13, 1908, 8. As George Chauncey and John D'Emilio argued, the "closet" and the notion of cross-dressing was not perceived as "dangerous" until the 1930s, when the closet was constructed by way of the red scare and the Great Depression. See John D'Emilio, "Capitalism and Gay Identity," in *Making Trouble: Essays on Gay History, Politics, and the University* (New York: Routledge, 1992), 3–16; George Chauncey, *Gay New York: Gender, Urban culture, and the Making of a Gay Male Work, 1890–1940* (New York: Basic Books, 1994).

8. There was a vast difference in how Scandinavians employed the term *Nordic* in comparison to Americans. "Nordic" could signal race and ethnic identity, as well as a shared nationality when used by Scandinavians. American race "scientists," however, used "Nordic" to denote the biological and physical characteristics of race and

202 • *Notes to Chapter 2*

"Scandinavian" to discuss ethnicity and difference. Some American immigration historians such as David Roediger employ a more comprehensive approach to the study of ethnic identity and whiteness in relation to Scandinavian, using "Nordic" to signal the notion of an "embraced" identity rather than a racial one. See Roediger, *Working toward Whiteness*, and Lunde, *Nordic Exposures*.

9. See A History of the World's Columbian Exposition Held in Chicago in 1893, ed. Rossiter Johnson (New York: Appleton, 1897–1898).

10. Lovoll, *A Century of Urban Life*, 185–186.

11. Eric Dregni, *Vikings in the Attic: In Search of Nordic America* (Minneapolis: University of Minnesota Press, 2011), 47–50; Brøndal, "The Fairest," 11.

12. On the "homemaking myth," see Øverland, *Immigrant Minds*, 144–173.

13. On the "invention" of ethnicity from a historical outlook, see "The Invention of Ethnicity: A Perspective from the U.S.A.," by Kathleen Neils Conzen et al., *Journal of American Ethnic History* 12, no. 1 (Fall 1992): 3–41; Clifford Geertz, *The Interpretation of Cultures* (New York: Basic Books, 1972); Herbert J. Gans, "Symbolic Ethnicity: The Future of Ethnic Groups and Cultures in America," in *On the Making of Americans: Essays in Honor of David Riesman*, ed. Herbert J. Gans (Philadelphia: University of Pennsylvania Press, 1979), 193–220; Richard Alba, *Ethnic Identity: The Transformation of White America* (New Haven: Yale University Press, 1990).

14. See Lovoll, *A Century of Urban Life*; Joy Lintelman, "Our Serving Sisters": Swedish-American Domestic Servants and Their Ethnic Community," *Social Science History* 15, no. 3 (Fall 1991): 381–395; Joy Lintelman, "More Freedom, Better Pay: Single Swedish Immigrant Women in the United States, 1880–1920" (PhD diss., University of Minnesota, 1991); *Swedes in America: New Perspectives*, ed. Ulf Beijbom (Växjö: Swedish Emigrant Institute, 1993).

15. The best recent historiographic analysis of the filiopietistic writers of the late nineteenth and early twentieth centuries is Jørn Brøndal's, "The Fairest among the So-Called White Races," whose title was adopted from Olaf Norlie, *History of the Norwegian People*, 19.

16. U.S. Immigration Commission, *Reports of the Immigration Commission: Statistical Review of Immigration 1820–1910*, vol. 3 (Washington, D.C.: Government Printing Office, 1911), 33, 36.

17. Beijbom, *Swedes in Chicago*, 121, 125, 142.

18. Lovoll, *A Century of Urban Life*, 152.

19. *Statistical Review of Immigration*, 33–38; Nelson, *History of the Scandinavians*, 254–255.

20. Burgess, *Census Data*, 5.

21. In a review of advertisements from both the *Chicago Daily Tribune* and the *Chicago Daily News*, classifieds between 1879 and into the 1890s reflected a substantial call for women of Scandinavian descent. *Chicago Daily Tribune*, Classified Ad. 11, November 21, 1880. See also Lovoll, *A Century of Urban Life*, 155.

22. *Statistical Review of Immigration*, 30–38.

Notes to Chapter 2 • 203

23. Maine Bureau of Industrial and Labor Statistics, Twenty-fourth Annual Report of the Bureau of Industrial and Labor Statistics for the State of Maine (Augusta: Kennebec Journal Print, 1910), 340; Minnesota Bureau of Labor Statistics, Biennial Report of the Bureau of Labor of the State of Minnesota (n.p., 1887), 154; David Katzman, *Seven Days a Week: Women and Domestic Service in Industrializing America* (New York: Oxford University Press, 1978), 49, 70.

24. William Graham Sumner, "Social Darwinism," 1880, in *The Challenge of Facts and Other Essays* by William Graham Sumner, ed. Albert G. Keller (New Haven: Yale University Press, 1914), 17–27.

25. John R. Commons, *Races and Immigrants in America* (New York: Macmillan, 1907), 224. Other works include Nelson, *History of the Scandinavians*; Prescott F. Hall, *Immigration and Its Effects upon the United States* (New York: H. Holt, 1906), 62; Henry Pratt Fairchild, *Immigration: A World Movement and Its American Significance* (New York: Macmillan, 1914), 94, 253; Babcock, *The Scandinavian Element*, 17.

26. "The Domain of Woman: Some Good Things Said of and by the Gentler Sex," *Chicago Daily Tribune*, September 25, 1886.

27. E. H. Thörnberg, *Lefnadsstandard och sparkraft. Med särskild hänsyn till den svenska befolkningen i Chicago* (Stockholm: Hugo Geber, 1915), 59.

28. "Union Maid the Kitchen Queen," *Chicago Daily Tribune*, July 28, 1901; "The Union Servant Girl," *Chicago Daily Tribune*, July 29, 1901. See also Vanessa H. May, *Unprotected Labor: Household Workers, Politics, and Middle-class Reform in New York, 1870–1940* (Chapel Hill: University of North Carolina Press, 2011); Faye E. Dudden, *Serving Women: Household Service in Nineteenth-Century America* (Middletown: Wesleyan University Press, 1983); Katzman, *Seven Days a Week*; Meyerowitz, *Women Adrift*.

29. Stina Hirsch, "The Swedish Maid: 1900–1915" (Master's thesis, DePaul University, 1985), 5.

30. See Lillian Pettengill, *Toilers of the Home: The Record of a College Woman's Experience as a Domestic Servant* (New York: Doubleday, 1903).

31. "Piga eller Fabriksflicka," *Svenska Nyheter*, June 23, 1903, 4.

32. Advertisement for Sapolio scouring soap, selected advertisements featured in Skandinaven and the *Chicago Daily Tribune* over the course of 1881.

33. "Swedish Girls Not Slow: They Have Been Working for Freedom if They Don't Say Much," *Chicago Daily Tribune*, February 14, 1891.

34. Lintelman, "Our Serving Sisters," 381–395.

35. Andrew L. Löfström, *Bland Kolingar och Kogubbar*, vols. 1 and 2 (Chicago: Andrew L. Löfström, 1908); Lintelman, "Our Serving Sisters," 384.

36. "Two Good Reasons," *Puck*, July 28, 1909, 13.

37. Ole and Lena jokes illustrate a long-lasting cultural legacy of joke-telling among Scandinavian Americans as a way of coping with a difference in American customs and are said to have originated around the turn of the twentieth century.

38. Katharine Lee Bates, "America. A Poem for July 4," 1897, *American Kitchen Magazine* 7 (Home Science Publishing, 1897): 151, accessed November 21, 2017, https://

204 · *Notes to Chapter 2*

books.google.com/books?id=uXbOAAAAMAAJ&pg=PA151#v=onepag&q&f=alse; Robert Rydell, *All the World's a Fair: Visions of Empire at American International Expositions* (Chicago: University of Chicago Press, 1987), 48.

39. Rydell, *All the World's a Fair*, 41.

40. Linnaeus did not use the term *race*, but instead preferred *homo variant* in Systema Naturae. See Carl Linnaeus, Systema naturæ per regna tria naturae, secundum classes, ordines, genera, species cum characteribus, differentiis, synonymis, locis, 13th ed. (Vienna: Trattnern 1767), 29, 34; John Jackson and Nadine M. Weidman, *Race, Racism, and Science: Social Impact and Interaction* (New Brunswick: Rutgers University Press, 2005), 39–41.

41. Rydell, *All the World's a Fair*, 55; Otis T. Mason, "Summary of Progress in Anthropology," in *Annual Reports of the Smithsonian Institution for the Year Ending July 1893* (Washington, D.C.: Government Printing Office, 1894), 605; William H. Dall, "Anthropology," *Nation* 57 (September 28, 1893): 226.

42. "Swedish Week in Edgewater," *Edgewater News*, September 4, 1935.

43. Dag Blanck, "Swedish Americans and the 1893 Columbian Exposition," in *Swedish-American Life in Chicago*, 292.

44. Rasmus Björn Anderson, *America Not Discovered by Columbus: A Historical Sketch of the Discovery of America by the Norsemen in the Tenth Century* (Chicago: S. C. Griggs, 1883), 51, 74; Brøndal, "The Fairest," 13–14.

45. Nelson, *History of the Scandinavians*, 6, 19, 22.

46. Ibid.

47. "Leif Erikson's Day, His Discovery of America Celebrated by Norwegians," *Chicago Tribune*, October 28, 1892.

48. "Sweden and the World's Fair," *Chicago Tribune*, December 29, 1891.

49. The Royal Swedish Commission, Swedish Catalogue, 15.

50. Ibid., 15–16.

51. Ibid., 13.

52. Ibid., 14.

53. Ibid., 192.

54. Amandus Johnson, *Swedish Contributions to American National Life 1638–1921* (New York: Committee of the Swedish Section of America's Making, 1921), 35.

55. Nelson, *History of the Scandinavians*, 33.

56. Ibid.

57. Swedish Ladies' Committee to the World's Columbian Exposition, *Reports from the Swedish Ladies' Committee to the World's Columbian Exposition at Chicago 1893* (Stockholm: Central-Tryckeriet, 1893), 20–23.

58. Ibid., 53.

59. The Royal Swedish Commission, Swedish Catalogue, 200.

60. Ibid., 201. This concept originates from a sizable literature on nudity and bathing in Western Europe, including Chad Ross, *Naked Germany: Health, Race, and the Nation* (New York: Berg, 2005); John Alexander Williams, *Turning to Nature in Germany: Hik-*

ing, Nudism, and Conservation, 1900–1940 (Palo Alto: Stanford University Press, 2007); Stephen L. Harp, *Au Naturel: Naturism, Nudism, and Tourism in Twentieth-Century France* (Baton Rouge: Louisiana State University Press, 2014).

61. The Royal Swedish Commission, Swedish Catalogue, 15–16.

62. Ibid., 44.

63. Commission for Sweden's Participation in the World Exposition in Chicago, *The Social Condition of the Swedish Woman* (Stockholm: A. L. Normans, 1893), 3.

64. Ibid.

65. Ibid., 4–7.

66. Ibid., 7.

67. Ibid., 27.

68. Brøndal, "The Fairest," 13; Nelson, *History of the Scandinavians*, vol. 1: 1–2, 4, 11–12. Scandinavian American Herbert N. Casson's "The Scandinavians in America" subscribed to the notion that nation approximated race. See Casson, "The Scandinavians in America," *Munsey's Magazine* 35 (August 1906): 613–618.

69. Nelson, *History of the Scandinavians*, vol. 1: 1–2.

70. Ibid.

71. Ibid., vol. 1: 53.

72. Whereas Nelson specified in his study that his source desired to remain anonymous, he noted in his text that the source was a prominent American scholar at the University of Minnesota. See Nelson, *History of the Scandinavians*, vol. 1: 65.

73. Ibid.

74. Ibid.

75. Banner, *American Beauty*, 5.

76. Historian Robert Allen noted the significance of burlesque's legacy as a cultural form as it established patterns of gender representation that changed the role and place of woman in American society. See Robert G. Allen, *Horrible Prettiness: Burlesque and American Culture* (Chapel Hill: University of North Carolina Press, 1991), 258–259; Banner, *American Beauty*, 124.

77. Charlotte Perkins Gilman, *Women and Economics: A Study of the Economic Relation between Men and Women as a Factor in Social Evolution* (Boston: Small, Maynard, 1898), 148.

78. Banner, *American Beauty*, 158.

79. For further discussion of the use of cosmetic goods by working-class consumers, see Kathy Peiss, *Hope in a Jar: The Making of America's Beauty Culture* (New York: Metropolitan Books, 1998), 4–5; Nan Enstad, *Ladies of Labor, Girls of Adventure: Working Women, Popular Culture, and Labor Politics at the Turn of the Twentieth Century* (New York: Columbia University Press, 1999), 61, 95, 215 n. 20, 229 n. 18; Peiss, *Cheap Amusements*, 56–87.

80. Sears Roebuck and Company, Sears Roebuck and Company Catalog (June 1896).

81. Peiss, *Hope in a Jar*, 31.

82. Advertisement, The Nordic Fairway [Periodicals 1925–29], MS6, Nordic Country Club Records, 1924–1931 (hereafter cited as NCC), box 1, folder 6, Swedish-American Archives of Greater Chicago, North Park University, Chicago.

206 · *Notes to Chapters 2 and 3*

83. "Other Gossip from Gotham: Nellie Neustretter in New York," *Chicago Tribune*, February 10, 1898.

84. "This Is My Birthday—A Romantic Marriage: Miss Lotten Lillieberg," *Chicago Tribune*, April 12, 1903.

85. "Marriageable Age for Swedish Women," *Chicago Tribune*, February 6, 1892; "The Wonderful Blonde Beauties of Denmark," *Chicago Tribune*, January 8, 1905.

86. Banner, *American Beauty*, 255–257.

87. For further discussion of the Congress of Beauty, see David Berg, *Chicago's White City of 1893* (Lexington: University of Kentucky Press, 1982), 218; Banner, *American Beauty*, 259; Ellen Strain, *Public Places, Private Journeys: Ethnography, Entertainment, and the Tourist Gaze* (New Brunswick: Rutgers University Press, 2003), 55.

88. "Paris Excited over a Beauty Contest of All Nations," *Chicago Tribune*, March 1, 1903.

89. "Judges Unable to Decide Swedish Beauty Contest; Embarrassment of Comeliness Results in a Deadlock and Young Women Must Wait for the Next Picnic," *Chicago Tribune*, June 29, 1903.

90. "Here Are the Rest of the 96 Prize Winning Beauties. Is the Most Beautiful of All among Them?" *Chicago Tribune*, February 10, 1907.

91. "Are These Chicago's Most Beautiful Working Girls? Do You Know of Any More Beautiful?" *Chicago Tribune*, March 10, 1912.

Chapter 3. The "Swedish Maid"

1. Johan Person, "Den Tjänande Systern" [Our Serving Sister], in *Svensk-Amerikanska Studier* (Rock Island: Augustana Book Concern, 1912), 106.

2. Ibid., 104.

3. U.S. Immigration Commission, *Reports of the Immigration Commission: Occupations of the First and Second Generation of Immigrants in the United States*, vol. 28 (Washington, D.C.: Governmental Printing Office, 1911), 71. Another localized study of Minnesota's immigrant workers reflected a similar preference for Scandinavian domestics among American employers. See Minnesota Bureau of Labor Statistics, *Biennial Report of the Bureau of Labor of the State of Minnesota* (St. Paul: Thos. A. Clark, 1888), 154, 157, 160, 165.

4. Wallengren, *Welcome Home Mr. Swanson*, 153.

5. Ulf Beijbom, *Utvandrarkvinnor: svenska kvinnoöden i Amerika* (Stockholm: Norstedts, 2006), 229.

6. Hirsch, "The Swedish Maid," 5.

7. The history of domestic service in America lends itself to focus on the negative aspects of the position including racial bias and discrimination, sexual harassment and abuse, and exploitation of workers. Domestic service is an occupation that is given a significant amount of attention within the historiography of women, immigration, and labor because the position lends itself to a vibrant discourse on various

themes, including class conflict, gender relations, and the effects of industrialization. The influence of David Katzman's 1978 monograph, *Seven Days a Week*, was notable, and throughout the 1980s and 1990s, a number of studies dedicated to the study of domestic work and household labor in America helped to expand the historiography of an occupation with great depth. Some useful studies include Daniel E. Sutherland, *Americans and Their Servants* (Baton Rogue: Louisiana State University Press, 1981); Susan Strasser, *Never Done: A History of American Housework* (New York: Pantheon Books, 1982); Phyllis Palmer, *Domesticity and Dirt: Housewives and Domestic Servants in the United States, 1920–1945* (Philadelphia: Temple University Press, 1989); Christine B. N. Chin, *In Service and Servitude: Foreign Female Domestic Workers and the Malaysian "Modernity" Project* (New York: Columbia University Press, 1998).

8. Roediger, *The Wages of Whiteness*, 47–48.

9. For further discussion on the birth of the cult of domesticity and true womanhood, see Nancy Cott, *The Bonds of Womanhood: "Women's Sphere" in New England, 1780–1835* (New Haven: Yale University Press, 1977).

10. "Bridget," *Harper's Bazar* 4, n. 11 (November 1871): 706. It was not until 1929 that the magazine changed the spelling of its name to its contemporary form, *Harper's Bazaar*. See also Andrew Urban, "Irish Domestic Servants, 'Biddy' and Rebellion in the American Home, 1850–1900," *Gender and History* 2, no. 2 (August 2009): 263–286.

11. Amy Kaplan, "Manifest Domesticity," *American Literature* 70, no. 3 (September 1998): 582.

12. Urban, "Irish Domestic Servants," 264.

13. While this chapter examines the role of work for men and women, I place more of an emphasis on female domestic servants and Nordic femininity in an effort to further the goals of women's history in replacing agency to the standard narrative. The stereotype of the hardworking, unproblematic (and therefore servile) Scandinavian in America trickled down to men just as it did women as the "Swedish maid" was the most readily assumed image of Nordics during the late nineteenth and early twentieth centuries.

14. In the 1990s, historians such as Ulf Beijbom, Joy Lintelman, and Margareta Matovic shifted the negative focus away from domestic service as a position rife with social stigmas by instead addressing the relative privilege given to Scandinavian servants at the turn of the century. See Beijbom, *Swedes in America*, 10; Lintelman, *I Go to America*.

15. U.S. Census Bureau, *The Eleventh Census of the United States: 1890* (Washington, D.C.: Government Printing Office, 1890–1896), 650–651; O. N. Nelson, *History of the Scandinavians*, 46.

16. Janson, *The Background of Swedish Immigration*, 22.

17. "The Emigration from Sweden and the Cause of It," *Svenska Tribunen*, June 7, 1882.

18. Beijbom, *Swedes in Chicago*, 141.

19. Nelson, *History of the Scandinavians*, 46.

208 · Notes to Chapter 3

20. U.S. Immigration Commission, *Statistical Review of Immigration*, 33–38.

21. U.S. Immigration Commission, *Reports of the Immigration Commission: Immigrants in Cities; A Study of the Population of Selected Districts in New York, Chicago, Philadelphia, Boston, Cleveland, Buffalo, and Milwaukee*, vol. 26 (Washington, D.C.: Government Printing Office, 1911), 262.

22. The report noted that of 141 foreign-born Swedish immigrants interviewed, 103 had lived in the area and 126 had lived in the city for over ten years—one of two groups exhibiting the highest percentages of entire residence in a single neighborhood. See U.S. Immigration Commission, *Immigrants in Cities*, 262–263, 268, 269, 328–330.

23. Ibid.

24. A number of historians, including Margareta Matovic, concluded that Scandinavians, like many other European immigrants, ceased work upon marriage. Yet, this assumption is more complex given the context of an American desire for Scandinavian domestic workers during the early twentieth century. See Matovic, "Embracing," in Harzig, *Peasant Maids*, 268–269.

25. U.S. Immigration Commission, *Immigrants in Cities*, 332–333.

26. Ibid., 315–316.

27. A. E. Strand, *The History of the Norwegians of Illinois: A Concise Record of the Struggles and Achievements of the Early Settlers Together with a Narrative of What Is Now Being Done by the Norwegian-Americans of Illinois in the Development of Their Adopted Country* (Chicago: John Anderson Publishing, 1905), 306–307.

28. "Go to School," *Skandinaven*, November 18, 1900.

29. Matovic, "Embracing," in Harzig, *Peasant Maids*, 268.

30. Ibid., 269.

31. Lilly and Lennart Stetterdahl, *Bror Johansson's Chicago; With Poems by Bror Johansson* (Moline: Lilly and Lennart Stetterdahl, 1985), 71.

32. Matovic, "Embracing," in Harzig, *Peasant Maids*, 265; Anita R. Olson, "The Community Created: Chicago Swedes 1880–1920," in *Swedish-American Life in Chicago*, 11.

33. U.S. Census Bureau, *The Twelfth Census of the United States: 1900* (Washington, D.C.: Government Printing Office, 1900–1907); Matovic, "Embracing," in Harzig, *Peasant Maids*, 271.

34. Christiane Harzig and Dirk Hoerder, "European Immigrant Women in Chicago at the Turn of the Century: A Comparative Approach," in *Swedes in America*, 98.

35. Ibid. See also Matovic, "Embracing," in Harzig, *Peasant Maids*, 270; U.S. Census Bureau, *Twelfth Census, 1900*.

36. Daniel A. Graff, "Domestic Work and Workers," *Encyclopedia of Chicago*, accessed July 14, 2015, http://www.encyclopedia.chicagohistory.org/pages/386.html. See also Dudden, *Serving Women*; Katzman, *Seven Days a Week*; Meyerowitz, *Women Adrift*.

37. Letter from Stina Wibäck in Chicago to her sister, Cari, January 1, 1871, in Beijbom, *Swedes in Chicago*, 173.

38. Isidor Kjellberg, *Amerika-bok* (Linköping: Isidor Kjellbergs Boktryckeri, 1892), 36.

Notes to Chapter 3 • 209

39. Coleen Browne Kilner, *Joseph Sears and his Kenilworth*, 2nd ed. (Kenilworth: Kenilworth Historical Society, 1990), 138.

40. Diary of Dorothy Sears, August 8, 1905, Joseph Sears Papers, Kenilworth Historical Society, Kenilworth, Ill.

41. Lot deed, 1893, Kenilworth Historical Society, Kenilworth, Ill.; Kilner, *Joseph Sears*, 143.

42. Hirsch, "The Swedish Maid," 1.

43. Kilner, *Joseph Sears*, vi.

44. "Help Wanted," *Svenska Tribunen Nyheter*, September 7, 1909.

45. "Help Wanted," *Chicago Tribune*, November 21, 1880.

46. "Help Wanted," *Chicago Tribune*, July 12, 1925.

47. Silke Wehner, "German Domestic Servants in America, 1850–1914: A New Look at German Immigrant Women's Experiences," in *People in Transit: German Migrations in Comparative Perspective, 1820–1930*, eds. Dirk Hoerder and Jörg Nagler (Washington, D.C.: German Historical Institute, Cambridge University Press, 1995), 278–279.

48. "Situations Wanted," *Chicago Tribune*, November 21, 1880.

49. Ibid.

50. In a select analysis of the *Chicago Tribune* between April 1909 and May 1910, the "situations wanted" section illustrated such acknowledgment of preference in service employment by Swedish, Norwegian, and Danish women and men.

51. Select advertisements from "situations wanted," *Chicago Tribune*, April 29, 1909.

52. Harzig and Hoerder, *Swedes in America*, 101; Katzman, *Seven Days a Week*, 139.

53. Hirsch, "The Swedish Maid," 29.

54. "Swedish National Association's Employment Bureau," *Svenska Nyheter*, June 9, 1903.

55. "The Norwegian Employment Office," *Skandinaven*, April 24, 1907.

56. Hirsch, "The Swedish Maid," 24, 25.

57. Ibid.

58. Robert Coles, "Introduction," in *To the Manor Born*, ed. Mary Lloyd Estin (New York: New York Graphic Society, 1979), 11. On the benefits provided to upper-class women by way of their domestic help, see Barbara Welter, "The Cult of True Womanhood: 1820–1860," *American Quarterly* 18, no. 2 (Summer 1966): 151–174; Kathryn Kish Sklar, *Catherine Beecher: A Study in American Domesticity* (New Haven: Yale University Press, 1973); and Flanagan, *Seeing with Their Hearts*.

59. Diary of Dorothy Sears, October 1905–January 1906, Joseph Sears Papers, Kenilworth Historical Society, Kenilworth, Ill.

60. "Marion Harland's Helping Hand," *Chicago Tribune*, January 2, 1916.

61. As a way of expediting the acculturation process of Swedish servants, the author translated this cookbook in both English and Swedish. See Carl Grimsköld, *Swedish-American Book of Cookery and Adviser for Swedish Servants in America* (New York: Otto Chils' Print, 1890), in English and Swedish, 1.

62. Ibid., 2.

210 · *Notes to Chapter 3*

63. See Sydney Stahl Weinberg, "The Treatment of Women in Immigration History: A Call for Change," in *Seeking Common Ground: Multidisciplinary Studies of Immigrant Women in the United States*, ed. Donna Gabaccia (Westport: Praeger, 1992), 3–22; Wolfgang Helbich and Ulrike Sommer, "Immigrant Letters as Sources," in *The Press of Labor Migrants in Europe and North America, 1880s to 1930s*, eds. Dirk Hoerder and Christiane Harzig (Bremen: Universitat Bremen, 1985), 39–58; H. Arnold Barton, *Letters from the Promised Land* (Minneapolis: University of Minnesota Press, 1975), 5.

64. Hirsch, "The Swedish Maid," 1, 47.

65. Hannah Mathison to Walter Franklin Newberry, letters sent from Trondheim, Norway, on June 18, 1895, and August 8, 1895, Oliver Perry Newberry papers, folder 1, Midwest Manuscript Series, Newberry Library, Chicago, Ill.

66. Ibid.

67. C. F. Peterson [under the pseudonym "Jeppe"], "The Servant Girl," *Svenska Tribunen*, December 10, 1891.

68. Ibid.

69. "Maid or Factory Girl?" *Svenska Nyheter*, June 23, 1903.

70. Ibid.

71. "The Swedish Women as Domestics," *New York Herald*, reprinted in *Svenska Tribunen*, September 21, 1892.

72. "For the Day," *Svenska Tribunen*, February 6, 1901.

73. O. W., "How I Kept My Housemaid for Three Years," *Harper's Bazar* 42, no. 4 (April 1908): 378.

74. Lucy Maynard Salmon, *Domestic Service* (New York: Macmillan, 1901), 92, 121.

75. Pettengill, *Toilers of the Home*, 5.

76. Ibid., 36–37, 55.

77. Inge Lund, *En piga i USA* [*A Maid in the USA*] (Stockholm: Åhlen and Åkerlund, 1917), 112–113.

78. Hirsch, "The Swedish Maid," 36.

79. Ibid.

80. Graff, "Domestic Work and Workers."

81. Lloyd Wendt and Herman Kogan, *Give the Lady What She Wants! The Story of Marshall Field and Company* (Chicago: Rand McNally, 1952), 223.

82. Ibid., 4–5.

83. Ibid., 5.

84. Marie Louise Obenauer, U.S. Bureau of Labor, *Wage Earning Women in Stores and Factories* (Washington, D.C.: Government Printing Office, 1910), 92, 114, 133–135, 187–188; Susan Porter Benson, *Counter Cultures: Saleswomen, Managers, and Customers in American Department Stores, 1890–1940* (Urbana: University of Illinois Press, 1987), 208–209.

85. Ibid.

86. Ibid.

87. Augustana Hospital of the Deaconess Institution of the Swedish Evangelical Lutheran Church, *Twenty-Ninth Annual Report* (Chicago: n.p., 1913), 3–4.

Notes to Chapters 3 and 4 • 211

88. Ibid., 57.

89. Ibid.

Chapter 4. Scandinavians Behaving Badly

1. Casson's reasoning was part of a larger racial construct that made Nordics exceptional above all other Europeans and therefore ignored their associations with vice. See Casson, "The Scandinavians in America," 618.

2. Walter C. Reckless, *Vice in Chicago* (Montclair: Patterson Smith, 1933), 38–39, Case 17, Chicago Vice Study File.

3. Ibid.

4. Ibid.

5. Some recent studies have begun to explore the "underside" of Scandinavian immigrant life; however, there remains a notable historiographic gap. Joy Lintelman pointed to the fact that individuals who led difficult lives did not leave behind records, nor did they write to their families about their troubles. Yet, the assumption that ethnic newspapers did not stress the negative elements of immigrant society appears not to be the case. On the experiences of "unfortunates" and the moral condition of Scandinavian women, see Joy Lintelman, "'Unfortunates' and 'City Guests': Swedish American Inmates and the Minneapolis City Workhouse, 1907," in *Swedes in the Twin Cities: Immigrant Life and Minnesota's Urban Frontier*, eds. Philip J. Anderson and Dag Blanck (Minnesota: Minnesota Historical Society Press, 2001), 57–76; Lintelman, "On My Own": Single, Swedish, and Female in Turn-of-the-Century Chicago," in *Swedish-American Life in Chicago*, 95–97; Wallengren, *Welcome Home Mr. Swanson*, 156–162.

6. On definitions of white slavery, urban space, and sexuality within Chicago, see Meyerowitz, *Women Adrift*, xvii–xxiii; Kevin Mumford, *Interzones: Black/White Sex Districts in Chicago and New York in the Early Twentieth Century* (New York: Columbia University Press, 1997); Amy R. Lagler, "For God's Sake Do Something": White Slavery Narratives and Moral Panic in Turn-of-the-Century American Cities" (PhD diss., Michigan State University, 2000); Karen Abbott, *Sin in the Second City: Madams, Ministers, Playboys, and the Battle for America's Soul* (New York: Random House, 2007). See also Janet E. Rasmussen, "'I Was Scared to Death When I Came to Chicago': White Slavery and the Woman Immigrant," in *Fin(s) de Siecle in Scandinavian Perspective: Studies in Honor of Harald S. Naess*, eds. Faith Ingwersen and Mary Kay Norseng (Columbia: Camden House, 1993), 195.

7. See Beijbom, "The Promised Land for Swedish Maids," in *Swedes in America*, 117–124; Rasmussen, "I Was Scared to Death"; Lintelman, "A Good Position," in *I Go to America*, 92–134.

8. "Offer Landsman," *Svenska Tribunen*, July 23, 1891.

9. "Förbrytelse Bland Skandinaver," *Skandinaven*, January 28, 1884.

10. "Kriminalitet," *Skandinaven*, December 15, 1891.

11. Lintelman, "'Unfortunates' and 'City Guests'," 57, 64–66.

12. Ibid., 68–69. Lintelman indicates that further analysis is needed into the question of whether men were also arrested for soliciting women, and if so, whether their sentences were comparable.

212 · *Notes to Chapter 4*

13. Meyerowitz, *Women Adrift*, 11–12; U.S. Census Bureau, *Tenth Census* (1880), 538–541.

14. On Italian and Jewish women and strong family and kin networks, see Virginia Yans-McLaughlin, *Family and Community: Italian Immigrants in Buffalo, 1880–1930* (Ithaca: Cornell University Press, 1977); Elizabeth Ewen, *Immigrant Women in the Land of Dollars: Life and Culture on the Lower East Side, 1890–1925* (New York: Monthly Review Press, 1985).

15. "Flickor Harmas Avgifter," *Skandinaven*, September 18, 1872.

16. Ibid.

17. The July 1873 exchange between the two newspapers was part of an ongoing debate over the position of the "Swedish" maid in Chicago's society. See *"Nya Verlden" och Tjensteflickorna," Svenska Amerikanaren*, July 5, 1873.

18. Ibid.

19. "Piga eller Fabrikenflicka?" *Svenska Nyheter*, June 23, 1903.

20. Pauline Hegborn Nelson, memoirs, younger years—1920s, MS39, HNF, box 2, folder 8, Swedish-American Archives of Greater Chicago, North Park University, Chicago.

21. George Wharton James, *Chicago's Dark Places: Investigations by a Corps of Specially Appointed Commissioners* (Chicago: Craig Press, 1891); William T. Stead, *If Christ Came to Chicago! A Plea for the Union of All Who Love in the Service of All Who Suffer* (London: Review of Reviews, 1894).

22. Ernest Bell, *Fighting the Traffic in Young Girls; or, War on the White Slave Trade: A Complete and Detailed Account of the Shameless Traffic in Young Girls* (Chicago: G. S. Ball, 1910), 258–259, 262.

23. Ibid, 57.

24. Konni Zilliacus, *Amerika-boken: hjälpreda for utvandrare: jämte en kort vägledning till engelska sprakets talande: med karta över Förenta staterna* (Stockholm: Albert Bonnier, 1893), 10–11; Johan Henrik Chronwall, *Utvandrare-boken. Om lyftet I och på Resan till Amerika* (Stockholm: Skandia, 1914), 26–27. See also Wallengren, *Welcome Home Mr. Swanson*, 156–162.

25. Lee Grieveson, "Policing the Cinema: *Traffic in Souls* at Ellis Island, 1913," *Screen* 38, no. 2 (July 1997): 149–171; Wallengren, *Welcome Home Mr. Swanson*, 158.

26. "Scandinavian Emigrants; Healthy and Spirited Emigrants Bound for the West," *Seattle Press-Times*, May 7, 1891.

27. Helga Pederson Watney, Oral History Interview, 1979, Pacific Lutheran University Archives and Special Collections, Tacoma, Wash.

28. "Vit Slav Flyr," *Skandinaven*, November 12, 1889.

29. Meyerowitz, *Women Adrift*, 41–42.

30. Thörnberg, *Lefnadsstandard och sparkraft*, 40, 43.

31. "Flickor som flyttar Hemifrån," *Skandinaven*, January 30, 1889.

32. "Kidnappade," *Skandinaven*, March 7, 1889; "Ungdomsbrottslighet," *Skandinaven*, September 24, 1889.

Notes to Chapter 4 • 213

33. "Ungdomsbrottslighet," *Skandinaven*, September 24, 1889.

34. "The City: General News," *Chicago Tribune*, August 21, 1880.

35. Matovic, "Embracing," in Harzig, *Peasant Maids*, 275–276; Matovic, "Illegitimacy and Marriage in Stockholm in the Nineteenth Century," in *Bastardy and Its Comparative History: Studies in the History of Illegitimacy and Marital Nonconformism in Britain, France, Germany, Sweden, North America, Jamaica, and Japan* (London: Edward Arnold, 1980), 336. For further discussion on illegitimacy within western Europe, see Peter Laslett, "Introduction: Comparing Illegitimacy over Time and between Cultures," in *Bastardy and Its Comparative History*, 1–68; R. F. Thomasson, "Premarital Permissiveness and Illegitimacy in the Nordic Countries," *Comparative Studies in Society and History* 8, no. 2 (April 1976): 252–270; Ann-Sofie Kälvemark, "Illegitimacy and Marriage in Three Swedish Parishes in the Nineteenth Century," in *Bastardy and Its Comparative History*, 330.

36. The Royal Swedish Commission for the World's Columbian Exposition, *Swedish Catalogue*, 17–19.

37. See Thörnberg, *Lefnadsstandard och Sparkraft*, 42–43; Castberg's Law in Illinois," *Skandinaven*, December 4, 1916; Cecilia Milow, "Till frågan om det moraliska tillståndet bland svenska tjänsteflickor i Amerika," *Dagny* 12 (1904): 293–294.

38. On illegitimacy, immigrants, and sexual double standards, see Marion E. Kenworthy, "The Mental Hygiene Aspects of Illegitimacy," *Mental Hygiene* 5 (July 1921): 499–508; U.S. Children's Bureau, *Children of Illegitimate Birth and Measures for Their Protection* (Washington, D.C.: Government Printing Office, 1926); Maud Morlock, "Wanted: A Square Deal for the Baby Born out of Wedlock," *Child* 10 (May 1946): 167–169; Regina G. Kunzel, *Fallen Women, Problem Girls: Unmarried Mothers and the Professionalization of Social Work, 1890–1945* (New Haven: Yale University Press, 1993); E. Wayne Carp, "Professional Social Workers, Adoption, and the Problem of Illegitimacy, 1915–1945," *Journal of Policy History* 6 (1994): 161–184; Linda Gordon, *Pitied but Not Entitled: Single Mothers and the History of Welfare, 1890–1935* (New York: The Free Press, 1994).

39. Robert L. Heuser, *Fertility Tables for Birth Cohorts by Color: United States, 1917–73* (Rockville: U.S. Dept. of Health, Education, and Welfare, 1976), 79–85.

40. Dorothy Francis Puttee and Mary Ruth Colby, *The Illegitimate Child in Illinois* (Chicago: The University of Chicago Press, 1937), 82–83, 85–86.

41. Ibid., 91–92.

42. Matovic, "Embracing," in Harzig, *Peasant Maids*, 277–278.

43. Puttee and Colby, *The Illegitimate Child*, 98–99; Matovic, "Embracing," in Harzig, *Peasant Maids*, 275–276.

44. "Romance Ended; The Norwegian Woman's Friend Arrested on Complaint of His Wife," *Chicago Tribune*, August 5, 1884.

45. "Fred Hanson Skyldig," *Svenska Tribunen*, April 3, 1901.

46. "Woman's Slayer Hanged," *Richmond Dispatch*, August 9, 1902.

47. "Eight Jurors Accepted in Thombs Murder Case," *Chicago Tribune*, March 29, 1902.

48. "Fallet med Thombs," *Skandinaven*, August 3, 1902.

214 · *Notes to Chapter 4*

49. Ibid.

50. "Tillkännagivande om ny Rättegång för John Nordgren," *Svenska Nyheter*, November 1, 1904.

51. "Avenges Her Own Home and Heart; Helga Anderson Shoots Thrice and Dangerously Wounds Julius C. Darby," *Chicago Tribune*, May 19, 1907.

52. "Minister Greps," *Skandinaven*, May 23, 1907.

53. Lintelman, *I Go to America*, 95–96.

54. See Lisa Fine, "Between Two Worlds: Business Women in a Chicago Boarding House 1900–1930," *Journal of Social History* 19, no. 3 (Spring 1986): 511–519; Advertisement for the Augustana Central Home and Inner Mission, which was located at 1346 N. Lasalle Street, in *The Swedish Blue Book: A Swedish-American Directory and Yearbook for Chicago, 1927* (Chicago: Swedish-American pub., 1927), 115.

55. Advertisement for the Augustana Central Home and Inner Mission, *Swedish Blue Book, 1927*.

56. Advertisement for the Susanna Wesley Home of the Swedish M.E. Church on 3143 S. Michigan Avenue, *Swedish Blue Book, 1927*, 120.

57. Booklet published by the Chicago Immanuel Woman's Home, *Historical Sketch of the Immanuel Woman's Home, Looking Back Twenty-five Years (1907–1932)*, 12. In The Immanuel Woman's Home Association Collection (hereafter IWHAC), Swenson Swedish Immigration Research Center, Augustana College, Rock Island, Ill.

58. Ibid., 9; "Immanuel Women's Home Observes Twenty-Fifth Anniversary," *Svenska Tribunen-Nyheter*, December 7, 1932.

59. Constitution and By-Laws for Immanuel Woman's Home Association, 1911 (IWHAC).

60. *Historical Sketch* (IWHAC), 9.

61. Ibid., 28.

62. Ibid., 11, 14–19.

63. *The Closing Chapter of the History of Immanuel Woman's Home Association* (CIWHM).

64. "En Skandinavisk Folkets Hus i Chicago," *Svenska Nyheter*, June 7, 1904; "Till Skandinaverna i Chicago," *Svenska Nyheter*, June 28, 1904.

65. Ibid.

66. "Till Skandinaverna i Chicago," *Svenska Nyheter*, June 28, 1904.

67. Pehr Nordahl, *Weaving the Ethnic Fabric: Social Networks among Swedish-American Radicals in Chicago 1890–1940* (Stockholm: Almquist and Wiksell, 1994), 13, 21.

68. Ibid.

69. *Ibid.*, 23, 25; Eric L. Hirsch, *Urban Revolt: Ethnic Politics in the Nineteenth-Century Chicago Labor Movement* (Berkeley: University of California Press, 1990); Conzen et al., "The Invention of Ethnicity."

70. Nordahl, *Weaving the Ethnic Fabric*, 61.

71. Ibid.

72. "Svält måste gå," *Skandinaven*, March 29, 1896; "Barn arbetar som slavar i Chicago," *Skandinaven*, September 12, 1907.

Notes to Chapters 4 and 5 • 215

73. "T. M. Swanson's 'Konserthus' Utsatt," *Scandia*, May 5, 1900.

74. Reckless, *Vice in Chicago*, 42–43.

75. Ibid., 44. See also The Vice Commission of Chicago, *The Social Evil in Chicago: A Study of Existing Conditions with Recommendations by the Vice Commission of Chicago* (Chicago: Gunthorp-Warren Printing, 1911).

76. Swedish Educational League, "Swedish Educational League: An Adult Education Experiment in Scandinavian Tradition [1924]," MS3, Swedish Educational League Records, box 1, folder 3, Swedish-American Archives of Greater Chicago, North Park University, Chicago, Ill.

77. Janson, *Background of the Immigration*, 18.

78. "Swedish Educational League."

Chapter 5. World War I, Nativist Rhetoric, and the "White Man Par Excellence"

1. Grant, *The Passing of the Great Race*, 79–80. In "The Fairest among the So-Called White Races," Jørn Brøndal emphasizes the influence of Grant's work in spite of the fact that only seventeen thousand copies were printed in the United States; the study was translated into German, French, and Norwegian and therefore found a large European audience. See Brøndal, "The Fairest," 17.

2. "Tolka Amerika," *Skandinaven*, July 13, 1918.

3. Ibid.

4. "Ett ord som är ägnat till Skandinaver," *Skandinaven*, August 23, 1917.

5. Russell Kazal's monograph, *Becoming Old Stock*, offers one of the most useful analyses on the German American experience during World War I and argues that German ethnicity never fully recovered from its subversion during the tumultuous period despite racial similarities that linked Germans to Scandinavians as Nordic "stock." Some notable sources on the subversion of ethnicity during wartime, and the concepts of assimilation and pluralism, include Kazal, *Becoming Old Stock*; Russell A. Kazal, "Revisiting Assimilation: The Rise, Fall, and Reappraisal of a Concept in American Ethnic History," *American Historical Review* 100, no. 2 (April 1995): 437–471; Philip Gleason, "The Odd Couple: Pluralism and Assimilation," in *Speaking to Diversity: Language and Ethnicity in Twentieth-Century America* (Baltimore: Johns Hopkins University Press, 1992), 47–90; John Higham, *Send These to Me: Immigrants in Urban America*, rev. ed. (Baltimore: Johns Hopkins University Press, 1984).

6. Jacobson, *Whiteness of a Different Color*, 93.

7. The wartime response of Scandinavian Americans in urban areas of Wisconsin and Minnesota, as well as urban areas of the Pacific Northwest, was similar to Scandinavians in Chicago; however, there was far less of an emphasis on *Nordic* as a unifying term. See Brøndal, *Ethnic Leadership and Midwestern Politics*; Lars Olsson, "Evelina Johansdotter, Textile Workers, and the Munsingwear Family: Class, Gender, and Ethnicity in the Political Economy of Minnesota at the End of World War I," in *Swedes in the Twin Cities*, 77–90; Lars Ljungmark, "The Northern Neighbor: Winnipeg, the Swedish Service Station in the 'Last Best West: 1890–1950,'" in *Swedes in the Twin*

216 · *Notes to Chapter 5*

Cities, 91–103; Ulf Jonas Björk, "*Svenska Amerikanska Posten*: An Immigrant Newspaper with American Accents," in *Swedes in the Twin Cities*, 210–222; Janet E. Rasmussen, *New Land, New Lives: Scandinavian Immigrants to the Pacific Northwest* (Seattle: University of Washington Press, 1998).

8. For representative works, see Anita Olson, "Swedish Chicago: The Extension and Transformation of an Urban Immigrant Community, 1880–1920" (PhD diss., Northwestern University, 1990); Lintelman, "More Freedom, Better Pay"; Barton, *A Folk Divided*; April Schultz, *Ethnicity on Parade: Inventing the Norwegian American through Celebration* (Amherst: University of Massachusetts Press, 1994).

9. Geoffrey G. Field, "Nordic Racism," *Journal of the History of Ideas* 38, no. 3 (July–September 1977): 523.

10. For further discussions of the distinctions between the public and private spheres for immigrant groups, see Peiss, *Cheap Amusements*. Quite possibly, the greatest attention to the dynamics of this intriguing hyphenated ethnic identity lies in works dedicated to the shifting prosperity of Jewish Americans during the same era. Some examples include Deborah Dash Moore, *At Home in America: Second Generation New York Jews* (New York: Columbia University Press, 1981); Beth Wegner, *New York Jews and the Great Depression: Uncertain Promise* (Syracuse: Syracuse University Press, 1999); Goldstein, *The Price of Whiteness*.

11. "Invandraren," *Svenska Tribunen-Nyheter*, September 28, 1921.

12. U.S. Census Bureau, The *Thirteenth Census of the United States: 1910* (Washington, D.C.: Government Printing Office, 1910); "Skandinaviska folkräkningen," *Skandinaven*, September 17, 1914; Burgess, *Census Data for the City of Chicago, 1920*, 19 (table 6).

13. *Thirteenth Census of the United States, 1910*; Barton, *A Folk Divided*, 210.

14. Barton, *A Folk Divided*, 241.

15. For further discussion of the importance of ethnic prevalence for Swedish Americans, in particular during the 1900s and 1910s, see ibid., *A Folk Divided*, 212.

16. "Scandia," *Scandia*, August 31, 1912.

17. "Redaktionell," *Scandia*, October 7, 1911.

18. Babcock, *The Scandinavian Element in the United States*, 9–11; see also Babcock, "The Scandinavian Element in the American Population," The *American Historical Review* 16, no. 2 (January 1911): 300–310.

19. Ibid.

20. "Krigstidsjusteringar," *Hemlandet*, August 6, 1914.

21. Barton, *A Folk Divided*, 246; see also Carl H. Chrislock, *Ethnicity Challenged: The Upper Midwest Norwegian-American Experience in World War I* (Northfield: Norwegian American Historical Association, 1981).

22. Björk, "*Svenska Amerikanska Posten*," 218.

23. Ibid.

24. "Vi Protesterar!" *Skandinaven*, February 16, 1915.

25. April Schultz pointed out that, in addition to opposition to the war, Norwegian Americans were vulnerable to attacks by anti-hyphenates because of their continued

use of the Norwegian language, their strong immigrant press, and their thriving ethnic organization. See Schultz, *Ethnicity on Parade*, 41; "En överklagande till Amerikanska folket," *Skandinaven*, April 7, 1915.

26. "Seize Seditious Papers in Raid on Lunde Home," *Chicago Daily Tribune*, November 8, 1917.

27. "Norska arresterade, laddade med spionage," *Skandinaven*, November 8, 1917.

28. "Den Nya Amerikanismen," *Svenska Kuriren*, June 22, 1916.

29. Ibid.

30. Jacobson, *Whiteness of a Different Color*, 77–85.

31. Kazal, *Becoming Old Stock*, 125.

32. Grant, *The Passing of the Great Race*, 10–12, 18, 69, 90, 124, 168–169, 177, 193, 206–211, 228, 236; John Higham, *Strangers in the Land: Patterns of American Nativism 1860–1925* (New Brunswick: Rutgers University Press, 1955), 155–157.

33. Grant, *The Passing of the Great Race*, 79.

34. "Metropolitan Council, John Ericssons liga för patriotisk service," *Ungdomsvännen*, October 7, 1918. See also Barton, *A Folk Divided*, 247.

35. Ibid.

36. "Ett ord som är ägnat till Skandinaver," *Skandinaven*, August 23, 1917.

37. Ibid.

38. Kazal, *Becoming Old Stock*, 170–171.

39. "Det Tredje Frihetslånet," *Skandinaven*, May 12, 1918.

40. "Den Norska Klubben," *Skandinaven*, October 20, 1918; "Utrikes Födda och Tredje Frihetslånet," *Svenska Kuriren*, September 19, 1918.

41. "Utrikes Födda och Tredje Frihetslånet," *Svenska Kuriren*, September 19, 1918.

42. The author of the article expressed an urgency to give credit where credit was due, stating that, "after considerable deliberation by leaders from the many Swedish societies, it was decided to urge our countrymen who subscribe to mark each subscription black with the words 'Swedish Division,' in order that the Swedish purchases can be properly credited and correctly accounted." See "Kampanjen för Fjärde Frihetslånet," *Svenska Kuriren*, October 3, 1918.

43. "Utländsk-språkdag; Liberty Loan Parade," *Skandinaven*, April 24, 1919.

44. William M. Tuttle, *Race Riot: Chicago in the Red Summer of 1919* (Urbana: University of Illinois Press, 1970), 5–10, 64.

45. Carl Sandburg, *The Letters of Carl Sandburg* (New York: Harcourt Brace, 1968), 166.

46. Aldon Nielsen, *Reading Race in American Poetry: An Area of "Act"* (Urbana: University of Illinois Press, 2000), 34.

47. "Angelsaksisk, ikke Latinsk," *Skandinaven*, October 24, 1917.

48. "Chicago Norsk Klubb er Sterk for Norsk Språk," *Skandinaven*, December 21, 1917.

49. "De Fremmedsprakene," *Skandinaven*, August 25, 1920.

50. U.S. Census Bureau, *The Fourteenth Census of the United States: 1920* (Washington, D.C.: Government Printing Office, 1920); "Folketelling," *Skandinaven*, March 27, 1920.

218 · Notes to Chapters 5 and 6

51. John Higham wrote that, although intended as a temporary legislation, the act "proved in the long run the most important turning-point in American immigration policy" because it imposed numerical limits on European immigration for the first time and established a nationality quota system. See Higham, *Strangers in the Land*, 311; Mae M. Ngai, "The Architecture of Race in American Immigration Law: A Reexamination of the Immigration Act of 1924," *Journal of American History* 86, no. 1 (June 1999): 69–70.

52. In 1923, no less than 24,948 Swedes came to the United States; however, during the next year, that number witnessed a drastic plummet to average slightly fewer than 8,400 immigrants a year between 1924 and 1929. During the course of the Great Depression, the number of annual immigrants from Sweden dropped to only 900 a year—far below the quota set for Sweden and far below return migration to Sweden. See U.S. Department of Commerce, *Statistical Abstract of the United States, 1922* (Washington, D.C.: Government Printing Office, 1923), 101 (table 74); Statistiska Centralbyrån, *Statistisk årsbok för Sverige, 1930* (Stockholm: Boktryckeriet, 1930), 65; Barton, *A Folk Divided*, 241.

53. Kenneth Roberts, "Editorial," *Saturday Evening Post*, November 18, 1922; "Förordningen om Invandring," *Svenska Tribunen-Nyheter*, November 22, 1922.

54. "Invandrare från Norr," *Svenska Tribunen-Nyheter*, January 31, 1923; "Invandringsräkningen," *Svenska Tribunen-Nyheter*, February 14, 1923.

55. "Svenska Nykomlingar," *Svenska Tribunen-Nyheter*, November 28, 1923.

56. Carl J. Bengston, "Opinion," *The Lutheran Companion*, October 26, 1929; Finis Herbert Capps, *From Isolationism to Involvement: The Swedish Immigrant Press in America, 1914–1945* (Chicago: Swedish Pioneer Historical Society, 1966), 112–113; Barton, *A Folk Divided*, 252.

57. "Varför Om Ansiktet?" *Svenska Tribunen-Nyheter*, March 20, 1929.

58. Barton, *A Folk Divided*, 252–253, 379.

59. Ibid., 242.

60. Schultz's study explores the meanings of community and ethnic identity through the cultural celebrations of Norwegian Americans. See Schultz, *Ethnicity on Parade*, 38.

61. Lydia Hedberg, *Reseminnen från U.S.A.* (Skövde: Isakssonska Boktryckeri-Aktiebolaget, 1925), 29, 81.

62. Anita Olson, "The Community Created," in *Swedish-American Life in Chicago*, 57.

63. Schultz, *Ethnicity on Parade*, 57; John R. Jenswold, "Becoming American, Becoming Suburban: Norwegians in the 1920s," *Norwegian-American Studies* 33 (1992): 5–6.

64. Lizabeth Cohen, *Making a New Deal: Industrial Workers in Chicago, 1919–1939* (Cambridge: Cambridge University Press, 1990); Jenswold, "Becoming American," 16–17.

Chapter 6. The New Nordic Man of the 1920s

1. See Anita R. Olson, "The Community Created: Chicago Swedes 1880–1920," in *Swedish-American Life in Chicago*, 49–59.

2. For further discussion, see Helen M. Lynd and Robert S. Lynd, *Middletown: A Study in American Culture* (New York: Harcourt Brace, 1929); *The Culture of Consumption*, eds.

Richard Wightman Fox and T. J. Jackson Lears (New York: Pantheon, 1983); Cohen, *Making a New Deal*.

3. See Anita Olson Gustafson, "North Park: Building a Swedish Community in Chicago," *Journal of American Ethnic History* 22, no. 2 (Winter 2003): 31–49.

4. Ibid., 32.

5. Nordic Country Club, publicity map of Itasca and the proposed Nordic Country Club, MS6, NCC, box 1, folder 8, Swedish-American Archives of Greater Chicago, North Park University, Chicago.

6. Nordic Country Club, commemorative booklet printed for the Nordic Country Club [mid-1920s], MS6, NCC, box 1, folder 7, Swedish-American Archives of Greater Chicago, North Park University, Chicago.

7. Within the announcement, the investors encouraged prospective members to purchase property in the subdivision of 1200 acres near the potential club, promising that it was "property which will greatly increase in value." See Nordic Country Club, Contract, MS6, NCC, box 1, folder 2, Swedish-American Archives of Greater Chicago, North Park University, Chicago.

8. Nordic Country Club, commemorative booklet.

9. Ibid.

10. Nordic Country Club, Membership List [1925], MS6, NCC, box 1, folder 4, Swedish-American Archives of Greater Chicago, North Park University, Chicago.

11. Ibid.

12. Matovic, "Embracing," in Harzig, *Peasant Maids*, 271.

13. Aldous Huxley, "The Importance of Being Nordic," in *Essays New and Old* (New York: The Forum Publishing, 1925), 239.

14. Ibid., 241.

15. F. Scott Fitzgerald, *The Great Gatsby* (New York: Simon and Schuster, 1925), 18.

16. Lothrop Stoddard, *The Rising Tide of Color against White World-Supremacy* (New York: Charles Scribner's Sons, 1922), v–vii.

17. *The Crack-Up, with Other Uncollected Pieces, Notebooks, and Unpublished Letters*, ed. Edmund Wilson (New York: New Directions, 1945), 326.

18. "New Nordic Country Club; Nordic Club Purchases 200 Acres," *Herald-Examiner*, April 19, 1925; "Country Club for Chicago Scandinavians," *Chicago Sunday Tribune*, April 19, 1925.

19. Nordic Country Club, Membership List [1925].

20. Nordic Country Club, Bylaws [Adopted April 13, 1925], MS6, NCC, box 1, folder 1, Swedish-American Archives of Greater Chicago, North Park University, Chicago.

21. Nordic Country Club, Membership Recommendation Card, MS6, NCC, box 1, folder 4, Swedish-American Archives of Greater Chicago, North Park University, Chicago.

22. Nordic Country Club, Bylaws.

23. Carl Hjalmar Lundquist, letter to the Nordic Country Club charter members, MS6, NCC, box 1, folder 4, Swedish-American Archives of Greater Chicago, North Park University, Chicago.

220 · *Notes to Chapter 6*

24. Article from the club's newsletter [October 1929], *The Nordic Fairway*, MS6, NCC, box 1, folder 6, Swedish-American Archives of Greater Chicago, North Park University, Chicago.

25. "Scandia Beach (Contributed)," *Scandia*, June 11, 1927.

26. Carl Hjalmar Lundquist, letter to Chas H. Fellowes [June 19, 1925], MS6, NCC, box 1, folder 4, Swedish-American Archives of Greater Chicago, North Park University, Chicago.

27. Nordic Country Club, commemorative booklet [1926], MS6, NCC, box 1, folder 6, Swedish-American Archives of Greater Chicago, North Park University, Chicago.

28. *Swedish Blue Book*, 1927.

29. *The Nordic Fairway* [October 1929].

30. Ibid.

31. *The Nordic Fairway* [September 1926], MS6, NCC, box 1, folder 6, Swedish-American Archives of Greater Chicago, North Park University, Chicago.

32. Ibid.

33. Ibid.

34. See Lintelman, "Our Serving Sisters," 384–386; W. R. Linneman, "Immigrant Stereotypes: 1880–1900," *Studies in American Humor* 1 (1974): 28–39.

35. *The Nordic Fairway* [September 1929], MS6, NCC, box 1, folder 6, Swedish-American Archives of Greater Chicago, North Park University, Chicago.

36. Ibid.

37. Chas Fellowes, legal document prepared by Fellowes, Lawrence and Fellowes LLP, MS6, NCC, box 1, folder 9, Swedish-American Archives of Greater Chicago, North Park University, Chicago.

38. Taken from a handwritten note by Lundquist in response to the tactics used by Fellowes in getting Scandinavians (mostly Swedes) to commit to purchasing land and joining the club. See Carl Hjalmar Lundquist, note to Chas Fellowes, MS6, NCC, box 1, folder 9, Swedish-American Archives of Greater Chicago, North Park University, Chicago.

39. NCC Board of Directors, notice of debt issued to Carl Hjalmar Lundquist [April 1, 1930], MS6, NCC, box 1, folder 4, Swedish-American Archives of Greater Chicago, North Park University, Chicago.

40. Ibid.

41. Ibid.; Legal papers filed by Carl Hjalmar Lundquist v. the board of directors, MS6, NCC, box 1, folder 7, Swedish-American Archives of Greater Chicago, North Park University, Chicago.

42. See Ulf Beijbom, *Utvandrarna och den stora depressionen: Svenskamerikaner i trettiotalers malström* (Stockholm: Carlsson Bokförlag, 2012).

43. "Nordic Golfers Begin Season," *Herald Examiner*, April 25, 1933.

44. Nordic Country Club, directories [1925–1930] MS6, NCC, box 1, folder 8, Swedish-American Archives of Greater Chicago, North Park University, Chicago.

45. Stetterdahl and Stetterdahl, *Bror Johansson's Chicago*, 11.

46. Ibid., 16.

Notes to Chapter 6 and Conclusion • 221

47. Ibid., 71.

48. Ibid., 75.

49. Ibid., 77, 91.

50. Ibid., 83.

51. Beijbom, *Utvandrarna och den stora depressionen*, 7.

52. Ibid., 85.

53. Ibid., 88–89.

54. Ibid., 92–93.

55. H. Arnold Barton, *The Old Country and the New: Essays on Swedes and America* (Carbondale: Southern Illinois University Press, 2007), 192.

56. Lane and Isaacson, *Andersonville*, 17.

57. Stetterdahl and Stetterdahl, *Bror Johansson's Chicago*, 81, 91.

58. Advertisement for the Skandinavien-Amerika Linien (Swedish America Line), printed in the *Swedish Blue Book, 1927*; American Daughters of Sweden, yearbooks [1927–1951], MS11, American Daughters of Sweden Records, box 11, folder 6, Swedish-American Archives of Greater Chicago, North Park University, Chicago.

59. Barton, *A Folk Divided*, 243.

Conclusion

1. "Rachel Dolezal: I Am Definitely Not White," interview by Savannah Guthrie, *NBC Nightly News*, June 16, 2015, accessed November 10, 2016, http://www.nbcnews.com/nightly-news/video/rachel-dolezal-i-definitely-am-not-white-465554499589.

2. Darryl E. Owens, "In One Week, a Poser and a Killer reveal U.S. Racial Dysfunction," *Orlando Sentinel*, June 22, 2015, accessed October 27, 2016, http://www.orlandosentinel.com/opinion/os-rachel-dolezal-dylann-roof-darryl-owens-20150622-column.html.

3. Nell Irvin Painter, "What Is Whiteness?" *New York Times*, June 20, 2015, accessed October 27, 2016, http://www.nytimes.com/2015/06/21/opimnion/sunday/what-is-whiteness.html?_r=0.

4. Jørn Brøndal and other scholars of race and ethnicity have begun to fill in the gaps of our historiographic knowledge in the early twenty-first century, and the goal of this book is to continue this introduction. For further discussion, see Brøndal, "The Fairest"; Ignatiev, *How the Irish Became White*; Guglielmo, *White on Arrival*, 15, 59–63; Goldstein, *The Price of Whiteness*. Russell Kazal's book, *Becoming Old Stock*, serves as an important counterpoint to this argument of the enduring importance of ethnic whiteness. Germans in American underwent a process by which their ethnic character and racial stock went under fire during World War I.

5. Erwin Baur, Eugen Fischer, and Fritz Lenz, *Human Heredity*, trans. Eden and Cedar Paul (London: Allen and Unwin, 1931), 191.

6. Ronald H. Bayor, "Another Look at 'Whiteness': The Persistence of Ethnicity in American Life," *Journal of American Ethnic History* 29, no. 1 (Fall 2009): 13–14. See also Peter Kolchin, "Whiteness Studies: The New History of Race in America," *Journal of American History* 89, no.1 (June 2002): 154–173; Øverland, "Becoming White in 1881."

7. See Kazal, *Becoming Old Stock*; Ignatiev, *How the Irish Became White*.

8. Jean Halley, Amy Eshleman, and Ramya Mahadevan Vijaya, *Seeing White: An Introduction to White Privilege and Race* (Lanham: Rowman and Littlefield, 2011), 4.

9. The highest household incomes as ranked according to ancestry are rather surprising when one takes into account the importance of whiteness in America today. The top ten highest median household incomes are as follows: Indian American, Taiwanese American, Filipino American, Australian American, Latvian American, British American, European American, Russian American, Lithuanian American, and Austrian American. See U.S. Census Bureau, "Median Household Income in the Past 12 Months (in 2015 Inflation-adjusted Dollars)," *American Community Survey*, accessed October 15, 2016, https://factfinder.census.gov/faces/tableservices/jsf/pages/productview.xhtml?src=bkmk.

10. Richard J. Herrnstein and Charles Murray, *The Bell Curve: Intelligence and Class Structure in American Life* (New York: Free Press Paperbacks, 1994).

11. Halley et al., *Seeing White*, 38–39.

12. Daniel Chandler and Rod Munday, *A Dictionary of Media and Communication* (Oxford: Oxford University Press, 2011), accessed December 1, 2016, www.oxfordreference.com/view/10.1093/acref/9780199568758.001.0001/acref-9780199568758-e-218.

13. American Anthropological Association Executive Board, "AAA Statement on Race," *American Anthropologist* 100, no. 3 (September 1998): 712–713.

14. Ibid.

15. This Ancestry.com television commercial first aired on television in 2015. According to performance analytics of this particular commercial, which aired on channels like TLC, CNN, PBS, and other channels likely viewed by a wide demographic, the commercial was very well received with a satisfaction rate of 90 percent. Ancestry DNA Commercial, "Testimonial: Kyle," advertisement aired on TLC, November 22, 2017, 30 seconds.

16. Matt Miller, "A DNA Test Won't Explain Elizabeth Warren's Ancestry," *Slate*, June 29, 2016, accessed October 27, 2016, http://www.slate.com/articles/technology/future _tense/2016/06/dna_testing_cannot_determine_ancestry_including_elizabeth _warren_s.html.

17. Ibid.

18. Jason Horowitz, "For Donald Trump's Family, an Immigrant's Tale with 2 Beginnings," *New York Times*, August 21, 2016, accessed August 31, 2016, http://www .nytimes.com/2016/08/22/us/politics/for-donald-trumps-family-an-immigrants-tale -with-2-beginnings.html?_r=0.

19. Ibid.

20. Charles M. Blow, "The Menace of Trumpism," *New York Times*, October 26, 2017, accessed December 6, 2017, https://www.nytimes.com/2017/10/26/opinion/menace -trumpism-flake-republicans.html; Nurith Aizenman, "Trump Wishes We Had More Immigrants from Norway. Turns Out We Once Did," *NPR*, January 18, 2018, https:// www.npr.org/sections/goatsandsoda/2018/01/12/577673191/trump-wishes-we-had -more-immigrants-from-norway-turns-out-we-once-did.

Index

Alpine(s), 3, 8, 82, 95
Americanism, 137, 139, 141, 143–44, 149, 153
Ancestry.com, 186–87, 222n15
Andersonville (Chicago), 42, 153, 157, 177, 182
Anglo-Saxon: and American social norms, 8, 124; as "old stock" race, 40, 41, 98, 141, 144, 161–62; and racial constructs, 6, 19–20, 149, 161–62, 180; and white protestants (WASPs), 20, 187
Armour Square (Chicago), 43
Aryan, 8, 16, 138, 181
Augustana: Book Concern, 130; Central Home, 128–29; College, 168, 184–85; Hospital of the City of Chicago, 107; Lutheran Mission Home, 128; Synod, 36, 128, 145; Women's Home, 128

Babcock, Kendrick, 55, 140, 141
Barnum, Phineas T., 2, 75, 76
bathing in nude, 67–68, 160, 204n60
beauty culture: context on, 73; historiography on, 191n2; Nordic whiteness and, 72; photographic newspaper contests, 1
Beecher, Lyman, 29, 198n27
Beery, Wallace, 48, 49, 50
Beijbom, Ulf, 34, 80, 83, 173, 175, 197n10

blondeness: and the British Blondes, 72–73; as desired by American women, 73–74; history of, 46, 50; and Nordic physicality, 2, 3, 4, 11, 15, 46, 50; and "Swedish" maids, 50, 59; and Vikings, 63
bohemians, 43, 86, 144
Bremer, Fredrika, 34, 69
Burnham, Daniel, 59, 93

Café Idrott. *See* temperance
Casson, Herbert, 109, 193n18
Chicago (Ill.): bachelor culture in, 32, 113; boosterism in, 1, 31; cholera epidemic, 33–34, 43; class divides, 32, 39; Color Riot of 1919, 147–48; context on, 5, 13–15, 19, 189; Depression era, 170, 174, 176–77; domestic service work, 56, 80, 91; elite of, 79, 82, 92–94, 98, 100, 155; ethnic tensions during WWI, 136; Gilded age, 55; illegitimacy rates in, 123; labor force, 41, 101, 106, 167; labor wars, 15, 132; migration and settlement of Scandinavians after 1890, 83–90, 132, 138; migration and settlement of Scandinavians before 1890, 13–14, 22, 23, 30, 42, 45, 53; movie industry, 48; multicultural population of, 5–6, 20, 54; neighborhood relations, 22;

224 · Index

Chicago (Ill.) (*continued*): nineteenth century, 19, 28, 35; in the 1920s, 134; overcrowding in, 39; post-WWI immigration, 150, 152, 174; Progressive era, 32, 39, 82, 128–30; Scandinavian American press, 11–12, 36, 133, 151; Scandinavian foreign-born population of, 45, 138; social clubs, 158–59, 167; suburbs of, 39, 56, 82, 93, 154–55, 177; vice in, 109, 11–12, 118, 120, 125, 133–34; women "adrift" in, 15, 42, 115, 128–29

Chicago Daily News, 12, 54, 148, 202n21

Chicago Daily Tribune: advertisements in, 54; articles on domestic workers, 56, 58; context on, 12; contribution to positive Nordic stereotypes, 15, 55; photographic newspaper contest, 1–3; rhetoric during WWI, 143

Chicago fire: context on, 19, 37; and ethnic tensions, 37; Scandinavian recovery from, 22, 38, 39

Chicago Immanuel Woman's Home, 129–30, 132

Chicago River, 30, 31, 33, 40, 43, 125

Chicago Times-Herald, 12

Chicago Tribune. See *Chicago Daily Tribune*

Collier, Carl, 160, 162

Columbian Exposition: and beauty pageants, 76; and birth of discourse on civilization, 9, 14, 15, 21, 45–46, 50–51, 61; context on, 14, 60; and the Ling method, 66, 73; and the Midway Plaisance, 61; and Nordic whiteness, 59, 61, 63, 70; and Norway's pavilion, 51; and Norwegian representation, 9, 15, 51, 61, 63; preparation for, 42; and Scandinavian representation, 52, 59, 61, 63, 69; and the *Swedish Catalogue*, 25, 28, 65, 66, 123; Swedish Government Building, 62, 64; and Swedish representation, 9, 62, 65; and Viking replica ship, 9, 51, 63; and the White City, 9, 60, 61; and the Women's Pavilion, 69

Columbus, Christopher, 9, 51, 61, 63–64, 149

Commons, John, 55

Conradi, P. A., 64

construction: of downtown Chicago, 34, 38, 45; industry, 39, 41, 44, 93; work for men, 24, 84

Dalkullan bookstore, 90, 175

Danes: and businesses, 113; in comparison to Swedes, 25–26; and fire relief aid, 38; immigrant population in the U.S. 1881–1890, 54; and intermarriage, 90; and liberty loans, 146; population of Chicago in 1890, 45, 54; population of Chicago in 1910, 138; population of Chicago in 1920, 150; population of Illinois in 1880, 198n29; population of Minnesota in 1880, 198n29; and Scandinavian newspapers, 11; as Scandinavians, 6, 36, 70, 131, 152; stereotypes of, 71; and vice, 114; in West Town (Chicago), 87

Daughters of Norway, 146

Den Danske Pioneer, 12

Deniker, Joseph, 72, 144, 161, 180

Denmark: literacy rates of, 66; and political break with Norway, 25; political ties with Sweden and Norway, 23, 26; progressive movement in, 68; rural population of, 35; short-distance migration into, 25, 28; similarities to Sweden and Norway, 24, 71, 80. *See also* Danes

DNA, 14, 185, 186–87

Dolezal, Rachel, 179–80, 186, 187

domestic service: and American domestic customs, 54, 56, 58, 67, 94, 99; context on, 24, 41, 44, 53–54, 80–81, 104–5; experiences of, 56, 83, 85, 98–100; and formal training, 67, 83, 101; historiography on, 15, 80–81, 206–7n7; and Irish women, 57, 80, 81–82, 94; and "manifest domesticity," 81; and Nordic whiteness, 58, 107; and Norwegian women, 97; and preparation for marriage, 95; and Scandinavian youth, 88; and *Sweedie, The Swedish Maid*, 48; undercover reporting on, 103–4; and wages, 56, 92, 97; as women "adrift," 48, 115–116, 121

domestic service (Scandinavian women), 24, 27, 41, 54, 69, 104; advertisements seeking, 94, 97; in the American press, 102; correspondence about, 100; employment bureaus for, 97; harsh treatment of, 83; and illegitimacy, 124–25; jokes about, 58–59; and leisure, 100; social mobility of, 91, 100–102, 105; statistics on, 79–80, 88–89, 91 domestic service (Swedish women), 54, 56–57, 75, 83; and pride of community, 79, 117; and sexual harassment, 104, 121; social mobility of, 92, 102; as "Swedish maids," 80, 92, 103–4, 201n6; and transportation to North Shore, 43

Elvig, A. J., 64
Englewood (Chicago), 43, 177
Erikson, Leif, 63–64, 147, 149
Evanston (Ill.), 93, 159

factory work, 24, 57, 81, 88, 101–2, 116
Fellowes, Chas, 165, 170–71
femininity: discourse on, 1, 11, 69, 72–73, 76–78, 103; ideals of, 74; and masculinity, 10, 73; and Nordic whiteness, 1, 55, 207n13; and Swedish women, 10–11; and Victorians, 82
filiopietistic studies, 6, 9, 70, 84, 140, 193n18
Finns, 28, 31, 131, 192n13
Fisk, John, 64
Franklin, Benjamin, 8, 18
fraternal organizations: context on, 36, 42–43, 131–32; and ethnic preservation, 11, 152; and the Nordic Country Club, 16, 155, 159, 163, 168; and Nordic whiteness, 168; Scandinavian Viking clubs, 26, 36, 167; and singing and athleticism, 139, 167
French, 18, 71, 72, 118

Gender: and American norms, 55; discourse on, 4–5, 9–10; in discourse on civilization, 15, 19, 46, 70; and divisions of labor, 96, 116; historiography on, 8, 10, 192n8, 194n33; and Janson, Florence Edith, 27; and manliness, 9, 19, 194n34, 196n45; and Nordic whiteness, 2, 4, 10–11, 17, 46; roles in the old country, 24, 86; and *Sweedie, The Swedish Maid*, 47–50; and women "adrift," 128. *See also* femininity; masculinity; womanhood
German(s): and anti-German rhetoric during WWI, 136–37, 140–41, 142, 143, 146; and Aryan whiteness, 8, 18, 35, 77, 180; context on, 19, 35, 38, 141; as department store workers, 106; and

domestic service, 54, 57, 94, 95, 103; and historiography, 138, 215n5, 221n4; and illegitimacy, 124; and immigration quotas, 151–52; and liberty loans, 146; and Lutheranism, 31, 137, 145–46; as manual workers, 39, 84–85, 86, 87, 175; negative viewpoints on, 15, 20, 29, 71, 181, 187–88; as neighbors of Scandinavians, 14, 35, 38, 43–44, 139; and New Trier (Ill.), 92; and the Nordic Country Club, 173; population in Chicago, 6, 22, 31, 35, 42, 54; and race, 29, 70, 141, 179, 186–87; and short-distance migration, 28; and unification movements, 26; and union affiliation, 15; and white slavery, 118
Gibson girl, 72, 73, 76
gilded age, 43, 53, 55, 56
Gold Coast and the Slum, The (Zorbaugh), 32, 42
Grant, Madison: and "nordic" categorization, 72, 138, 148, 180, 201n5; and *Passing of the Great Race, The*, 51, 136, 140, 144, 160–61
Great Gatsby, The (Fitzgerald), 161–62

Harper's Bazaar, 81, 102, 207n10
Hegborn, Pauline Nelson, 44–45, 106–7, 117, 118
Hemlandet, 12, 36, 37, 141
Hirsch, Stina, 56, 80, 98
Humboldt Park (Chicago), 6, 43
Hyde Park (Chicago), 43

Idun, 1, 2
illegitimacy, 113, 121, 122–25
Irish: and ancestry, 186–87; and the Chicago fire, 37; and domestic service, 57, 80, 81–82, 94; and ethnic conflict with Scandinavians, 32, 34; and Kilgubben (Chicago), 32; negative viewpoints on, 15, 20, 29, 36, 45, 113; as neighbors to Scandinavians, 14, 22, 40–41, 43, 44–45, 173; population of Chicago in 1890, 54; population of Chicago in 1900, 5–6; and union affiliation, 15; and vice, 114, 115, 125; as wage earners, 87; and whiteness, 3, 7, 10, 20, 29, 152; women as workers, 54, 85, 86

226 · *Index*

Italian(s): and ethnic conflict with Scandinavians, 40; and family networks, 115;
and the "homemaking myth," 51; and
illegitimacy, 124; and literacy rates, 66;
as neighbors to Scandinavians, 14, 22,
40; percentage of manual workers in
1900, 85; use of the ethnic press, 5; and
whiteness, 7, 18, 36, 113, 147, 152; and
white slavery, 118, 134; women as workers, 86, 95
Itasca (Ill.), 155, 159

Janson, Florence Edith, 27, 83, 134–35
Jansson, Erik, 30–31
Jews, 10, 95, 115, 118, 140
Johansson, Bror, 174–77
Johnson-Reed Act of 1924, 161
jokes stereotyping Scandinavians, 49–50,
58–59, 82, 168–69, 203n37

Kenilworth (Ill.), 92–94
Kjellberg, Isidor, 92

Lake Michigan, 30, 43, 60, 164
Lake View (Chicago): background of, 86,
88, 89, 90, 139, 174–75; commercial
district of, 89–90, 96–97, 139, 174–75,
176; compared to the Townsend street
district, 86, 88; ethnic makeup of, 89; fe-
male residents of, 89; generational shift
by 1910s, 101, 132; settlement houses in,
105, 113, 128–33
Lange, Olaf Gottfrid, 30
Larigelando, Kund, 116
Larson, Carrie, 125–26
liberty loan campaigns, 146–47
Lillieberg, Lotten, 75
Lincoln Park (Chicago), 128, 130
Lind, Jenny, 76
Ling, Pehr Henrik, 66. *See also* Columbian
Exposition
Linnaeus, Carl, 60–61, 204n40
Little Norway (Chicago), 6, 13
Lund, Inge, 103–4, 105
Lunde, Theodore H., 142–43
Lundquist, Carl Hjalmar: background on,
21; investment in the Nordic Coun-
try Club, 170–71, 172; leadership of the
Nordic Country Club, 163, 164, 165, 172;

rise to professional success, 171, 173; on
Swedish stubbornness, 35–36; use of
"Scandinavian stock," 20
Lusitania, The, 139, 142
Lutheranism: American perceptions of, 30,
45; context on, 31, 40, 168; and ethnic
connections to Germans, 35, 137, 145;
and immigrants, 31, 40; and literacy, 11;
and Lutheran churches, 87, 89, 91, 107,
128–29; and *Lutheran Companion, The*, 152;
and ministers, 6; and settlement homes,
128–29, 130; and Swedish language
newspapers, 12, 36, 112, 141, 145 (*see also
Hemlandet);* and temperance, 68, 113

Manz, Doris, 77
Marshall Fields, 105
masculinity: and bachelor culture, 32, 36;
and cross-dressing, 50; discourse on,
10, 16, 26; and femininity, 10, 73, 74; and
male desire, 126; and the "new" Nordic man, 16, 160, 168, 174; and Nordic
whiteness, 9, 66, 70–71, 96; and Vikings,
9, 10, 26, 63. *See also* gender
Mathison, Hannah, 100
Mediterranean, 3, 8
Midwest, 5, 11–12, 13, 20, 22, 28–29
Minneapolis (Minn.): and Scandinavian
newspapers, 137, 141, 142; and Scandinavian population, 5, 30, 115, 125, 189; and
white slavery, 119
Minneapolis City Workhouse, 115
Minnesota, 12, 29, 168, 184, 198n29
Missions-Vännen, 12
Montgomery Wards, 106, 107

National Origins Act of 1927, 151, 152
nativism: and anthropological discussions
of race, 3–8, 12, 51, 72, 141, 144; and competition with, fear of European immigrants, 18, 20, 29, 30; and cultural preservation, 12; and ethnic preservation, 6, 70,
137, 142, 145, 152–54; and *The Rising Tide of
Color against White World-Supremacy* (Stoddard), 161–62; and Trump, Donald, 187;
and wartime press discourse, 136, 140,
143; after WWI, 147–50, 156, 174, 180
Nelson, Olaf N.: and construction of Nordic whiteness, 31, 55, 63, 70–71; on

emigration, 26–27; and filiopietistic discourse, 70–71, 84, 193n18; and *History of the Scandinavians*, 21–22

Newberry, Walter Franklin, 100

New York Times, 11, 49, 51, 187, 188

Nordic Country Club: background on, 155–56, 164, 172–74; as a fraternal club, 16, 158, 163, 164, 168–69, 173; and leadership of, 165, 170, 171; and the "new" Nordic man, 16, 160, 163–64, 168, 174; *Nordic Fairway, The*, 164, 168–70, 171, 173; and Norwegians, 164; planning, 156, 158, 159, 166; promotion of, 159, 162, 165, 173. *See also* Carl Hjalmar Lundquist

nordicism, 5, 47, 51, 181

Nordic whiteness: and American cultural constructions, 107, 182, 184; definition of, 3–4; discourse on, 3, 51, 52, 69, 180–81; and domestic servants, 58; and gender, 4, 5, 10; historiography on, 6, 192n9; in *History of Scandinavians, The* (Nelson), 70–71; importance and benefits of, 3, 23, 70, 152, 153, 180–81; and marriage patterns, 91; and nativism, 149, 150, 160; and othering, 82; and physicality, 11, 65, 72, 75, 78; and Scandinavian representation, 3, 13, 15, 31, 63–64, 156; and social construction, 2, 14, 40, 53, 67, 89; and white slavery, 118

Norsk Familie Journal of Christiania, 1

North Park College, 66,

North Shore (Chicago): background on, 54, 56–57, 92, 94, 100, 104; and domestic servants, 56–57, 80, 82, 94–95, 98–100; and elite families, 82, 94, 97–98, 104, 155

Norway, 1, 2, 23, 26, 68, 71

Norwegian National League Employment Office, 97

Norwegian(s): and aid following the Chicago fire, 38–39; and ancestry, 182, 183; churches, 38; Club, 146, 149; context on, 36, 70, 71, 113, 131; deaths from cholera, 33; and disputes with other Scandinavians, 71; and emigration from Norway, 25, 26, 37; establishment of "the Sands," 30; group dynamics with Scandinavians, 6, 11, 26, 71; historiography of, 52, 192n13, 193n18; history of, 22, 25–26; language, 1, 12, 31, 87, 90, 142, 149; and

liberty loans, 146; and literacy rates, 66; National League, 133; newspapers, 12, 114, 139; and the 1925 Centennial, 153; in Norway, 24, 35; population of Chicago before 1900, 29, 31, 35, 45, 53–54, 84; population of Chicago in 1900, 6, 90; population of Chicago in 1910, 138–39, 145; population of Chicago in 1920, 150; and racial constructs, 71, 149, 152; and Scandia Community Beach, 164; and short-term migration, 28; and vice, 114, 115, 122, 125, 126–27; Viking replica ship, 9, 51; women, 80, 84, 116, 130, 146

nursing, 68–69

"old stock." *See* Anglo-Saxon

Olmsted, Frederick Law, 39

Person, Johan, 79

Pettengill, Lillian, 103

Peyton, John Lewis, 19, 23, 24

Polish: population of Chicago, 40, 43, 85, 134, 147, 152; women, 54, 86, 95

Prairie Avenue (Chicago), 54, 92

Progressive ideology: context on, 15, 36, 48, 69, 71, 113, 135; and the middle-class, 82, 133; and reformers, 15, 32, 38–39, 68, 118, 120; and Sandburg, Carl, 148; Scandinavian reform groups, 68, 112; and women "adrift," 128, 129, 130, 132

Prostitution: and anti-prostitution reformers, 118; context on, 109, 112, 113, 115–16, 119–20, 124. *See also* white slavery

racial fitness: for American citizenship, 3, 14, 20; discourse on, 19, 50–51; and European immigrants, 46, 69; and social achievement, 20; and Swedes, 2, 66; during WWI, 136–38, 144

racial hierarchy: discourse on, 1, 5, 6, 46, 47; and illegitimacy, 124; and the Johnson-Reed Act of 1924, 161; middle-class notions of, 50; and nationalism, 160; after the World's Columbian Exposition, 69

Reckless, Walter, 111, 133–34

Ripley, William Z., 3, 51, 71–72, 144, 160–61, 180

Roe, Clifford, 109, 111

228 · *Index*

Royal Swedish Commission, 25, 64, 67–68
Russians: and literacy, 66; and nativism, 147; and negative media, 15; and race, 18, 119, 152; and women at work, 86

Salmon, Lucy Maynard, 103
Sandburg, Carl, 148
"The Sands," (Chicago), 30, 31, 32, 34, 35
Sapolio soap, 57
Scandinavian People's Home, 131–32
Scandinavian(s). *See* Danes; Nordic whiteness; Norwegian(s); Swede(s); Swedish
Scandinavism, 9, 47
scientific racism, 14, 46, 136, 147, 162
Sears, Dorothy, 98–99
Sears, Joseph, 92, 93, 98
settlement homes, 105, 113, 128–33
"shop girls," 101, 105–7, 116
singing societies, 43, 114, 139, 147, 168
Skandinaven: advertising in, 57; and anti-Italian rhetoric, 40; background on, 11, 12, 36, 87, 97; and Conradi, P. A., 64; on culture of Swede Town, 37; and Nordic unity, 37, 87; on pay for domestic servants, 97; reporting during WWI, 137, 142, 143, 145–46, 147, 149; on white slavery, 114, 116, 120–22, 126, 133
social Darwinism, 19, 46, 50, 55, 144
Social Evil in Chicago, The. See Vice Commission of Chicago
St. Ansgarius Church, 32, 33
Stoddard, Lothrop, 51, 138, 160, 162
Svea Hall, 40
Svenska Amerikanaren, 12, 36, 37, 117, 137, 141
Svenska Kuriren, 12, 97, 143, 146
Svenska Tribunen: advertising in, 94; background on, 12, 36, 133; on benefits of assimilation, 102; and domestic service, 102; on ethnic preservation, 138; on immigration quotas, 152; and Lundquist, Carl Hjalmar, 171; and Peterson, C. F., 100; on work ethic, 8, 151
Svithiod Singing Club, 167, 171
Sweden. *See* Swedes
Swedes: and aid following the Chicago fire, 38–39; and alcohol consumption, 68; and church membership, 33, 132;
and citizenship, 145; and conflict with Italians, 40; context on, 19, 113, 131; and emigration from Sweden, 25, 27–28, 37; and ethnic stereotypes, 35–36, 67–68, 70–71; group dynamics with Scandinavians, 6, 11, 36, 43, 71; hegemony of, 25, 40; historiography of, 52, 192n13, 193n18; intermarriage rates of, 90; and liberty loans, 146; in the Midwest, 29, 36; population of Chicago before 1900, 35, 45, 53–54; population of Chicago in 1900, 5; population of Chicago in 1910, 138–39; population of Chicago in 1920, 150; and racial constructs, 18, 25, 65, 71, 152; in Sweden, 24, 37; and vice, 114, 115, 125, 126; as wage earners, 87, 156
Swede Town (Chicago): context on, 35, 39, 43; culture of, 37; as described by Bremer, Fredrika, 34; improvements to, 34; and Larsson, Anders, 30; replacement by Little Sicily (Chicago), 41
Swedish: ancestry, 75, 182; femininity, 10; language, 11–12, 25, 31, 87, 90; newspapers, 12, 36–37, 57, 114, 116; women, 2, 54, 57–58, 69, 75, 78, 130. *See also* domestic service; Nordic Country Club; Swede(s); white slavery
Swedish Blue Book, The, 167, 177
Swedish Catalogue, 25, 27
Swedish Educational League, 134–35
Swedish Ladies' Committee, 67, 69
Swedish National League, 126, 133
Sweedie, The Swedish Maid, 47–50

Taylor, Bayard, 23, 24, 197n11
temperance: and Café Idrott, 90, 175; as a social issue, 22, 68, 157, 169; and the Women's Christian Temperance Union, 118
Teutonic, 3, 20, 70, 144
Thörnberg, E. H., 56, 121, 123
Trinity Lutheran Church, 89, 91

Unonius, Gustaf, 32, 34

Vice Commission of Chicago, 111, 133, 134
vice in Chicago, 16, 112, 125; and drunkenness, 114; and kidnapping, 122; and

murder, 125–26. *See also* Vice Commission of Chicago; white slavery

Victorian culture: context on, 2, 27; and femininity, 72, 76, 82; and race science, 46, 60; and separate spheres, 20, 24, 58, 98

Watney, Helga Pederson, 119–20

West Town (Chicago), 44, 87, 88

whiteness studies, 7, 10, 16, 192n8

white slavery: cases of, 110, 134; context on, 109, 111–12, 118, 124, 211n6; narratives, 109, 110, 111; in the Pacific Northwest, 119–20; panic in Chicago, 15, 111, 118, 133; and racial contrasts, 110. See also *Skandinaven*

womanhood, 57, 121

women "adrift," 48, 112, 115, 128. *See also* white slavery

World's Columbian Exposition. *See* Columbian Exposition

Yankee, 19, 28, 187. *See also* Anglo-Saxon

ERIKA K. JACKSON is an associate professor of history at Colorado Mesa University.

The University of Illinois Press
is a founding member of the
Association of American University Presses.

University of Illinois Press
1325 South Oak Street
Champaign, IL 61820-6903
www.press.uillinois.edu